SHOE DOG

SHOE DOG

A Memoir by the Creator of Nike

PHIL KNIGHT

**SIMON &
SCHUSTER**

London · New York · Sydney · Toronto · New Delhi

A CBS COMPANY

First published in Great Britain by Simon & Schuster UK Ltd, 2016
A CBS COMPANY

11

Simon & Schuster UK Ltd
1st Floor
222 Gray's Inn Road
London WC1X 8HB

www.simonandschuster.co.uk

Simon & Schuster Australia, Sydney
Simon & Schuster India, New Delhi

Interior design by Kyle Kabel

A CIP catalogue record for this book is available
from the British Library.

ISBN: 978-1-4711-4670-1
Trade paperback ISBN: 978-1-4711-4671-8
Ebook ISBN: 978-1-4711-4673-2

Printed and bound by CPI Group (UK) Ltd, Croydon, CR0 4YY

Simon & Schuster UK Ltd are committed to sourcing paper
that is made from wood grown in sustainable forests and support the Forest
Stewardship Council, the leading international forest certification organisation.
°Our books displaying the FSC logo are printed on FSC certified paper.

For my grandchildren,
so they will know

In the beginner's mind there are many possibilities, but in the expert's mind there are few.

—Shunryu Suzuki, *Zen Mind, Beginner's Mind*

SHOE DOG

DAWN

I was up before the others, before the birds, before the sun. I drank a cup of coffee, wolfed down a piece of toast, put on my shorts and sweatshirt, and laced up my green running shoes. Then slipped quietly out the back door.

I stretched my legs, my hamstrings, my lower back, and groaned as I took the first few balky steps down the cool road, into the fog. Why is it always so hard to get started?

There were no cars, no people, no signs of life. I was all alone, the world to myself—though the trees seemed oddly aware of me. Then again, this was Oregon. The trees always seemed to know. The trees always had your back.

What a beautiful place to be from, I thought, gazing around. Calm, green, tranquil—I was proud to call Oregon my home, proud to call little Portland my place of birth. But I felt a stab of regret, too. Though beautiful, Oregon struck some people as the kind of place where nothing big had ever happened, or was ever likely to. If we Oregonians were famous for anything, it was an old, old trail we'd had to blaze to get here. Since then, things had been pretty tame.

The best teacher I ever had, one of the finest men I ever knew, spoke of that trail often. It's our birthright, he'd growl. Our character, our fate—our DNA. "The cowards never started," he'd tell me, "and the weak died along the way—that leaves us."

Us. Some rare strain of pioneer spirit was discovered along that

I

trail, my teacher believed, some outsized sense of possibility mixed with a diminished capacity for pessimism—and it was our job as Oregonians to keep that strain alive.

I'd nod, showing him all due respect. I loved the guy. But walking away I'd sometimes think: Jeez, it's just a dirt road.

That foggy morning, that momentous morning in 1962, I'd recently blazed my own trail—back home, after seven long years away. It was strange being home again, strange being lashed again by the daily rains. Stranger still was living again with my parents and twin sisters, sleeping in my childhood bed. Late at night I'd lie on my back, staring at my college textbooks, my high school trophies and blue ribbons, thinking: This is me? *Still?*

I moved quicker down the road. My breath formed rounded, frosty puffs, swirling into the fog. I savored that first physical awakening, that brilliant moment before the mind is fully clear, when the limbs and joints first begin to loosen and the material body starts to melt away. Solid to liquid.

Faster, I told myself. Faster.

On paper, I thought, I'm an adult. Graduated from a good college—University of Oregon. Earned a master's from a top business school—Stanford. Survived a yearlong hitch in the U.S. Army—Fort Lewis and Fort Eustis. My résumé said I was a learned, accomplished soldier, a twenty-four-year-old man in full . . . So why, I wondered, why do I still feel like a kid?

Worse, like the same shy, pale, rail-thin kid I'd always been.

Maybe because I still hadn't experienced anything of life. Least of all its many temptations and excitements. I hadn't smoked a cigarette, hadn't tried a drug. I hadn't broken a rule, let alone a law. The 1960s were just under way, the age of rebellion, and I was the only person in America who hadn't yet rebelled. I couldn't think of one time I'd cut loose, done the unexpected.

I'd never even been with a girl.

If I tended to dwell on all the things I wasn't, the reason was simple. Those were the things I knew best. I'd have found it diffi-cult to say what or who exactly I was, or might become. Like all my friends I wanted to be successful. Unlike my friends I didn't know what that meant. Money? Maybe. Wife? Kids? House? Sure, if I was lucky. These were the goals I was taught to aspire to, and part of me did aspire to them, instinctively. But deep down I was searching for something else, something more. I had an aching sense that our time is short, shorter than we ever know, short as a morning run, and I wanted mine to be meaningful. And purposeful. And creative. And important. Above all . . . different.

I wanted to leave a mark on the world.

I wanted to win.

No, that's not right. I simply didn't want to lose.

And then it happened. As my young heart began to thump, as my pink lungs expanded like the wings of a bird, as the trees turned to greenish blurs, I saw it all before me, exactly what I wanted my life to be. Play.

Yes, I thought, that's it. That's the word. The secret of happiness, I'd always suspected, the essence of beauty or truth, or all we ever need to know of either, lay somewhere in that moment when the ball is in midair, when both boxers sense the approach of the bell, when the runners near the finish line and the crowd rises as one. There's a kind of exuberant clarity in that pulsing half second before winning and losing are decided. I wanted that, whatever that was, to be my life, my daily life.

At different times I'd fantasized about becoming a great novelist, a great journalist, a great statesman. But the ultimate dream was al-ways to be a great athlete. Sadly, fate had made me good, not great. At twenty-four I was finally resigned to that fact. I'd run track at Oregon, and I'd distinguished myself, lettering three of four years. But that was that, the end. Now, as I began to clip off one brisk six-minute mile after another, as the rising sun set fire to the lowest needles of the pines, I asked myself: What if there were a way, without being an athlete, to feel what athletes feel? To play all the time, instead of working? Or else to enjoy work so much that it becomes essentially the same thing.

The world was so overrun with war and pain and misery, the daily grind was so exhausting and often unjust—maybe the only answer, I thought, was to find some prodigious, improbable dream that seemed worthy, that seemed fun, that seemed a good fit, and chase it with an athlete's single-minded dedication and purpose. Like it or not, life is a game. Whoever denies that truth, whoever simply refuses to play, gets left on the sidelines, and I didn't want that. More than anything, that was the thing I did not want.

Which led, as always, to my Crazy Idea. Maybe, I thought, just maybe, I need to take one more look at my Crazy Idea. Maybe my Crazy Idea just might . . . work?

Maybe.

No, no, I thought, running faster, faster, running as if I were chasing someone *and* being chased all at the same time. It *will* work. By God I'll *make* it work. No maybes about it.

I was suddenly smiling. Almost laughing. Drenched in sweat, moving as gracefully and effortlessly as I ever had, I saw my Crazy Idea shining up ahead, and it didn't look all that crazy. It didn't even look like an idea. It looked like a place. It looked like a person, or some life force that existed long before I did, separate from me, but also part of me. Waiting for me, but also hiding from me. That might sound a little high-flown, a little *crazy*. But that's how I felt back then.

Or maybe I didn't. Maybe my memory is enlarging this eureka moment, or condensing many eureka moments into one. Or maybe, if there was such a moment, it was nothing more than runner's high. I don't know. I can't say. So much about those days, and the months and years into which they slowly sorted themselves, has vanished, like those rounded, frosty puffs of breath. Faces, numbers, decisions that once seemed pressing and irrevocable, they're all gone.

What remains, however, is this one comforting certainty, this one anchoring truth that will never go away. At twenty-four I *did* have a Crazy Idea, and somehow, despite being dizzy with existential angst, and fears about the future, and doubts about myself, as all young men and women in their midtwenties are, I *did* decide that the world is made up of crazy ideas. History is one long processional of crazy ideas. The things I loved most—books, sports, democracy, free enterprise—started as crazy ideas.

For that matter, few ideas are as crazy as my favorite thing, running. It's hard. It's painful. It's risky. The rewards are few and far from guaranteed. When you run around an oval track, or down an empty road, you have no real destination. At least, none that can fully justify the effort. The act itself becomes the destination. It's not just that there's no finish line; it's that you define the finish line. Whatever pleasures or gains you derive from the act of running, you must find them within. It's all in how you frame it, how you sell it to yourself.

Every runner knows this. You run and run, mile after mile, and you never quite know why. You tell yourself that you're running toward some goal, chasing some rush, but really you run because the alternative, stopping, scares you to death.

So that morning in 1962 I told myself: Let everyone else call your idea crazy . . . just keep going. Don't stop. Don't even think about stopping until you get there, and don't give much thought to where "there" is. Whatever comes, just don't stop.

That's the precocious, prescient, urgent advice I managed to give myself, out of the blue, and somehow managed to take. Half a century later, I believe it's the best advice—maybe the only advice—any of us should ever give.

PART ONE

Now, *here*, you see, it takes all the running *you* can do,
to keep in the same place. If you want to get somewhere
else, you must run at least twice as fast as that.

—Lewis Carroll, *Through the Looking-Glass*

1962

When I broached the subject with my father, when I worked up the nerve to speak to him about my Crazy Idea, I made sure it was in the early evening. That was always the best time with Dad. He was relaxed then, well fed, stretched out in his vinyl recliner in the TV nook. I can still tilt back my head and close my eyes and hear the sound of the audience laughing, the tinny theme songs of his favorite shows, *Wagon Train* and *Rawhide*.

His all-time favorite was Red Buttons. Every episode began with Red singing: *Ho ho, hee hee . . . strange things are happening*.

I set a straight-backed chair beside him and gave a wan smile and waited for the next commercial. I'd rehearsed my spiel, in my head, over and over, especially the opening. *Sooo, Dad, you remember that Crazy Idea I had at Stanford . . . ?*

It was one of my final classes, a seminar on entrepreneurship. I'd written a research paper about shoes, and the paper had evolved from a run-of-the-mill assignment to an all-out obsession. Being a runner, I knew something about running shoes. Being a business buff, I knew that Japanese cameras had made deep cuts into the camera market, which had once been dominated by Germans. Thus, I argued in my paper that Japanese running shoes might do the same thing. The idea interested me, then inspired me, then captivated me. It seemed so obvious, so simple, so potentially huge.

I'd spent weeks and weeks on that paper. I'd moved into the

library, devoured everything I could find about importing and exporting, about starting a company. Finally, as required, I'd given a formal presentation of the paper to my classmates, who reacted with formal boredom. Not one asked a single question. They greeted my passion and intensity with labored sighs and vacant stares.

The professor thought my Crazy Idea had merit: He gave me an A. But that was that. At least, that was supposed to be that. I'd never really stopped thinking about that paper. Through the rest of my time at Stanford, through every morning run and right up to that moment in the TV nook, I'd pondered going to Japan, finding a shoe company, pitching *them* my Crazy Idea, in the hopes that they'd have a more enthusiastic reaction than my classmates, that they'd want to partner with a shy, pale, rail-thin kid from sleepy Oregon.

I'd also toyed with the notion of making an exotic detour on my way to and from Japan. How can I leave my mark on the world, I thought, unless I get out there first and *see* it? Before running a big race, you always want to walk the track. A backpacking trip around the globe might be just the thing, I reasoned. No one talked about bucket lists in those days, but I suppose that's close to what I had in mind. Before I died, became too old or consumed with everyday minutiae, I wanted to visit the planet's most beautiful and wondrous places.

And its most sacred. Of course I wanted to taste other foods, hear other languages, dive into other cultures, but what I really craved was connection with a capital C. I wanted to experience what the Chinese call Tao, the Greeks call Logos, the Hindus call Jñāna, the Buddhists call Dharma. What the Christians call Spirit. Before setting out on my own personal life voyage, I thought, let me first understand the greater voyage of humankind. Let me explore the grandest temples and churches and shrines, the holiest rivers and mountaintops. Let me feel the presence of . . . God?

Yes, I told myself, yes. For want of a better word, God.

But first, I'd need my father's approval.

More, I'd need his cash.

I'd already mentioned making a big trip, the previous year, and my father seemed open to it. But surely he'd forgotten. And surely I was pushing it, adding to the original proposal this Crazy Idea, this outrageous side trip—to Japan? To launch a company? Talk about boondoggles.

Surely he'd see this as a bridge too far.

And a bridge too darned expensive. I had some savings from the Army, and from various part-time jobs over the last several summers. On top of which, I planned to sell my car, a cherry black 1960 MG with racing tires and a twin cam. (The same car Elvis drove in *Blue Hawaii*.) All of which amounted to fifteen hundred dollars, leaving me a grand short, I now told my father. He nodded, uh-huh, mm-hmm, and flicked his eyes from the TV to me, and back again, while I laid it all out.

Remember how we talked, Dad? How I said I want to see the World?

The Himalayas? The pyramids?

The Dead Sea, Dad? The Dead *Sea*?

Well, haha, I'm also thinking of stopping off in Japan, Dad. Remember my Crazy Idea? Japanese running shoes? Right? It could be huge, Dad. Huge.

I was laying it on thick, putting on the hard sell, extra hard, because I always hated selling, and because this particular sell had zero chance. My father had just forked out hundreds of dollars to the University of Oregon, thousands more to Stanford. He was the publisher of the *Oregon Journal*, a solid job that paid for all the basic comforts, including our spacious white house on Claybourne Street, in Portland's quietest suburb, Eastmoreland. But the man wasn't made of money.

Also, this was 1962. The earth was bigger then. Though humans were beginning to orbit the planet in capsules, 90 percent of Americans still had never been on an airplane. The average man or woman had never ventured farther than one hundred miles from his or her own front door, so the mere mention of global travel by airplane would unnerve any father, and especially mine, whose predecessor at the paper had died in an air crash.

Setting aside money, setting aside safety concerns, the whole thing was just so impractical. I was aware that twenty-six of twenty-seven new companies failed, and my father was aware, too, and the idea of taking on such a colossal risk went against everything he stood for. In many ways my father was a conventional Episcopalian, a believer in Jesus Christ. But he also worshipped another secret deity—respectability. Colonial house, beautiful wife, obedient kids, my father enjoyed having these things, but what he really cherished was his friends and neighbors *knowing* he had them. He liked being admired. He liked doing a vigorous backstroke each day in the mainstream. Going around the world on a lark, therefore, would simply make no sense to him. It wasn't done. Certainly not by the respectable sons of respectable men. It was something other people's kids did. Something beatniks and hipsters did.

Possibly, the main reason for my father's respectability fixation was a fear of his inner chaos. I felt this, viscerally, because every now and then that chaos would burst forth. Without warning, late at night, the phone in the front hall would jingle, and when I answered there would be that same gravelly voice on the line. "Come getcher old man."

I'd pull on my raincoat—it always seemed, on those nights, that a misting rain was falling—and drive downtown to my father's club. As clearly as I remember my own bedroom, I remember that club. A century old, with floor-to-ceiling oak bookcases and wing-backed chairs, it looked like the drawing room of an English country house. In other words, eminently respectable.

I'd always find my father at the same table, in the same chair. I'd always help him gently to his feet. "You okay, Dad?" "Course I'm okay." I'd always guide him outside to the car, and the whole way home we'd pretend nothing was wrong. He'd sit perfectly erect, almost regal, and we'd talk sports, because talking sports was how I distracted myself, soothed myself, in times of stress.

My father liked sports, too. Sports were always respectable.

For these and a dozen other reasons I expected my father to greet my pitch in the TV nook with a furrowed brow and a quick put-down. "Haha, Crazy Idea. Fat chance, Buck." (My given name was Philip, but my father always called me Buck. In fact he'd been calling me Buck since before I was born. My mother told me he'd been in the habit of patting her stomach and asking, "How's little Buck today?") As I stopped talking, however, as I stopped pitching, my father rocked forward in his vinyl recliner and shot me a funny look. He said that he always regretted not traveling more when he was young. He said a trip might be just the finishing touch to my education. He said a lot of things, all of them focused more on the trip than the Crazy Idea, but I wasn't about to correct him. I wasn't about to complain, because in sum he was giving his blessing. And his cash.

"Okay," he said. "Okay, Buck. Okay."

I thanked my father and fled the nook before he had a chance to change his mind. Only later did I realize with a spasm of guilt that my father's lack of travel was an ulterior reason, perhaps the main reason, that I wanted to go. This trip, this Crazy Idea, would be one sure way of becoming someone other than him. Someone less respectable.

Or maybe not less respectable. Maybe just less obsessed with respectability.

The rest of the family wasn't quite so supportive. When my grandmother got wind of my itinerary, one item in particular appalled her. "Japan!" she cried. "Why, Buck, it was only a few years ago the Japs were out to kill us! Don't you *remember*? Pearl Harbor! The Japs tried to conquer the world! Some of them still don't know they lost! They're in hiding! They might take you prisoner,

Buck. Gouge out your eyeballs. They're known for that—your *eyeballs*."

I loved my mother's mother, whom we all called Mom Hatfield. And I understood her fear. Japan was about as far as you could get from Roseburg, Oregon, the farm town where she was born and where she'd lived all her life. I'd spent many summers down there with her and Pop Hatfield. Almost every night we'd sat out on the porch, listening to the croaking bullfrogs compete with the console radio, which in the early 1940s was always tuned to news of the war.

Which was always bad.

The Japanese, we were told repeatedly, hadn't lost a war in twenty-six hundred years, and it sure didn't seem they were going to lose this one, either. In battle after battle, we suffered defeat after defeat. Finally, in 1942, Mutual Broadcasting's Gabriel Heatter opened his nightly radio report with a shrill cry. "Good evening, everyone—there's *good news* tonight!" The Americans had won a decisive battle at last. Critics skewered Heatter for his shameless cheerleading, for abandoning all pretense of journalistic objectivity, but the public hatred of Japan was so intense, most people hailed Heatter as a folk hero. Thereafter he opened all broadcasts the same way. "*Good news* tonight!"

It's one of my earliest memories. Mom and Pop Hatfield beside me on that porch, Pop peeling a Gravenstein apple with his pocket-knife, handing me a slice, then eating a slice, then handing me a slice, and so on, until his apple-paring pace slowed dramatically. Heatter was coming on. *Sssh! Hush up!* I can still see us all chewing apples and gazing at the night sky, so Japan-obsessed that we half expected to see Japanese Zeros crisscrossing the Dog Star. No wonder my first time on an airplane, right around five years old, I asked: "Dad, are the Japs going to shoot us down?"

Though Mom Hatfield got the hair on my neck standing up, I told her not to worry, I'd be fine. I'd even bring her back a kimono.

My twin sisters, Jeanne and Joanne, four years younger than

me, didn't seem to care one way or another where I went or what I did.

And my mother, as I recall, said nothing. She rarely did. But there was something different about her silence this time. It equaled consent. Even pride.

I SPENT WEEKS reading, planning, preparing for my trip. I went for long runs, musing on every detail while racing the wild geese as they flew overhead. Their tight V formations—I'd read somewhere that the geese in the rear of the formation, cruising in the backdraft, only have to work 80 percent as hard as the leaders. Every runner understands this. Front runners always work the hardest, and risk the most.

Long before approaching my father, I'd decided it would be good to have a companion on my trip, and that companion should be my Stanford classmate Carter. Though he'd been a hoops star at William Jewell College, Carter wasn't your typical jock. He wore thick glasses and read books. Good books. He was easy to talk to, and easy not to talk to—equally important qualities in a friend. Essential in a travel companion.

But Carter laughed in my face. When I laid out the list of places I wanted to see—Hawaii, Tokyo, Hong Kong, Rangoon, Calcutta, Bombay, Saigon, Kathmandu, Cairo, Istanbul, Athens, Jordan, Jerusalem, Nairobi, Rome, Paris, Vienna, West Berlin, East Berlin, Munich, London—he rocked back on his heels and guffawed. Mortified, I looked down and began to make apologies. Then Carter, still laughing, said: "What a swell idea, Buck!"

I looked up. He wasn't laughing at me. He was laughing with joy, with glee. He was impressed. It took balls to put together an itinerary like that, he said. Balls. He wanted in.

Days later he got the okay from his parents, plus a loan from his father. Carter never did mess around. See an open shot, take it—that was Carter. I told myself there was much I could learn from a guy like that as we circled the earth.

We each packed one suitcase and one backpack. Only the bare necessities, we promised each other. A few pairs of jeans, a few T-shirts. Running shoes, desert boots, sunglasses, plus one pair of suntans—the 1960s word for khakis.

I also packed one good suit. A green Brooks Brothers two-button. Just in case my Crazy Idea came to fruition.

SEPTEMBER 7, 1962. Carter and I piled into his battered old Chevy and drove at warp speed down I-5, through the Willamette Valley, out the wooded bottom of Oregon, which felt like plunging through the roots of a tree. We sped into the piney tip of California, up and over tall green mountain passes, then down, down, until long after midnight we swept into fog-cloaked San Francisco. For several days we stayed with some friends, sleeping on their floor, and then we swung by Stanford and fetched a few of Carter's things out of storage. Finally we stopped at a liquor store and bought two discounted tickets on Standard Airlines to Honolulu. One-way, eighty bucks.

It felt like only minutes later that Carter and I were stepping onto the sandy tarmac of Oahu Airport. We wheeled and looked at the sky and thought: That is not the sky back home.

A line of beautiful girls came toward us. Soft-eyed, olive-skinned, barefoot, they had double-jointed hips, with which they twitched and swished their grass skirts in our faces. Carter and I looked at each other and slowly grinned.

We took a cab to Waikiki Beach and checked into a motel directly across the street from the sea. In one motion we dropped our bags and pulled on our swim trunks. Race you to the water!

As my feet hit the sand I whooped and laughed and kicked off my sneakers, then sprinted directly into the waves. I didn't stop until I was up to my neck in the foam. I dove to the bottom, all the way to the bottom, and then came up gasping, laughing, and rolled onto my back. At last I stumbled onto the shore and plopped onto the sand, smiling at the birds and the clouds. I must have looked like an escaped mental patient. Carter, sitting beside me now, wore the same daffy expression.

"We should stay here," I said. "Why be in a hurry to leave?"

"What about The Plan?" Carter said. "Going around the world?"

"Plans change."

Carter grinned. "Swell idea, Buck."

So we got jobs. Selling encyclopedias door to door. Not glamorous, to be sure, but heck. We didn't start work until 7:00 p.m., which gave us plenty of time for surfing. Suddenly nothing was more important than learning to surf. After only a few tries I was able to stay upright on a board, and after a few weeks I was good. Really good.

Gainfully employed, we ditched our motel room and signed a lease on an apartment, a furnished studio with two beds, one real, one fake—a sort of ironing board that folded out from the wall. Carter, being longer and heavier, got the real bed, and I got the ironing board. I didn't care. After a day of surfing and selling encyclopedias, followed by a late night at the local bars, I could have slept in a luau fire pit. The rent was one hundred bucks a month, which we split down the middle.

Life was sweet. Life was heaven. Except for one small thing. I couldn't sell encyclopedias.

I couldn't sell encyclopedias to save my life. The older I got, it seemed, the shier I got, and the sight of my extreme discomfort often made strangers uncomfortable. Thus, selling anything would have been challenging, but selling *encyclopedias*, which were about as popular in Hawaii as mosquitoes and mainlanders, was an ordeal. No matter how deftly or forcefully I managed to deliver the key phrases drilled into us during our brief training session ("Boys, tell the folks you ain't selling encyclopedias—you're selling a Vast Compendium of Human Knowledge . . . the Answers to Life's Questions!"), I always got the same response.

Beat it, kid.

If my shyness made me bad at selling encyclopedias, my nature made me despise it. I wasn't built for heavy doses of rejection. I'd known this about myself since high school, freshman year, when I got cut from the baseball team. A small setback, in the grand scheme, but it knocked me sideways. It was my first real awareness that not everyone in this world will like us, or accept us, that we're often cast aside at the very moment we most need to be included.

I will never forget that day. Dragging my bat along the sidewalk, I staggered home and holed up in my room, where I grieved, and moped, for about two weeks, until my mother appeared on the edge of my bed and said, "Enough."

She urged me to try something else. "Like what?" I groaned into my pillow. "How about track?" she said. "Track?" I said. "You can run fast, Buck." "I can?" I said, sitting up.

So I went out for track. And I found that I *could* run. And no one could take that away.

Now I gave up selling encyclopedias, and all the old familiar rejection that went with it, and I turned to the want ads. In no time I spotted a small ad inside a thick black border. *Wanted: Securities Salesmen.* I certainly figured to have better luck selling securities. After all, I had an MBA. And before leaving home I'd had a pretty successful interview with Dean Witter.

I did some research and found that this job had two things going for it. First, it was with Investors Overseas Services, which was headed by Bernard Cornfeld, one of the most famous businessmen of the 1960s. Second, it was located in the top floor of a beautiful beachside tower. Twenty-foot windows overlooking that turquoise sea. Both of these things appealed to me, and made me press hard in the interview. Somehow, after weeks of being unable to talk anyone into buying an encyclopedia, I talked Team Cornfeld into taking a flyer on me.

* * *

CORNFELD'S EXTRAORDINARY SUCCESS, plus that breathtaking view, made it possible most days to forget that the firm was nothing more than a boiler room. Cornfeld was notorious for asking his employees if they *sincerely* wanted to be rich, and every day a dozen wolfish young men demonstrated that they did, they *sincerely* did. With ferocity, with abandon, they crashed the phones, cold-calling prospects, scrambling desperately to arrange face-to-face meetings.

I wasn't a smooth talker. I wasn't any kind of talker. Still, I knew numbers, and I knew the product: Dreyfus Funds. More, I knew how to speak the truth. People seemed to like that. I was quickly able to schedule a few meetings, and to close a few sales. Inside a week I'd earned enough in commissions to pay my half of the rent for the next six months, with plenty left over for surfboard wax.

Most of my discretionary income went to the dive bars along the water. Tourists tended to hang out in the luxe resorts, the ones with names like incantations—the Moana, the Halekulani—but Carter and I preferred the dives. We liked to sit with our fellow beachniks and surf bums, seekers and vagabonds, feeling smug about the one thing we had in our favor. Geography. Those poor suckers back home, we'd say. Those poor saps sleepwalking through their humdrum lives, bundled against the cold and rain. Why can't they be more like us? Why can't they seize the day?

Our sense of carpe diem was heightened by the fact that the world was coming to an end. A nuclear standoff with the Soviets had been building for weeks. The Soviets had three dozen missiles in Cuba, the United States wanted them out, and both sides had made their final offer. Negotiations were over and World War III was set to begin any minute. According to the newspapers, missiles would fall from the sky later today. Tomorrow at the latest. The world was Pompeii, and the volcano was already spitting ash. Ah well, everyone in the dive bars agreed, when humanity ends, this will be as good a place as any to watch the rising mushroom clouds. Aloha, civilization.

And then, surprise, the world was spared. The crisis passed. The sky seemed to sigh with relief as the air turned suddenly crisper, calmer. A perfect Hawaiian autumn followed. Days of contentment and something close to bliss.

Followed by a sharp restlessness. One night I set my beer on the bar and turned to Carter. "I think maybe the time has come to leave Shangri-La," I said.

I didn't make a hard pitch. I didn't think I had to. It was clearly time to get back to The Plan. But Carter frowned and stroked his chin. "Gee, Buck, I don't know."

He'd met a girl. A beautiful Hawaiian teenager with long brown legs and jet-black eyes, the kind of girl who'd greeted our airplane, the kind I dreamed of having and never would. He wanted to stick around, and how could I argue?

I told him I understood. But I was cast low. I left the bar and went for a long walk on the beach. Game over, I told myself.

The last thing I wanted was to pack up and return to Oregon. But I couldn't see traveling around the world alone, either. Go home, a faint inner voice told me. Get a normal job. Be a normal person.

Then I heard another faint voice, equally emphatic. No, don't go home. Keep going. Don't stop.

The next day I gave my two weeks' notice at the boiler room. "Too bad, Buck," one of the bosses said, "you had a real future as a salesman." "God forbid," I muttered.

That afternoon, at a travel agency down the block, I purchased an open plane ticket, good for one year on any airline going any-where. A sort of Eurail Pass in the sky. On Thanksgiving Day, 1962, I hoisted my backpack and shook Carter's hand. "Buck," he said, "don't take any wooden nickels."

THE CAPTAIN ADDRESSED the passengers in rapid-fire Japanese, and I started to sweat. I looked out the window at the blazing red circle on the wing. Mom Hatfield was right, I thought. We were *just* at war with these people. Corregidor, the Bataan Death March, the Rape of Nanking—and now I was going there on some sort of *business* venture?

Crazy Idea? Maybe I was, *in fact*, crazy.

If so, it was too late to seek professional help. The plane was screeching down the runway, roaring above Hawaii's cornstarch beaches. I looked down at the massive volcanoes growing smaller and smaller. No turning back.

Since it was Thanksgiving, the in-flight meal was turkey, stuffing, and cranberry sauce. Since we were bound for Japan, there was also raw tuna, miso soup, and hot sake. I ate it all, while reading the paperbacks I'd stuffed into my backpack. *The Catcher in the Rye* and *Naked Lunch*. I identified with Holden Caulfield, the teenage introvert seeking his place in the world, but Burroughs went right over my head. *The junk merchant doesn't sell his product to the consumer, he sells the consumer to his product.*

Too rich for my blood. I passed out. When I woke we were in a steep, rapid descent. Below us lay a startlingly bright Tokyo. The Ginza in particular was like a Christmas tree.

Driving to my hotel, however, I saw only darkness. Vast sections of the city were total liquid black. "War," the cabdriver said. "Many building still bomb."

American B-29s. Superfortresses. Over a span of several nights in the summer of 1944, waves of them dropped 750,000 pounds of bombs, most filled with gasoline and flammable jelly. One of the world's oldest cities, Tokyo was made largely of wood, so the bombs set off a hurricane of fire. Some three hundred thousand people were burned alive, instantly, four times the number who died in Hiroshima. More than a million were gruesomely injured. And nearly 80 percent of the buildings were vaporized. For long, solemn stretches the cabdriver and I said nothing. There was nothing to say.

Finally the driver stopped at the address written in my notebook. A dingy hostel. Beyond dingy. I'd made the reservation through American Express, sight unseen, a mistake, I now realized. I crossed the pitted sidewalk and entered a building that seemed about to implode.

An old Japanese woman behind the front desk bowed to me. I realized she wasn't bowing, she was bent by age, like a tree that's weathered many storms. Slowly she led me to my room, which was more a box. Tatami mat, lopsided table, nothing else. I didn't care. I barely noticed that the tatami mat was wafer thin. I bowed to the bent old woman, bidding her good night. *Oyasumi nasai.* I curled up on the mat and passed out.

HOURS LATER I woke in a room flooded with light. I crawled to the window. Apparently I was in some kind of industrial district on the city's fringe. Filled with docks and factories, this district must have been a primary target of the B-29s. Everywhere I looked was desolation. Buildings cracked and broken. Block after block simply leveled. Gone.

Luckily my father knew people in Tokyo, including a group of American guys working at United Press International. I took a cab there and the guys greeted me like family. They gave me coffee and a breakfast ring and when I told them where I'd spent the night they laughed. They booked me into a clean, decent hotel. Then they wrote down the names of several good places to eat.

What in God's name are you doing in Tokyo? I explained that I was going around the world. Then I mentioned my Crazy Idea. "Huh," they said, giving a little eye roll. They mentioned two ex-GIs who ran a monthly magazine called *Importer*. "Talk to the fellas at *Importer*," they said, "before you do anything rash."

I promised I would. But first I wanted to see the city.

Guidebook and Minolta box camera in hand, I sought out the

few landmarks that had survived the war, the oldest temples and shrines. I spent hours sitting on benches in walled gardens, reading about Japan's dominant religions, Buddhism and Shinto. I marveled at the concept of *kensho*, or satori—enlightenment that comes in a flash, a blinding pop. Sort of like the bulb on my Minolta. I liked that. I wanted that.

But first I'd need to change my whole approach. I was a linear thinker, and according to Zen linear thinking is nothing but a delusion, one of the many that keep us unhappy. Reality is nonlinear, Zen says. No future, no past. All is now.

In every religion, it seemed, self is the obstacle, the enemy. And yet Zen declares plainly that the self doesn't exist. Self is a mirage, a fever dream, and our stubborn belief in its reality not only wastes life, but shortens it. Self is the bald-faced lie we tell ourselves daily, and happiness requires seeing through the lie, debunking it. *To study the self,* said the thirteenth-century Zen master Dogen, *is to forget the self.* Inner voice, outer voices, it's all the same. No dividing lines.

Especially in competition. Victory, Zen says, comes when we forget the self and the opponent, who are but two halves of one whole. In *Zen and the Art of Archery*, it's all laid out with crystal clarity. *Perfection in the art of swordsmanship is reached . . . when the heart is troubled by no more thought of I and You, of the opponent and his sword, of one's own sword and how to wield it. . . . All is emptiness: your own self, the flashing sword, and the arms that wield it. Even the thought of emptiness is no longer there.*

My head swimming, I decided to take a break, to visit a very un-Zen landmark, in fact the most anti-Zen place in Japan, an enclave where men focused on self and nothing but self—the Tokyo Stock Exchange. Housed in a marble Romanesque building with great big Greek columns, the Tosho looked from across the street like a stodgy bank in a quiet town in Kansas. Inside, however, all was bedlam. Hundreds of men waving their arms, pulling their hair, screaming. A more depraved version of Cornfeld's boiler room.

I couldn't look away. I watched and watched, asking myself, Is this what it's all about? Really? I appreciated money as much as the next guy. But I wanted my life to be about so much more.

After the Tosho I needed peace. I went deep into the silent heart of the city, to the garden of the nineteenth-century emperor Meiji and his empress, a space thought to possess immense spiritual power. I sat, contemplative, reverent, beneath swaying ginkgo trees, beside a beautiful torii gate. I read in my guidebook that a torii gate is usually a portal to sacred places, and so I basked in the sacredness, the serenity, trying to soak it all in.

The next morning I laced up my running shoes and jogged to Tsukiji, the world's largest fish market. It was the Tosho all over again, with shrimp instead of stocks. I watched ancient fishermen spread their catches onto wooden carts and haggle with leather-faced merchants. That night I took a bus up to the lakes region, in the northern Hakone Mountains, an area that inspired many of the great Zen poets. *You cannot travel the path until you have become the path yourself*, said the Buddha, and I stood in awe before a path that twisted from the glassy lakes to cloud-ringed Mount Fuji, a perfect snow-clad triangle that looked to me exactly like Mount Hood back home. The Japanese believe climbing Fuji is a mystical experience, a ritual act of celebration, and I was overcome with a desire to climb it, right then. I wanted to ascend into the clouds. I decided to wait, however. I would return when I had something to celebrate.

I WENT BACK to Tokyo and presented myself at *Importer*. The two ex-GIs in charge, thick-necked, brawny, very busy, looked as if they might chew me out for intruding and wasting their time. But within minutes their gruff exterior dissolved and they were warm, friendly, pleased to meet someone from back home. We talked mostly about sports. Can you believe the Yankees won it all again? How about that Willie Mays? None better. Yessir, none better.

Then they told me their story.

They were the first Americans I ever met who loved Japan. Stationed there during the Occupation, they fell under the spell of the culture, the food, the women, and when their hitch was up they simply couldn't bring themselves to leave. So they'd launched an import magazine, when no one anywhere was interested in importing anything Japanese, and somehow they'd managed to keep it afloat for seventeen years.

I told them my Crazy Idea and they listened with some interest. They made a pot of coffee and invited me to sit down. Was there a particular line of Japanese shoes I'd considered importing? they asked.

I told them I liked Tiger, a nifty brand manufactured by Onitsuka Co., down in Kobe, the largest city in southern Japan.

"Yes, yes, we've seen it," they said.

I told them I was thinking of heading down there, meeting the Onitsuka people face to face.

In that case, the ex-GIs said, you'd better learn a few things about doing business with the Japanese.

"The key," they said, "is don't be pushy. Don't come on like the typical asshole American, the typical gaijin—rude, loud, aggressive, not taking no for an answer. The Japanese do not react well to the hard sell. Negotiations here tend to be soft, sinewy. Look how long it took the Americans and Russians to coax Hirohito into surrendering. And even when he did surrender, when his country was reduced to a heap of ashes, what did he tell his people? 'The war situation hasn't developed to Japan's advantage.' It's a culture of indirection. No one ever turns you down flat. No one ever says, straight out, no. But they don't say yes, either. They speak in circles, sentences with no clear subject or object. Don't be discouraged, but don't be cocky. You might leave a man's office thinking you've blown it, when in fact he's ready to do a deal. You might leave thinking you've closed a deal, when in fact you've just been rejected. *You never know.*"

I frowned. Under the best of circumstances I was not a great negotiator. Now I was going to have to negotiate in some kind of funhouse with trick mirrors? Where normal rules didn't apply?

After an hour of this baffling tutorial, I shook hands with the ex-GIs and said my good-byes. Feeling suddenly that I couldn't wait, that I needed to strike quickly, while their words were fresh in my mind, I raced back to my hotel, threw everything into my little suitcase and backpack, and phoned Onitsuka to make an appointment.

Later that afternoon I boarded a train south.

JAPAN WAS RENOWNED for its impeccable order and extreme cleanliness. Japanese literature, philosophy, clothing, domestic life, all were marvelously pure and spare. Minimalist. *Expect nothing, seek nothing, grasp nothing*—the immortal Japanese poets wrote lines that seemed polished and polished until they gleamed like the blade of a samurai's sword, or the stones of a mountain brook. Spotless.

So why, I wondered, is this train to Kobe so filthy?

The floors were strewn with newspapers and cigarette butts. The seats were covered with orange rinds and discarded newspapers. Worse, every car was packed. There was barely room to stand.

I found a strap by a window and hung there for seven hours as the train rocked and inched past remote villages, past farms no bigger than the average Portland backyard. The trip was long, but neither my legs nor my patience gave out. I was too busy going over and over my tutorial with the ex-GIs.

When I arrived I took a small room in a cheap *ryokan*. My appointment at Onitsuka was early the next morning, so I lay down immediately on the tatami mat. But I was too excited to sleep. I rolled around on the mat most of the night, and at dawn I rose wearily and stared at my gaunt, bleary reflection in the mirror. After shaving, I put on my green Brooks Brothers suit and gave myself a pep talk.

You are capable. You are confident. You can do this.

You can DO this.

Then I went to the wrong place.

I presented myself at the Onitsuka showroom, when in fact I was expected at the Onitsuka *factory*—across town. I hailed a taxi and raced there, frantic, arriving half an hour late. Unfazed, a group of four executives met me in the lobby. They bowed. I bowed. One stepped forward. He said his name was Ken Miyazaki, and he wished to give me a tour.

The first shoe factory I'd ever seen. I found everything about it interesting. Even musical. Each time a shoe was molded, the metal last would fall to the floor with a silvery tinkle, a melodic CLING-*clong*. Every few seconds, CLING-*clong*, CLING-*clong*, a cobbler's concerto. The executives seemed to enjoy it, too. They smiled at me and each other.

We passed through the accounting department. Everyone in the room, men and women, leaped from their chairs, and in unison bowed, a gesture of *kei*, respect for the American tycoon. I'd read that "tycoon" came from *taikun*, Japanese for "warlord." I didn't know how to acknowledge their *kei*. To bow or not bow, that is always the question in Japan. I gave a weak smile and a half bow, and kept moving.

The executives told me that they churned out fifteen thousand pairs of shoes each month. "Impressive," I said, not knowing if that was a lot or a little. They led me into a conference room and pointed me to the chair at the head of a long round table. "Mr. Knight," someone said, "*here*."

Seat of honor. More *kei*. They arranged themselves around the table and straightened their ties and gazed at me. The moment of truth had arrived.

I'd rehearsed this scene in my head so many times, as I'd rehearsed every race I'd ever run, long before the starting pistol. But now I realized this was no race. There is a primal urge to compare everything—life, business, adventures of all sorts—to a race. But the metaphor is often inadequate. It can take you only so far.

Unable to remember what I'd wanted to say, or even why I was here, I took several quick breaths. Everything depended on my rising to this occasion. Everything. If I didn't, if I muffed this, I'd be doomed to spend the rest of my days selling encyclopedias, or mutual funds, or some other junk I didn't really care about. I'd be a disappointment to my parents, my school, my hometown. Myself.

I looked at the faces around the table. Whenever I'd imagined this scene, I'd omitted one crucial element. I'd failed to foresee how present World War II would be in that room. The war was right *there*, beside us, between us, attaching a subtext to every word we spoke. *Good evening, everyone—there's good news tonight!*

And yet it also *wasn't* there. Through their resilience, through their stoic acceptance of total defeat, and their heroic reconstruction of their nation, the Japanese had put the war cleanly behind them. Also, these executives in the conference room were young, like me, and you could see that they felt the war had nothing to do with them.

On the other hand, their fathers and uncles had tried to kill mine.

On the other hand, the past was past.

On the other hand, that whole question of Winning and Losing, which clouds and complicates so many deals, gets even more complicated when the potential winners and losers have recently been involved, albeit via proxies and ancestors, in a global conflagration.

All of this interior static, this seesawing confusion about war and peace, created a low-volume hum in my head, an awkwardness for which I was unprepared. The realist in me wanted to acknowledge it, the idealist in me pushed it aside. I coughed into my fist. "Gentlemen," I began.

Mr. Miyazaki interrupted. "Mr. Knight—what company are you with?" he asked.

"Ah, yes, good question."

Adrenaline surging through my blood, I felt the flight response, the longing to run and hide, which made me think of the safest place in the world. My parents' house. The house had been built decades before, by people of means, people with much more money than my parents, and thus the architect had included servants' quarters at the back of the house, and these quarters were my bedroom, which I'd filled with baseball cards, record albums, posters, books—all things holy. I'd also covered one wall with my blue ribbons from track, the one thing in my life of which I was unabashedly proud. And so? "Blue Ribbon," I blurted. "Gentlemen, I represent Blue Ribbon Sports of Portland, Oregon."

Mr. Miyazaki smiled. The other executives smiled. A murmur went around the table. *Blueribbon, blueribbon, blueribbon.* The executives folded their hands and fell silent again and resumed staring at me. "Well," I began again, "gentlemen, the American shoe market is enormous. And largely untapped. If Onitsuka can penetrate that market, if Onitsuka can get its Tigers into American stores, and price them to undercut Adidas, which most American athletes now wear, it could be a hugely profitable venture."

I was simply quoting my presentation at Stanford, verbatim, speaking lines and numbers I'd spent weeks and weeks researching and memorizing, and this helped to create an illusion of eloquence. I could see that the executives were impressed. But when I reached the end of my pitch there was a prickling silence. Then one man broke the silence, and then another, and now they were all speaking over one another in loud, excited voices. Not to me, but to each other.

Then, abruptly, they all stood and left.

Was this the customary Japanese way of rejecting a Crazy Idea? To stand in unison and leave? Had I squandered my *kei*—just like that? Was I dismissed? What should I do? Should I just . . . leave?

After a few minutes they returned. They were carrying sketches, samples, which Mr. Miyazaki helped to spread before me. "Mr. Knight," he said, "we've been thinking long time about American market."

"You have?"

"We already sell wrestling shoe in United States. In, eh, Northeast? But we discuss many time bringing other lines to other places in America."

They showed me three different models of Tigers. A training shoe, which they called a Limber Up. "Nice," I said. A high-jump shoe, which they called a Spring Up. "Lovely," I said. And a discus shoe, which they called a Throw Up.

Do not laugh, I told myself. Do not . . . laugh.

They barraged me with questions about the United States, about American culture and consumer trends, about different kinds of athletic shoes available in American sporting goods stores. They asked me how big I thought the American shoe market was, how big it could be, and I told them that ultimately it could be $1 billion. To this day I'm not sure where that number came from. They leaned back, gazed at each other, astonished. Now, to my astonishment, they began pitching *me*. "Would Blue Ribbon . . . be interested . . . in representing Tiger shoes? In the United States?" "Yes," I said. "Yes, it *would*."

I held forth the Limber Up. "This is a good shoe," I said. "This shoe—I can sell this shoe." I asked them to ship me samples right away. I gave them my address and promised to send them a money order for fifty dollars.

They stood. They bowed deeply. I bowed deeply. We shook hands. I bowed again. They bowed again. We all smiled. The war had never happened. We were partners. We were brothers. The meeting, which I'd expected to last fifteen minutes, had gone two hours.

From Onitsuka I went straight to the nearest American Express office and sent a letter to my father. *Dear Dad: Urgent. Please wire fifty dollars right away to Onitsuka Corp of Kobe.*

Ho ho, hee hee . . . strange things are happening.

BACK IN MY hotel I walked in circles around my tatami mat, trying to decide. Part of me wanted to race back to Oregon, wait for those samples, get a jump on my new business venture.

Also, I was crazed with loneliness, cut off from everything and everyone I knew. The occasional sight of a *New York Times*, or a *Time* magazine, gave me a lump in my throat. I was a castaway, a kind of modern Crusoe. I wanted to be home again. Now.

And yet. I was still aflame with curiosity about the world. I still wanted to see, to explore.

Curiosity won.

I went to Hong Kong and walked the mad, chaotic streets, horrified by the sight of legless, armless beggars, old men kneeling in filth, alongside pleading orphans. The old men were mute, but the children had a cry they repeated: *Hey, rich man, hey, rich man, hey, rich man.* Then they'd weep or slap the ground. Even after I gave them all the money in my pockets, the cry never stopped.

I went to the edge of the city, climbed to the top of Victoria Peak, gazed off into the distance at China. In college I'd read the analects of Confucius—*The man who moves a mountain begins by carrying away small stones*—and now I felt strongly that I'd never have a chance to move this particular mountain. I'd never get any closer to that walled-off mystical land, and it made me feel unaccountably sad. Incomplete.

I went to the Philippines, which had all the madness and chaos of Hong Kong, and twice the poverty. I moved slowly, as if in a nightmare, through Manila, through endless crowds and fathomless gridlock, toward the hotel where MacArthur once occupied the penthouse. I was fascinated by all the great generals, from Alexander the Great to George Patton. I hated war, but I loved the warrior spirit. I hated the sword, but loved the samurai. And of all the great fighting men in history I found MacArthur the most compelling. Those Ray-Bans, that corncob pipe—the man didn't lack for confidence. Brilliant tactician, master motivator, he also went on to head the U.S. Olympic Committee. How could I not love him?

Of course, he was deeply flawed. But he knew that. *You are remembered*, he said, prophetically, *for the rules you break*.

I wanted to book a night in his former suite. But I couldn't afford it.

One day, I vowed. One day I shall return.

I went to Bangkok, where I rode a long pole boat through murky swamps to an open-air market that seemed a Thai version of Hieronymous Bosch. I ate birds, and fruits, and vegetables I'd never seen before, and never would again. I dodged rickshaws, scooters, *tuk-tuks*, and elephants to reach Wat Phra Kaew, and one of the most sacred statues in Asia, an enormous six-hundred-year-old Buddha carved from a single hunk of jade. Standing before its placid face I asked, *Why am I here? What is my purpose?*

I waited.

Nothing.

Or else the silence was my answer.

I went to Vietnam, where streets were bristling with American soldiers, and thrumming with fear. Everyone knew that war was coming, and that it would be very ugly, very different. It would be a Lewis Carroll war, the kind in which a U.S. officer would declare: *We had to destroy the village in order to save it*. Days before Christmas, 1962, I went on to Calcutta, and rented a room the size of a coffin. No bed, no chair: there wasn't enough space. Just a hammock suspended above a fizzing hole—the toilet. Within hours I fell ill. An airborne virus, probably, or food poisoning. For one whole day I believed that I wouldn't make it. I knew that I was going to die.

But I rallied, somehow, forced myself out of that hammock, and the next day I was walking unsteadily with thousands of pilgrims and dozens of sacred monkeys down the steep staircase of Varanasi temple. The steps led directly into the hot seething Ganges. When the water was at my waist I looked up—a mirage? No, a funeral, taking place in the middle of the river. In fact, several funerals. I watched mourners wade out into the current and place their loved ones atop tall wooden biers, then set them afire. Not twenty yards away, others were calmly bathing. Still others were slaking their thirst with the same water.

The Upanishads say, *Lead me from the unreal to the real.* So I fled the unreal. I flew to Kathmandu and hiked straight up the clean white wall of the Himalayas. On the descent I stopped at a crowded *chowk* and devoured a bowl of buffalo meat, blood rare. The Tibetans in the *chowk*, I noted, wore boots of red wool and green flannel, with upturned wooden toes, not unlike the runners on sleds. Suddenly I was *noticing* everyone's shoes.

I went back to India, spent New Year's Eve wandering the streets of Bombay, weaving in and out among oxen and long-horned cows, feeling the start of an epic migraine—the noise and the smells, the colors and the glare. I went on to Kenya, and took a long bus ride deep into the bush. Giant ostriches tried to outrun the bus, and storks the size of pit bulls floated just outside the windows. Every time the driver stopped, in the middle of nowhere, to pick up a few Masai warriors, a baboon or two would try to board. The driver and warriors would then chase the baboons off with machetes. Before stepping off the bus, the baboons would always glance over their shoulders and give me a look of wounded pride. Sorry, old man, I thought. If it were up to me.

I went to Cairo, to the Giza plateau, and stood beside desert nomads and their silk-draped camels at the foot of the Great Sphinx, all of us squinting up into its eternally open eyes. The sun hammered down on my head, the same sun that hammered down on the thousands of men who built these pyramids, and the millions of visitors who came after. Not one of them was remembered, I thought. All is vanity, says the Bible. All is now, says Zen. All is dust, says the desert.

I went to Jerusalem, to the rock where Abraham prepared to kill his son, where Muhammad began his heavenward ascent. The Koran says the rock wanted to join Muhammad, and tried to follow, but Muhammad pressed his foot to the rock and stopped it. His footprint is said to be still visible. Was he barefoot or wearing a shoe? I ate a terrible midday meal in a dark tavern, surrounded by soot-faced laborers. Each looked bone-tired. They chewed slowly, absently, like zombies. Why must we work so hard? I thought. *Consider the lilies of the field . . . they neither toil nor spin.* And yet the first-century rabbi Eleazar ben Azariah said our work is the holiest part of us. *All are proud of their craft. God speaks of his work; how much more should man.*

I went on to Istanbul, got wired on Turkish coffee, got lost on the twisty streets beside the Bosphorus. I stopped to sketch the glowing minarets, and toured the golden labyrinths of Topkapi Palace, home of the Ottoman sultans, where Muhammad's sword is now kept. *Don't go to sleep one night*, wrote Rūmī, the thirteenth-century Persian poet. *What you most want will come to you then.*

Warmed by a sun inside you'll see wonders.

I went to Rome, spent days hiding in small trattorias, scarfing mountains of pasta, gazing upon the most beautiful women, and shoes, I'd ever seen. (Romans in the age of the Caesars believed that putting on the right shoe before the left brought prosperity and good luck.) I explored the grassy ruins of Nero's bedroom, the gorgeous rubble of the Coliseum, the vast halls and rooms of the Vatican. Expecting crowds, I was always out the door at dawn, determined to be first in line. But there was never a line. The city was mired in a historic cold snap. I had it all to myself.

Even the Sistine Chapel. Alone under Michelangelo's ceiling, I was able to wallow in my disbelief. I read in my guidebook that Michelangelo was miserable while painting his masterpiece. His back and neck ached. Paint fell constantly into his hair and eyes.

He couldn't wait to be finished, he told friends. If even Michel-angelo didn't like his work, I thought, what hope is there for the rest of us?

I went to Florence, spent days seeking Dante, reading Dante, the angry, exiled misanthrope. Did the misanthropy come first—or after? Was it the cause or the effect of his anger and exile?

I stood before the David, shocked at the anger in his eyes. Goliath never had a *chance*.

I went by train up to Milan, communed with Da Vinci, consid-ered his beautiful notebooks, and wondered at his peculiar obses-sions. Chief among them, the human foot. *Masterpiece of engineering*, he called it. *A work of art*.

Who was I to argue?

On my last night in Milan I attended the opera at La Scala. I aired out my Brooks Brothers suit and wore it proudly amid the *uomini* poured into custom-tailored tuxedos and the *donne* molded into bejeweled gowns. We all listened in wonder to *Turandot*. As Calaf sang "Nessun dorma"—*Set, stars! At dawn I will win, I will win, I will win!*—my eyes welled, and with the fall of the curtain I leaped to my feet. *Bravissimo!*

I went to Venice, spent a few languorous days walking in the footsteps of Marco Polo, and stood I don't know how long before the palazzo of Robert Browning. *If you get simple beauty and naught else, you get about the best thing God invents.*

My time was running out. Home was calling to me. I hurried to Paris, descended far belowground to the Pantheon, put my hand lightly on the crypts of Rousseau—and Voltaire. *Love truth, but par-don error.* I took a room in a seedy hotel, watched sheets of winter rain sluice the alley below my window, prayed at Notre Dame, got lost in the Louvre. I bought a few books at Shakespeare and Company, and I stood in the spot where Joyce slept, and F. Scott Fitzgerald. I then walked slowly down the Seine, stopping to sip a cappuccino at the café where Hemingway and Dos Passos read the New Testament aloud to each other. On my last day I sauntered up the Champs-Élysées, tracing the liberators' path, thinking all the while of Patton. *Don't tell people how to do things, tell them what to do and let them surprise you with their results.*

Of all the great generals, he was the most shoe-obsessed: *A soldier in shoes is only a soldier. But in boots he becomes a warrior.*

I flew to Munich, drank an ice-cold stein of beer at the Bür-gerbräukeller, where Hitler fired a gun into the ceiling and started everything. I tried to visit Dachau, but when I asked for directions people looked away, professing not to know. I went to Berlin and presented myself at Checkpoint Charlie. Flat-faced Russian guards in heavy topcoats examined my passport, patted me down, asked what business I had in communist East Berlin. "None," I said. I was terrified that they'd somehow find out I'd attended Stanford. Just before I arrived two Stanford students had tried to smuggle a teen-ager out in a Volkswagen. They were still in prison.

But the guards waved me through. I walked a little ways and stopped at the corner of Marx-Engels-Platz. I looked around, all directions. Nothing. No trees, no stores, no life. I thought of all the poverty I'd seen in every corner of Asia. This was a different kind of poverty, more willful, somehow, more preventable. I saw three children playing in the street. I walked over, took their picture. Two boys and a girl, eight years old. The girl—red wool hat, pink coat—smiled directly at me. Will I ever forget her? Or her shoes? They were made of cardboard.

I went to Vienna, that momentous, coffee-scented crossroads, where Stalin and Trotsky and Tito and Hitler and Jung and Freud all lived, at the same historical moment, and all loitered in the same steamy cafés, plotting how to save (or end) the world. I walked the cobblestones Mozart walked, crossed his graceful Danube on the most beautiful stone bridge I ever saw, stopped before the towering spires of St. Stephen's Church, where Beethoven discovered he was deaf. He looked up, saw birds fluttering from the bell tower, and to his horror . . . he did not hear the bells.

At last I flew to London. I went quickly to Buckingham Palace, Speakers' Corner, Harrods. I granted myself a bit of extra time at Commons. Eyes closed, I conjured the great Churchill. *You ask, What is our aim? I can answer in one word. It is victory, victory at all costs, victory in spite of all terror, victory . . . without victory, there is no survival.* I wanted desperately to hop a bus to Stratford, to see Shakespeare's house. (Elizabethan women wore a red silk rose on the toe of each shoe.) But I was out of time.

I spent my last night thinking back over my trip, making notes in my journal. I asked myself, What was the highlight?

Greece, I thought. No question. Greece.

When I first left Oregon I was most excited about two things on my itinerary.

I wanted to pitch the Japanese my Crazy Idea.

And I wanted to stand before the Acropolis.

Hours before boarding my flight at Heathrow, I meditated on that moment, looking up at those astonishing columns, experiencing that bracing shock, the kind you receive from all great beauty, but mixed with a powerful sense of—recognition?

Was it only my imagination? After all, I was standing at the birthplace of Western civilization. Maybe I merely *wanted* it to be familiar. But I didn't think so. I had the clearest thought: I've been here before.

Then, walking up those bleached steps, another thought: This is where it all begins.

On my left was the Parthenon, which Plato had watched the teams of architects and workmen build. On my right was the Temple of Athena Nike. Twenty-five centuries ago, per my guidebook, it had housed a beautiful frieze of the goddess Athena, thought to be the bringer of "nike," or victory.

It was one of many blessings Athena bestowed. She also rewarded the dealmakers. In the *Oresteia* she says: "I admire . . . the eyes of persuasion." She was, in a sense, the patron saint of negotiators.

I don't know how long I stood there, absorbing the energy and power of that epochal place. An hour? Three? I don't know how long after that day I discovered the Aristophanes play, set in the Temple of Nike, in which the warrior gives the king a gift—a pair of new shoes. I don't know when I figured out that the play was called *Knights*. I do know that as I turned to leave I noticed the temple's marble façade. Greek artisans had decorated it with several haunting carvings, including the most famous, in which the goddess inexplicably leans down . . . to adjust the strap of her shoe.

FEBRUARY 24, 1963. My twenty-fifth birthday. I walked through the door on Claybourne Street, hair to my shoulders, beard three inches long. My mother let out a cry. My sisters blinked as if they didn't recognize me, or else hadn't realized I'd been gone. Hugs, shouts, bursts of laughter. My mother made me sit, poured me a cup of coffee. She wanted to hear everything. But I was exhausted. I set my suitcase and backpack in the hall and went to my room. I stared blearily at my blue ribbons. Mr. Knight, what is the name of your company?

I curled up on the bed and sleep came down like the curtain at La Scala.

An hour later I woke to my mother calling out, "Dinner!"

My father was home from work, and he embraced me as I came into the dining room. He, too, wanted to hear every detail. And I wanted to tell him.

But first I wanted to know one thing.

"Dad," I said. "Did my shoes come?"

1963

My father invited all the neighbors over for coffee and cake and a special viewing of "Buck's slides." Dutifully, I stood at the slide projector, savoring the darkness, listlessly clicking the advance button and describing the pyramids, the Temple of Nike, but I wasn't there. I was at the pyramids, I was at the Temple of Nike. I was wondering about my shoes.

Four months after the big meeting at Onitsuka, after I'd connected with those executives, and won them over, or so I thought—and still the shoes hadn't arrived. I fired off a letter. *Dear Sirs, Re our meeting of last fall, have you had a chance to ship the samples . . . ?* Then I took a few days off, to sleep, wash my clothes, catch up with friends.

I got a speedy reply from Onitsuka. "Shoes coming," the letter said. "In just a little more days."

I showed the letter to my father. He winced. *A little more days?* "Buck," he said, chuckling, "that fifty bucks is long gone."

MY NEW LOOK—CASTAWAY hair, caveman beard—was too much for my mother and sisters. I'd catch them staring, frowning. I could hear them thinking: bum. So I shaved. Afterward I stood before the little mirror on my bureau in the servants' quarters and told myself, "It's official. You're back."

And yet I wasn't. There was something about me that would never return.

My mother noticed it before anyone else. Over dinner one night she gave me a long, searching look. "You seem more . . . worldly."

Worldly, I thought. Gosh.

UNTIL THE SHOES arrived, whether or not the shoes ever arrived, I'd need to find some way to earn cash money. Before my trip I'd had that interview with Dean Witter. Maybe I could go back there. I ran it by my father, in the TV nook. He stretched out in his vinyl recliner and suggested I first go have a chat with his old friend Don Frisbee, CEO of Pacific Power & Light.

I knew Mr. Frisbee. In college I'd done a summer internship for him. I liked him, and I liked that he'd graduated from Harvard Business School. When it came to schools, I was a bit of a snob. Also, I marveled that he'd gone on, rather quickly, to become CEO of a New York Stock Exchange company.

I recall that he welcomed me warmly that spring day in 1963, that he gave me one of those double-handed handshakes and led me into his office, into a chair across from his desk. He settled into his big high-backed leather throne and raised his eyebrows. "So . . . what's on your mind?"

"Honestly, Mr. Frisbee, I don't know what to do . . . about . . . or with . . . a job . . . or career . . ."

Weakly, I added: "My life."

I said I was thinking of going to Dean Witter. Or else maybe coming back to the electric company. Or else maybe working for some large corporation. The light from Mr. Frisbee's office window glinted off his rimless glasses and into my eyes. Like the sun off the Ganges. "Phil," he said, "those are all bad ideas."

"Sir?"

"I don't think you should do any of those things."

"Oh."

"Everyone, but everyone, changes jobs at least three times. So if you go to work for an investment firm now, you'll eventually leave, and then at your next job you'll have to start all over. If you go work for some big company, son, same deal. No, what you want to do, while you're young, is get your CPA. That, along with your MBA, will put a solid floor under your earnings. Then, when you change jobs, which you will, trust me, at least you'll maintain your salary level. You won't go backward."

That sounded practical. I certainly didn't want to go backward.

I hadn't majored in accounting, however. I needed nine more hours to even qualify to take the exam. So I quickly enrolled in three accounting classes at Portland State. "*More* school?" my father grumbled.

Worse, the school in question wasn't Stanford or Oregon. It was puny little Portland State.

I wasn't the only school snob in the family.

AFTER GETTING MY nine hours I worked at an accounting firm, Lybrand, Ross Bros. & Montgomery. It was one of the Big Eight national firms, but its Portland branch office was small. One partner, three junior accountants. Suits me, I thought. Smallness meant the firm would be intimate, conducive to learning.

And it did start out that way. My first assignment was a Beaverton company, Reser's Fine Foods, and as the solo man on the job I got to spend quality time with the CEO, Al Reser, who was just three years older than me. I picked up some important lessons from him, and enjoyed my time poring over his books. But I was too overworked to fully enjoy it. The trouble with a small satellite branch within a big accounting firm is the workload. Whenever extra work came rolling in, there was no one to take up the slack. During the busy season, November through April, we found ourselves up to our ears, logging twelve-hour days, six days a week, which didn't leave much time to learn.

Also, we were watched. Closely. Our minutes were counted, to the second. When President Kennedy was killed that November I asked for the day off. I wanted to sit in front of the TV with the rest of the nation and mourn. My boss, however, shook his head. Work first, mourn second. *Consider the lilies of the field . . . they neither toil nor spin.*

I had two consolations. One was money. I was earning five hundred dollars a month, which enabled me to buy a new car. I couldn't justify another MG, so I bought a Plymouth Valiant. Reliable, but with some pizzazz. And a dash of color. The salesman called it seafoam green. My friends called it vomit green.

It was actually the green of newly minted money.

My other consolation was lunch. Each day at noon I'd walk down the street to the local travel agency and stand like Walter Mitty before the posters in the window. Switzerland. Tahiti. Moscow. Bali. I'd grab a brochure and leaf through it while eating a peanut butter and jelly sandwich on a bench in the park. I'd ask the pigeons: Can you believe it was only a year ago that I was surfing Waikiki? Eating water buffalo stew after an early morning hike in the Himalayas?

Are the best moments of my life behind me?

Was my trip around the world . . . my peak?

The pigeons were less responsive than the statue at Wat Phra Kaew.

This is how I spent 1963. Quizzing pigeons. Polishing my Valiant. Writing letters.

Dear Carter, Did you ever leave Shangri-La? I'm an accountant now and giving some thought to blowing my brains out.

1964

The notice arrived right around Christmas, so I must have driven down to the waterfront warehouse the first week of 1964. I don't recall exactly. I know it was early morning. I can see myself getting there before the clerks unlocked the doors.

I handed them the notice and they went into the back and returned with a large box covered in Japanese writing.

I raced home, scurried down to the basement, ripped open the box. Twelve pairs of shoes, creamy white, with blue stripes down the sides. God, they were beautiful. They were more than beautiful. I'd seen nothing in Florence or Paris that surpassed them. I wanted to put them on marble pedestals, or in gilt-edged frames. I held them up to the light, caressed them as sacred objects, the way a writer might treat a new set of notebooks, or a baseball player a rack of bats.

Then I sent two pairs to my old track coach at Oregon, Bill Bowerman.

I did so without a second thought, since it was Bowerman who'd first made me think, really *think*, about what people put on their feet. Bowerman was a genius coach, a master motivator, a natural leader of young men, and there was one piece of gear he deemed crucial to their development. Shoes. He was obsessed with how human beings are shod.

In the four years I'd run for him at Oregon, Bowerman was constantly sneaking into our lockers and stealing our footwear. He'd spend days tearing them apart, stitching them back up, then hand them back with some minor modification, which made us either run like deer or bleed. Regardless of the results, he never stopped. He was determined to find new ways of bolstering the instep, cushioning the midsole, building out more room for the forefoot. He always had some new design, some new scheme to make our shoes sleeker, softer, lighter. Especially lighter. One ounce sliced off a pair of shoes, he said, is equivalent to 55 pounds over one mile. He wasn't kidding. His math was solid. You take the average man's stride of six feet, spread it out over a mile (5,280 feet), you get 880 steps. Remove one ounce from each step—that's 55 pounds on the button. Lightness, Bowerman believed, directly translated to less burden, which meant more energy, which meant more speed. And speed equaled winning. Bowerman didn't like to lose. (I got it from him.) Thus lightness was his constant goal.

Goal is putting it kindly. In quest of lightness he was willing to try anything. Animal, vegetable, mineral, any material was eligible if it might improve on the standard shoe leather of the day. That sometimes meant kangaroo skin. Other times, cod. You haven't lived until you've competed against the fastest runners in the world wearing shoes made of cod.

There were four or five of us on the track team who were Bowerman's podiatry guinea pigs, but I was his pet project. Something about my feet spoke to him. Something about my stride. Also, I afforded a wide margin of error. I wasn't the best on the team, not by a long shot, so he could afford to make mistakes on me. With my more talented teammates he didn't dare take undue chances.

As a freshman, as a sophomore, as a junior, I lost count of how many races I ran in flats or spikes modified by Bowerman. By my senior year he was making all my shoes from scratch.

Naturally I believed this new Tiger, this funny little shoe from

Japan that had taken more than a full year to reach me, would intrigue my old coach. Of course, it wasn't as light as his cod shoes. But it had potential: the Japanese were promising to improve it. Better yet, it was inexpensive. I knew this would appeal to Bowerman's innate frugality.

Even the shoe's name struck me as something Bowerman might flip for. He usually called his runners "Men of Oregon," but every once in a while he'd exhort us to be "tigers." I can see him pacing the locker room, telling us before a race, "Be *TIGERS* out there!" (If you weren't a tiger, he'd often call you a "hamburger.") Now and then, when we complained about our skimpy prerace meal, he'd growl: "A tiger hunts best when he's hungry."

With any luck, I thought, Coach will order a few pairs of Tigers for his tigers.

But whether or not he placed an order, impressing Bowerman would be enough. That alone would constitute success for my fledgling company.

It's possible that everything I did in those days was motivated by some deep yearning to impress, to please, Bowerman. Besides my father there was no man whose approval I craved more, and besides my father there was no man who gave it less often. Frugality carried over to every part of the coach's makeup. He weighed and hoarded words of praise, like uncut diamonds.

After you'd won a race, if you were lucky, Bowerman *might* say: "Nice race." (In fact, that's precisely what he said to one of his milers after the young man became one of the very first to crack the mythical four-minute mark in the United States.) More likely Bowerman would say nothing. He'd stand before you in his tweed blazer and ratty sweater vest, his string tie blowing in the wind, his battered ball cap pulled low, and nod once. Maybe stare. Those ice-blue eyes, which missed nothing, gave nothing. Everyone talked about Bowerman's dashing good looks, his retro crew cut, his ramrod posture and planed jawline, but what always got *me* was that gaze of pure violet blue.

It got me on Day One. From the moment I arrived at the University of Oregon, in August 1955, I loved Bowerman. And feared him. And neither of these initial impulses ever went away, they were always there between us. I never stopped loving the man, and I never found a way to shed the old fear. Sometimes the fear was less, sometimes more, sometimes it went right down to my shoes, which he'd probably cobbled with his bare hands. Love and fear—the same binary emotions governed the dynamic between me and my father. I wondered sometimes if it was mere coincidence that Bowerman and my father—both cryptic, both alpha, both inscrutable—were both named Bill.

And yet the two men were driven by different demons. My father, the son of a butcher, was always chasing respectability, whereas Bowerman, whose father had been governor of Oregon, didn't give a darn for respectability. He was also the grandson of legendary pioneers, men and women who'd walked the full length of the Oregon Trail. When they stopped walking they founded a tiny town in eastern Oregon, which they called Fossil. Bowerman spent his early days there, and compulsively returned. Part of his mind was always back in Fossil, which was funny, because there was something distinctly fossilized about him. Hard, brown, ancient, he possessed a prehistoric strain of maleness, a blend of grit and integrity and calcified stubbornness that was rare in Lyndon Johnson's America. Today it's all but extinct.

He was a war hero, too. Of course he was. As a major in the Tenth Mountain Division, stationed high in the Italian Alps, Bowerman had shot at men, and plenty had shot back. (His aura was so intimidating, I don't recall anyone ever asking if he'd actually killed a man.) In case you were tempted to overlook the war and the Tenth Mountain Division and their central role in his psyche, Bowerman always carried a battered leather briefcase with a Roman numeral X engraved in gold on the side.

The most famous track coach in America, Bowerman never

considered himself a track coach. He detested being called Coach. Given his background, his makeup, he naturally thought of track as a means to an end. He called himself a "Professor of Competitive Responses," and his job, as he saw it, and often described it, was to get you ready for the struggles and competitions that lay ahead, far beyond Oregon.

Despite this lofty mission, or perhaps because of it, the facilities at Oregon were Spartan. Dank wooden walls, lockers that hadn't been painted in decades. The lockers had no door, just slats to separate your stuff from the next guy's. We hung our clothes on nails. *Rusty* nails. We sometimes ran without socks. Complaining never crossed our minds. We saw our coach as a general, to be obeyed quickly and blindly. In my mind he was Patton with a stopwatch.

That is, when he wasn't a god.

Like all the ancient gods, Bowerman lived on a mountaintop. His majestic ranch sat on a peak high above the campus. And when reposing on his private Olympus, he could be vengeful as the gods. One story, told to me by a teammate, brought this fact pointedly home.

Apparently there was a truck driver who often dared to disturb the peace on Bowerman Mountain. He took turns too fast, and frequently knocked over Bowerman's mailbox. Bowerman scolded the trucker, threatened to punch him in the nose, and so forth, but the trucker paid no heed. He drove as he pleased, day after day. So Bowerman rigged the mailbox with explosives. Next time the trucker knocked it over—boom. When the smoke cleared, the trucker found his truck in pieces, its tires reduced to ribbons. He never again touched Bowerman's mailbox.

A man like that—you didn't want to get on his wrong side. Especially if you were a gangly middle-distance runner from the Portland suburbs. I always tiptoed around Bowerman. Even so, he'd often lose patience with me, though I remember only one time when he got really sore.

I was a sophomore, being worn down by my schedule. Class all morning, practice all afternoon, homework all night. One day, fearing that I was coming down with the flu, I stopped by Bowerman's office to say that I wouldn't be able to practice that afternoon. "Uh-huh," he said. "Who's the coach of this team?"

"You are."

"Well, as coach of this team I'm telling you to get your ass out there. And by the way . . . we're going to have a time trial today."

I was close to tears. But I held it together, channeled all my emotion into my run, and posted one of my best times of the year. As I walked off the track I glowered at Bowerman. *Happy now, you son of a—?* He looked at me, checked his stopwatch, looked at me again, nodded. He'd tested me. He'd broken me down and remade me, just like a pair of shoes. And I'd held up. Thereafter, I was truly one of his Men of Oregon. From that day on, I was a tiger.

I heard back right away from Bowerman. He wrote to say he was coming to Portland the following week, for the Oregon Indoor. He invited me to lunch at the Cosmopolitan Hotel, where the team would be staying.

January 25, 1964. I was terribly nervous as the waitress showed us to our table. I recall that Bowerman ordered a hamburger, and I said croakily: "Make it two."

We spent a few minutes catching up. I told Bowerman about my trip around the world. Kobe, Jordan, the Temple of Nike. Bowerman was especially interested in my time in Italy, which, despite his brushes with death, he remembered fondly.

At last he came to the point. "Those Japanese shoes," he said. "They're pretty good. How about letting me in on the deal?"

I looked at him. In? Deal? It took me a moment to absorb and understand what he was saying. He didn't merely want to buy a dozen Tigers for his team, he wanted to become—my partner? Had God spoken from the whirlwind and asked to be my partner, I wouldn't have been more surprised. I stammered, and stuttered, and said yes.

I put out my hand.

But then I pulled it back. "What kind of partnership did you have in mind?" I asked.

I was daring to negotiate with God. I couldn't believe my nerve. Nor could Bowerman. He looked bemused. "Fifty-fifty," he said.

"Well, you'll have to put up half the money."

"Of course."

"I figure the first order will be for a thousand dollars. Your half will be five hundred."

"I'm good for that."

When the waitress dropped off the check for the two hamburgers, we split that, too. Fifty-fifty.

I REMEMBER IT as the next day, or maybe sometime in the next few days or weeks, and yet all the documents contradict my memory. Letters, diaries, appointment books—they all definitively show it taking place much later. But I remember what I remember, and there must be a reason why I remember it the way I do. As we left the restaurant that day, I can *see* Bowerman putting on his ball cap, I can *see* him straightening his string tie, I can *hear* him saying: "I'll need you to meet my lawyer, John Jaqua. He can help us get this in writing."

Either way. Days later, weeks later, years later, the meeting happened like this.

I pulled up to Bowerman's stone fortress and marveled, as I always did, at the setting. Remote. Not many folks made it out there. Along Coburg Road to Mackenzie Drive until you found a winding dirt lane that went a couple miles up the hills into the woods. Eventually you came to a clearing with rosebushes, solitary trees, and a pleasant house, small but solid, with a stone face. Bowerman had built it with his bare hands. As I slipped my Valiant into park, I wondered how on earth he'd managed all that backbreaking labor by himself. *The man who moves a mountain begins by carrying away small stones.*

Wrapped around the house was a wide wooden porch, with several camp chairs—he'd built that by himself, too. It afforded sweeping views of the McKenzie River, and it wouldn't have taken much convincing to have me believing Bowerman had laid the river between its banks as well.

Now I saw Bowerman standing on the porch. He squinted and strode down the steps toward my car. I don't remember a lot of small talk as he got in. I just slammed it into drive and set a course for his lawyer's house.

Besides being Bowerman's lawyer and best friend, Jaqua was his next-door neighbor. He owned fifteen hundred acres at the base of Bowerman's mountain, prime bottomland right on the McKenzie. Driving there, I couldn't imagine how this was going to be good for me. I got along fine with Bowerman, sure, and we had ourselves a deal, but lawyers always messed things up. Lawyers specialized in messing things up. And best friend–lawyers . . . ?

Bowerman, meanwhile, was doing nothing to put my mind at ease. He sat ramrod straight and watched the scenery.

Amid the booming silence I kept my eyes on the road and mulled over Bowerman's eccentric personality, which carried over to everything he did. He always went against the grain. Always. For example, he was the first college coach in America to emphasize rest, to place as much value on recovery as on work. But when he worked you, brother, he worked you. Bowerman's strategy for running the mile was simple. Set a fast pace for the first two laps, run the third as hard as you can, then triple your speed on the fourth. There was a Zen-like quality to this strategy, because it was impossible. And yet it worked. Bowerman coached more sub-four-minute milers than anybody, ever. I wasn't one of them, however, and this day I wondered if I was going to fall short once again in that crucial final lap.

We found Jaqua standing out on his porch. I'd met him before, at a track meet or two, but I'd never gotten a really good look at him. Though bespectacled, and sneaking up on middle age, he didn't square with my idea of a lawyer. He was too sturdy, too well made. I learned later that he'd been a star tailback in high school, and one of the best hundred-meter men ever at Pomona College. He still had that telltale athletic power. It came right through his handshake. "Buckaroo," he said, grabbing me by the arm and guiding me into his living room, "I was going to wear your shoes today but I got cow shit all over 'em!"

The day was typical for Oregon in January. Along with the spitting rain, a deep, wet cold permeated everything. We arranged ourselves on chairs around Jaqua's fireplace, the biggest fireplace I ever saw, big enough to roast an elk. Roaring flames were spinning around several logs the size of hydrants. From a side door came Jaqua's wife carrying a tray. Mugs of hot chocolate. She asked if I'd like whipped cream or marshmallows. *Neither, thank you, ma'am.* My voice was two octaves higher than normal. She tilted her head and gave me a pitying look. *Boy, they're going to skin you alive.*

Jaqua took a sip, wiped the cream from his lips, and began. He talked a bit about Oregon track, and about Bowerman. He was wearing dirty blue jeans and a wrinkled flannel shirt, and I couldn't stop thinking how unlawyerly he looked.

Now Jaqua said he'd never seen Bowerman this pumped up about an idea. I liked the sound of that. "But," he added, "fifty-fifty is not so hot for the Coach. He doesn't want to be in charge, and he doesn't want to be at loggerheads with you, ever. How about we make it fifty-one–forty-nine? We give you operating control?"

His whole demeanor was that of a man trying to help, to make this situation a win for everyone. I trusted him.

"Fine by me," I said. "That . . . all?"

He nodded. "Deal?" he said. "Deal," I said. We all shook hands, signed the papers, and I was now officially in a legal and binding partnership with Almighty Bowerman. Mrs. Jaqua asked if I'd care for more hot chocolate. Yes, please, ma'am. And do you have any marshmallows?

*   *   *

LATER THAT DAY I wrote Onitsuka and asked if I could be the exclusive distributor of Tiger shoes in the western United States. Then I asked them to send three hundred pairs of Tigers, ASAP. At $3.33 a pair that was roughly $1,000 worth of shoes. Even with Bowerman's kick-in, that was more than I had on hand. Again I put the touch on my father. This time he balked. He didn't mind getting me started, but he didn't want me coming back to him year after year. Besides, he'd thought this shoe thing was a lark. He hadn't sent me to Oregon and Stanford to become a door-to-door shoe salesman, he said. "Jackassing around," that's what he called it. "Buck," he said, "how long do you think you're going to keep jackassing around with these shoes?"

I shrugged. "I don't know, Dad."

I looked at my mother. As usual, she said nothing. She simply smiled, vaguely, prettily. I got my shyness from her, that was plain. I often wished I'd also gotten her looks.

The first time my father laid eyes on my mother, he thought she was a mannequin. He was walking by the only department store in Roseburg and there she was, standing in the window, modeling an evening gown. Realizing that she was flesh-and-blood, he went straight home and begged his sister to find out the name of that gorgeous gal in the window. His sister found out. That's Lota Hatfield, she said.

Eight months later my father made her Lota Knight.

At the time my father was on his way to becoming an established lawyer, on his way to escaping the terrible poverty that defined his childhood. He was twenty-eight years old. My mother, who had just turned twenty-one, had grown up even poorer than he had. (Her father was a railroad conductor.) Poverty was one of the few things they had in common.

In many ways they were the classic case of opposites attracting. My mother, tall, stunning, a lover of the outdoors, was always seeking places to regain some lost inner peace. My father, small, average with thick rimless glasses to correct his 20-450 vision, was engaged in a daily, noisome battle to overcome his past, to become respectable, mainly through academics and hard work. Second in his law school class, he never tired of complaining about the one C on his transcript. (He felt the professor penalized him for his political beliefs.)

When their diametrically opposed personalities caused problems, my parents would fall back on the thing they had most deeply in common, their belief that family comes first. When that consensus didn't work, there were difficult days. And nights. My father turned to drink. My mother turned to stone.

Her façade could be deceiving, however. Dangerously so. People assumed from her silence that she was meek, and she'd often remind them, in startling ways, that she was not. For instance, there was the time my father refused to cut back on his salt, despite a doctor's warnings that his blood pressure was up. My mother simply filled all the saltshakers in the house with powdered milk. And there was the day my sisters and I were bickering and clamoring for lunch, despite her pleas for quiet. My mother suddenly let out a savage scream and hurled an egg salad sandwich against the wall. She then walked out of the house, across the lawn, and disappeared. I'll never forget the sight of that egg salad slowly dripping down the wall while my mother's sundress dissolved in the distant trees.

Perhaps nothing ever revealed my mother's true nature like the frequent drills she put me through. As a young girl she'd witnessed a house in her neighborhood burn to the ground; one of the people inside had been killed. So she often tied a rope to the post of my bed and made me use it to rappel out of my second-floor window. While she timed me. What must the neighbors have thought? What must I have thought? Probably this: Life is dangerous. And this: We must always be prepared.

And this: My mother loves me.

When I was twelve, Les Steers and his family moved in across the street, next to my best friend Jackie Emory. One day Mr. Steers set up a high-jump course in Jackie's backyard, and Jackie and I did battle. Each of us maxed out at four feet six inches. "Maybe one of you will break the world record one day," Mr. Steers said. (I learned later that the world record at that time, six feet eleven inches, belonged to Mr. Steers.)

Out of nowhere my mother appeared. (She was wearing gardening slacks and a summery blouse.) Uh-oh, I thought, we're in trouble. She looked over the scene, looked at me and Jackie. Looked at Mr. Steers. "Move the bar up," she said.

She slipped off her shoes, toed her mark, and burst forward, clearing five feet easily.

I don't know if I ever loved her more.

In the moment I thought she was cool. Soon after, I realized she was also a closet track-ophile.

It happened my sophomore year. I developed a painful wart on the bottom of my foot. The podiatrist recommended surgery, which would mean a lost season of track. My mother had two words for that podiatrist. "Un. Acceptable." She marched down to the drugstore and bought a vial of wart remover, which she applied each day to my foot. Then, every two weeks, she took a carving knife and pared away a sliver of the wart, until it was all gone. That spring I posted the best times of my life.

So I shouldn't have been too surprised by my mother's next move when my father accused me of jackassing around. Casually she opened her purse and took out seven dollars. "I'd like to purchase one pair of Limber Ups, please," she said, loud enough for him to hear.

Was it my mother's way of digging at my father? A show of loyalty to her only son? An affirmation of her love of track? I don't know. But no matter. It never failed to move me, the sight of her standing at the stove or the kitchen sink, cooking dinner or washing dishes in a pair of Japanese running shoes, size 6.

*　　*　　*

PROBABLY BECAUSE HE didn't want any trouble with my mother, my father loaned me the thousand bucks. This time the shoes came right away.

April 1964. I rented a truck, drove down to the warehouse district, and the customs clerk handed over ten enormous cartons. Again I hurried home, carried the cartons down to the basement, ripped them open. Each carton held thirty pairs of Tigers, and each pair was wrapped in cellophane. (Shoe boxes would have been too costly.) Within minutes the basement was filled with shoes. I admired them, studied them, played with them, rolled around on top of them. Then I stacked them out of the way, arranging them neatly around the furnace and under the Ping-Pong table, as far as possible from the washer and dryer, so my mother could still do laundry. Lastly I tried on a pair. I ran circles around the basement. I jumped for joy.

Days later came a letter from Mr. Miyazaki. Yes, he said, *you* can be the distributor for Onitsuka in the West.

That was all I needed. To my father's horror, and my mother's subversive delight, I quit my job at the accounting firm, and all that spring I did nothing but sell shoes out of the trunk of my Valiant.

MY SALES STRATEGY was simple, and I thought rather brilliant. After being rejected by a couple of sporting goods stores ("Kid, what this world does not need is another track shoe!"), I drove all over the Pacific Northwest, to various track meets. Between races I'd chat up the coaches, the runners, the fans, and show them my wares. The response was always the same. I couldn't write orders fast enough.

Driving back to Portland I'd puzzle over my sudden success at selling. I'd been unable to sell encyclopedias, and I'd despised it to boot. I'd been slightly better at selling mutual funds, but I'd felt dead inside. So why was selling shoes so different? Because, I realized, it wasn't selling. I *believed* in running. I believed that if people got out and ran a few miles every day, the world would be a better place, and I believed these shoes were better to run in. People, sensing my belief, wanted some of that belief for themselves.

Belief, I decided. Belief is irresistible.

Sometimes people wanted my shoes so badly that they'd write me, or phone me, saying they'd heard about the new Tigers and just had to have a pair, could I please send them, COD? Without my even trying, my mail order business was born.

Sometimes people would simply show up at my parents' house. Every few nights the doorbell would ring, and my father, grumbling, would get up from his vinyl recliner and turn down the TV and wonder who in the world. There on the porch would be some skinny kid with oddly muscular legs, shifty-eyed and twitchy, like a junky looking to score. "Buck here?" the kid would say. My father would call through the kitchen to my room in the servants' quarters. I'd come out, invite the kid in, show him over to the sofa, then kneel before him and measure his foot. My father, hands jammed into his pockets, would watch the whole transaction, incredulous.

Most people who came to the house had found me through word of mouth. Friend of a friend. But a few found me through my first attempt at advertising—a handout I'd designed and produced at a local print shop. Along the top, in big type, it said: *Best news in flats! Japan challenges European track shoe domination!* The handout then went on to explain: *Low Japanese labor costs make it possible for an exciting new firm to offer these shoes at the low low price of $6.95.* Along the bottom was my address and phone number. I nailed them up all over Portland.

On July 4, 1964, I sold out my first shipment. I wrote to Tiger and ordered nine hundred more. That would cost roughly three thousand dollars, which would wipe out my father's petty cash, and patience. The Bank of Dad, he said, is now closed. He did agree, grudgingly, to give me a letter of guarantee, which I took down to the First National Bank of Oregon. On the strength of my father's reputation, and nothing more, the bank approved the loan. My father's vaunted respectability was finally paying dividends, at least for me.

I HAD A venerable partner, a legitimate bank, and a product that was selling itself. I was on a roll.

In fact, the shoes sold so well, I decided to hire another salesman. Maybe two. In California.

The problem was, how to get to California? I certainly couldn't afford airfare. And I didn't have time to drive. So every other weekend I'd load a duffel bag with Tigers, put on my crispest army uniform, and head out to the local air base. Seeing the uniform, the MPs would wave me onto the next military transport to San Francisco or Los Angeles, no questions asked. When I went to Los Angeles I'd save even more money by crashing with Chuck Cale, a friend from Stanford. A good friend. When I'd presented my running-shoe paper to my entrepreneurship class, Cale showed up, for moral support.

During one of those Los Angeles weekends I attended a meet at Occidental College. As always, I stood on the infield grass, letting the shoes do their magic. Suddenly a guy sauntered up and held out his hand. Twinkly eyes, handsome face. In fact, very handsome—though also sad. Despite the enameled calm of his expression, there was something sorrowful, almost tragic, around the eyes. Also, something vaguely familiar. "Phil," he said. "Yes?" I said. "Jeff Johnson," he said.

Of course! Johnson. I'd known him at Stanford. He'd been a runner, a pretty fair miler, and we'd competed against each other at several all-comer meets. And sometimes he'd gone for a run with me and Cale, then for a bite after. "Heya, Jeff," I said, "what are you up to these days?" "Grad school," he said, "studying anthro." The plan was to become a social worker. "No kidding," I said, arching an eyebrow. Johnson didn't seem the social worker type. I couldn't see him counseling drug addicts and placing orphans. Nor did he seem the anthropologist type. I couldn't imagine him chatting up cannibals in New Guinea, or scouring Anasazi campsites with a toothbrush, sifting through goat dung for pottery shards.

But these, he said, were merely his daytime drudgeries. On weekends he was following his heart, selling shoes. "No!" I said. "Adidas," he said. "Screw Adidas," I said, "you should work for me, help me sell these new Japanese running shoes."

I handed him a Tiger flat, told him about my trip to Japan, my meeting with Onitsuka. He bent the shoe, examined the sole. Pretty cool, he said. He was intrigued, but no. "I'm getting married," he said. "Not sure I can take on a new venture right now."

I didn't take his rejection to heart. It was the first time I'd heard the word "no" in months.

LIFE WAS GOOD. Life was grand. I even had a sort of girlfriend, though I didn't have much time for her. I was happy, maybe as happy as I'd ever been, and happiness can be dangerous. It dulls the senses. Thus, I wasn't prepared for that dreadful letter.

It was from a high school wrestling coach in some benighted town back east, some little burg on Long Island called Valley Stream or Massapequa or Manhasset. I had to read it twice before I understood. The coach claimed that he was just back from Japan, where he'd met with top executives at Onitsuka, who'd anointed him their exclusive American distributor. Since he'd heard that I was selling Tigers, I was therefore poaching, and he ordered me—ordered me!—to stop.

Heart pounding, I phoned my cousin, Doug Houser. He'd graduated from Stanford Law School and was now working at a respected firm in town. I asked him to look into this Mr. Manhasset, find out what he could, then back the guy off with a letter. "Saying what, exactly?" Cousin Houser asked. "That any attempt to interfere with Blue Ribbon will be met with swift legal reprisal," I said.

My "business" was two months old and I was embroiled in a legal battle? Served me right for daring to call myself happy.

Next I sat down and dashed off a frantic letter to Onitsuka. *Dear Sirs, I was very distressed to receive a letter this morning from a man in Manhasset, New York, who claims . . . ?*

I waited for a response.

And waited.

I wrote again.

Nani mo.

Nothing.

COUSIN HOUSER FOUND out that Mr. Manhasset was something of a celebrity. Before becoming a high school wrestling coach, he'd been a model—one of the original Marlboro Men. Beautiful, I thought. Just what I need. A pissing match with some mythic American cowboy.

I went into a deep funk. I became such a grouch, such poor company, the girlfriend fell away. Each night I'd sit with my family at dinner, moving my mother's pot roast and vegetables around my plate. Then I'd sit with my father in the nook, staring glumly at the TV. "Buck," my father said, "you look like someone hit you in the back of the head with a two-by-four. Snap out of it."

But I couldn't. I kept going over my meeting at Onitsuka. The executives had shown me such *kei*. They'd bowed to me, and vice versa. I'd been straightforward with them, honest—for the most part. Sure, I hadn't "technically" owned a "business" called "Blue Ribbon." But that was splitting hairs. I owned one now, and it had single-handedly brought Tigers to the West Coast, and it could sell Tigers ten times faster if Onitsuka gave me half a chance. Instead the company was going to cut me out? Throw me over for the fricking Marlboro Man? Come to where the flavor is.

*   *   *

TOWARD SUMMER'S END I still hadn't heard from Onitsuka, and I'd all but given up on the idea of selling shoes. Labor Day, however, I had a change of heart. I couldn't give up. Not yet. And not giving up meant flying back to Japan. I needed to force a showdown with Onitsuka.

I ran the idea by my father. He still didn't like me jackassing around with shoes. But what he really didn't like was someone mistreating his son. He furrowed his brow. "You should probably go," he said.

I talked it over with my mother. "No probablys about it," she said. In fact, she'd drive me to the airport.

FIFTY YEARS LATER I can see us in that car. I can recall every detail. It was a bright, clear day, no humidity, temperature in the low eighties. Both of us, quietly watching the sunlight play across the windshield, said nothing. The silence between us was like the silence on the many days she drove me to meets. I was too busy fighting my nerves to talk, and she, better than anyone, understood. She respected the lines we draw around ourselves in crisis.

Then, as we neared the airport, she broke the silence. "Just be yourself," she said.

I looked out the window. Be myself. Really? Is that my best option? *To study the self is to forget the self.*

I looked down. I certainly wasn't dressed like myself. I was wearing a new suit, a proper charcoal gray, and toting a small suitcase. In the side pocket was a new book: *How to Do Business with the Japanese.* Heaven only knows how or where I'd heard about it. And now I grimace to remember this last detail: I was also wearing a black bowler hat. I'd bought it expressly for this trip, thinking it made me look older. In fact it made me look mad. Stark, staring mad. As if I'd escaped from a Victorian insane asylum inside a painting by Magritte.

* * *

I SPENT MOST of the flight memorizing *How to Do Business with the Japanese*. When my eyes grew tired I shut the book and stared out the window. I tried to talk to myself, to coach myself up. I told myself that I needed to put aside hurt feelings, put aside all thoughts of injustice, which would only make me emotional and keep me from thinking clearly. Emotion would be fatal. I needed to remain cool.

I thought back on my running career at Oregon. I'd competed with, and against, men far better, faster, more physically gifted. Many were future Olympians. And yet I'd trained myself to forget this unhappy fact. People reflexively assume that competition is always a good thing, that it always brings out the best in people, but that's only true of people who can forget the competition. The art of competing, I'd learned from track, was the art of forgetting, and I now reminded myself of that fact. You must forget your limits. You must forget your doubts, your pain, your past. You must forget that internal voice screaming, begging, "Not one more step!" And when it's not possible to forget it, you must negotiate with it. I thought over all the races in which my mind wanted one thing, and my body wanted another, those laps in which I'd had to tell my body, "Yes, you raise some excellent points, but let's keep going anyway . . ."

Despite all my negotiations with that voice, the skill had never come naturally, and now I feared that I was out of practice. As the plane swooped down toward Haneda Airport I told myself that I'd need to summon the old skill quickly, or lose.

I could not bear the thought of losing.

THE 1964 OLYMPICS were about to be held in Japan, so I had my pick of brand-new, reasonably priced lodgings in Kobe. I got a room right downtown, at the Newport, which featured a revolving restaurant on the top. Just like the one atop the Space Needle—a touch of the Great Northwest to settle my nerves. Before unpacking, I phoned Onitsuka and left a message. *I'm here and I request a meeting.*

Then I sat on the edge of the bed and stared at the phone.

At last it rang. A prim-sounding secretary informed me that my contact at Onitsuka, Mr. Miyazaki, no longer worked there. Bad sign. His replacement, Mr. Morimoto, did not wish me to come to the company's headquarters. Very bad sign. Instead, she said, Mr. Morimoto would meet me for tea in my hotel's revolving restaurant. Tomorrow morning.

I went to bed early, slept fitfully. Dreams of car chases, prison, duels—the same dreams that always plagued me the night before a big meet, or date, or exam. I rose at dawn, ate a breakfast of raw egg poured over hot rice, and some grilled fish, and washed it down with a pot of green tea. Then, reciting memorized passages from *How to Do Business with the Japanese*, I shaved my pale jaws. I cut myself once or twice, and had trouble stopping the bleeding. I must have been a sight. Finally I put on my suit and shambled onto the elevator. As I pressed the button for the top floor I noticed that my hand was white as bone.

Morimoto arrived on time. He was about my age, but far more mature, more self-assured. He wore a rumpled sport coat and had a kind of rumpled face. We sat at a table by the window. Immediately, before the waiter came to take our order, I launched into my pitch, saying everything I'd vowed not to say. I told Morimoto how distressed I was by this Marlboro Man encroaching on my turf. I said I'd been under the impression that I'd made a personal connection with the executives I'd met the previous year, and the impression was underscored by a letter from Mr. Miyazaki saying the thirteen western states were exclusively mine. I was therefore at a loss to explain this treatment. I appealed to Morimoto's sense of fairness, to his sense of honor. He looked uncomfortable, so I took a breath, paused. I raised it from the personal to the professional. I cited my robust sales. I dropped the name of my partner, the legendary coach whose reputation had cachet even on the other side of the Pacific. I emphasized all that I might do for Onitsuka in the future, if given a chance.

Morimoto took a sip of tea. When it was clear that I'd talked myself out, he set down his cup and looked out the window. Slowly we rotated above Kobe. "I will get back to you."

ANOTHER FITFUL NIGHT. I got up several times, went to the window, watched the ships bobbing on Kobe's dark purple bay. Beautiful place, I thought. Too bad all beauty is beyond me. The world is without beauty when you lose, and I was about to lose, big-time.

I knew that in the morning Morimoto would tell me he was sorry, nothing personal, it was just business, but they were going with the Marlboro Man.

At 9:00 a.m. the phone by the bed rang. Morimoto. "Mr. Onitsuka . . . *himself* . . . wishes to see you," he said.

I put on my suit and took a taxi to Onitsuka headquarters. In the conference room, the familiar conference room, Morimoto pointed me to a chair in the middle of the table. The middle this time, not the head. No more *kei*. He sat across from me and stared at me as the room slowly filled with executives. When everyone was there, Morimoto nodded to me. "*Hai*," he said.

I plunged in, essentially repeating what I'd said to him the previous morning. As I built to my crescendo, as I prepared to close, all heads swiveled toward the door, and I stopped midsentence. The temperature of the room dropped ten degrees. The founder of the company, Mr. Onitsuka, had arrived.

Dressed in a dark blue Italian suit, with a head of black hair as thick as shag carpet, he filled every man in the conference room with fear. He seemed oblivious, however. For all his power, for all his wealth, his movements were deferential. He came forward haltingly, with a shuffling gait, giving no sign that he was the boss of all bosses, the shogun of shoes. Slowly he made his way around the table, making brief eye contact with each executive. Eventually he came to me. We bowed to each other, shook hands. Now he took the seat at the head of the table and Morimoto tried to summarize my reason for being there. Mr. Onitsuka raised a hand, cut him off.

Without preamble he launched into a long, passionate monologue. Some time ago, he said, he'd had a vision. A wondrous glimpse of the future. "Everyone in the world wear athletic shoes all the time," he said. "I know this day come." He paused, looking around the table at each person, to see if they also knew. His gaze rested on me. He smiled. I smiled. He blinked twice. "You remind me of myself when I am young," he said softly. He stared into my eyes. One second. Two. Now he turned his gaze to Morimoto. "This about those thirteen western states?" he said. "Yes," Morimoto said. "Hm," Onitsuka said. "Hmmmm." He narrowed his eyes, looked down. He seemed to be meditating. Again he looked up at me. "Yes," he said, "all right. You have western states."

The Marlboro Man, he said, could continue selling his wrestling shoes nationwide, but would limit his track shoe sales to the East Coast.

Mr. Onitsuka would personally write to the Marlboro Man and inform him of this decision.

He rose. I rose. Everyone rose. We all bowed. He left the conference room.

Everyone remaining in the conference room exhaled. "So . . . it is decided," Morimoto said.

For one year, he added. Then the subject would be revisited.

I thanked Morimoto, assured him that Onitsuka wouldn't regret its faith in me. I went around the table shaking everyone's hand, bowing, and when I came back to Morimoto I gave his hand an extra-vigorous shake. I then followed a secretary into a side room, where I signed several contracts, and placed an order for a whopping thirty-five hundred dollars' worth of shoes.

I RAN ALL the way back to my hotel. Halfway there I started skipping, then leaping through the air like a dancer. I stopped at a railing and looked out at the bay. None of its beauty was lost on me now. I watched the boats gliding before a brisk wind and decided that I would hire one. I would take a ride on the Inland Sea. An hour later I was standing in the prow of a boat, wind in my hair, sailing into the sunset and feeling pretty good about myself.

The next day I boarded a train to Tokyo. It was time, at last, to ascend into the clouds.

ALL THE GUIDEBOOKS said to climb Mount Fuji at night. A proper climb, they said, must culminate with a view of sunrise from the summit. So I arrived at the base of the mountain promptly at dusk. The day had been muggy, but the air was growing cooler, and right away I rethought my decision to wear Bermuda shorts, a T-shirt, and Tigers. I saw a man coming down the mountain in a rubberized coat. I stopped him and offered him three dollars for his coat. He looked at me, looked at the coat, nodded.

I was negotiating successful deals all over Japan!

As night fell hundreds of natives and tourists appeared and began streaming up the mountain. All, I noticed, were carrying long wooden sticks with tinkling bells attached. I spotted an older British couple and asked them about these sticks. "They ward off evil spirits," the woman said.

"There are *evil spirits* on this mountain?" I asked.

"Presumably."

I bought a stick.

I then noticed people gathering at a roadside stand and buying straw shoes. The British woman explained that Fuji was an active volcano, and its ash and soot were guaranteed to ruin shoes. Climbers therefore wore disposable straw sandals.

I bought sandals.

Poorer, but properly outfitted at last, I set off.

There were many ways down Mount Fuji, according to my guidebook, but only one way up. Life lesson in that, I thought. Signs along the upward path, written in many languages, said there would be nine stations before the summit, each offering food and a place to rest. Within two hours, however, I'd passed Station 3 several times. Did the Japanese count differently? Alarmed, I wondered if thirteen western states might actually mean three?

At Station 7 I stopped and bought a Japanese beer and a cup of noodles. While eating my dinner I fell to talking with another couple. They were Americans, younger than me—students, I assumed. He was preppy, in a ridiculous sort of way. Golf slacks and tennis shirt and cloth belt—he was all the colors of an Easter egg. She was pure beatnik. Torn jeans, faded T-shirt, wild dark hair. Her wide-set eyes were brown-black. Like little cups of espresso.

Both were sweating from the climb. They mentioned that I wasn't. I shrugged and said that I'd run track at Oregon. "Half-miler." The young man scowled. His girlfriend said, "Wow." We finished our beers and resumed climbing together.

Her name was Sarah. She was from Maryland. Horse country, she said. Rich country, I thought. She'd grown up riding, and jumping, and showing, and still spent much of her time in saddles and show rings. She talked about her favorite ponies and horses as if they were her closest friends.

I asked about her family. "Daddy owns a candy bar company," she said. She mentioned the company and I laughed. I'd eaten many of her family's candy bars, sometimes before a race. The company was founded by her grandfather, she said, though she hastened to add that she had no interest in money.

I caught her boyfriend scowling again.

She was studying philosophy at Connecticut College for Women. "Not a great school," she said apologetically. She'd wanted to go to Smith, where her sister was a senior, but she didn't get in.

"You sound as if you haven't gotten over the rejection," I said.

"Not even close," she said.

"Rejection is never easy," I said.

"You can say that again."

Her voice was peculiar. She pronounced certain words oddly, and I couldn't decide if it was a Maryland accent or a speech impediment. Whichever, it was adorable.

She asked what brought me to Japan. I explained that I'd come to save my shoe company. "Your *company*?" she said. Clearly she was thinking about the men in her family, founders of companies, captains of industry. Entrepreneurs. "Yes," I said, "my company." "And did you . . . save it?" she asked. "I did," I said. "All the boys back home are going to business school," she said, "and then they all plan to become *bankers*." She rolled her eyes, adding: "Everyone does the same thing—so boring."

"Boredom scares me," I said.

"Ah. That's because you're a rebel."

I stopped climbing, stabbed my walking stick into the ground. Me—a rebel? My face grew warm.

As we neared the summit, the path grew narrow. I mentioned that it reminded me of a trail I'd hiked in the Himalayas. Sarah and the boyfriend stared. *Himalayas?* Now she was really impressed. And he was really put out. As the summit came slowly into view, the climb became tricky, treacherous. She seized my hand. "The Japanese have a saying," her boyfriend shouted over his shoulder, to us, to everyone. "A wise man climbs Fuji once. A fool climbs it twice."

No one laughed. Though I wanted to, at his Easter egg clothing.

On the very top we came to a large wooden torii gate. We sat beside it and waited. The air was strange. Not quite dark, not quite light. Then the sun crept above the horizon. I told Sarah and her boyfriend that the Japanese place torii gates at sacral borderlands, portals between this world and the world beyond. "Wherever you pass from the profane to the sacred," I said, "you'll find a torii gate." Sarah liked that. I told her that Zen masters believed mountains "flow," but that we can't always perceive the flow with our limited senses, and indeed, in that moment, we did feel as if Fuji was flowing, as if we were riding a wave across the world.

Unlike the climb up, the climb down took no effort, and no time. At the bottom I bowed and said good-bye to Sarah and the Easter egg. "*Yoroshiku ne.*" Nice meeting you. "Where you headed?" Sarah asked. "I think I'm going to stay at the Hakone Inn tonight," I said. "Well," she said, "I'm coming with you."

I took a step back. I looked at the boyfriend. He scowled. I realized at last that he wasn't her boyfriend. Happy Easter.

WE SPENT TWO days at the inn, laughing, talking, falling. Beginning. If only this could never end, we said, but of course it had to. I had to go back to Tokyo, to catch a flight home, and Sarah was determined to move on, see the rest of Japan. We made no plans to see each other again. She was a free spirit, she didn't believe in plans. "Good-bye," she said. "*Hajimemashite*," I said. Lovely meeting you.

Hours before I boarded my plane, I stopped at the American Express office. I knew she'd have to stop there, too, at some point, to get money from the Candy Bar People. I left her a note: "You've got to fly over Portland to get to the East Coast . . . why not stop for a visit?"

MY FIRST NIGHT home, over dinner, I told my family the good news. I'd met a girl.

Then I told them the other good news. I'd saved my company.

I turned and looked hard at my twin sisters. They spent half of every day crouched beside the telephone, waiting to pounce on it at the first ring. "Her name is Sarah," I said. "So if she calls, please . . . be nice."

* * *

WEEKS LATER I came home from running errands and there she was, in my living room, sitting with my mother and sisters. "Surprise," she said. She'd gotten my note and decided to take me up on my offer. She'd phoned from the airport and my sister Joanne had answered and shown what sisters are for. She promptly drove out to the airport and fetched Sarah.

I laughed. We hugged, awkwardly, my mother and sisters watching. "Let's go for a walk," I said.

I got her a jacket from the servants' quarters and we walked in a light rain to a wooded park nearby. She saw Mount Hood in the distance and agreed that it looked astonishingly like Fuji, which made us both reminisce.

I asked where she was staying. "Silly boy," she said. The second time she'd invited herself into my space.

For two weeks she lived in my parents' guestroom, just like one of the family, which I began to think she might one day be. I watched in disbelief as she charmed the uncharmable Knights. My protective sisters, my shy mother, my autocratic father, they were no match for her. Especially my father. When she shook his hand, she melted something hard at his core. Maybe it was growing up among the Candy Bar People, and all their mogul friends—she had the kind of self-confidence you run across once or twice in a lifetime.

She was certainly the only person I'd ever known who could casually drop Babe Paley and Hermann Hesse into the same conversation. She admired them both. But especially Hesse. She was going to write a book about him one day. "It's like Hesse says," she purred over dinner one night, "happiness is a *how*, not a *what*." The Knights chewed their pot roast, sipped their milk. "Very interesting," my father said.

I brought Sarah down to the worldwide headquarters of Blue Ribbon, in the basement, and showed her the operation. I gave her a pair of Limber Ups. She wore them when we drove out to the coast. We went hiking up Humbug Mountain, and crabbing along the scalloped coastline, and huckleberry picking in the woods. Standing under an eighty-foot spruce we shared a huckleberry kiss.

When it was time for her to fly back to Maryland, I was bereft. I wrote her every other day. My first-ever love letters. *Dear Sarah, I think about sitting beside that torii gate with you . . .*

She always wrote back right away. She always expressed her undying love.

THAT CHRISTMAS, 1964, she returned. This time I picked her up at the airport. On the way to my house she told me that there had been a terrible row before she got on the plane. Her parents forbade her to come. They didn't approve of me. "My father screamed," she said.

"What did he scream?" I asked.

She imitated his voice. "You can't meet a guy on Mount Fuji who's going to amount to anything."

I winced. I knew I had two strikes against me, but I didn't realize climbing Mount Fuji was one of them. What was so bad about climbing Mount Fuji?

"How did you get away?" I asked.

"My brother. He snuck me out of the house early this morning and drove me to the airport."

I wondered if she really loved me, or just saw me as a chance to rebel.

DURING THE DAY, while I was busy working on Blue Ribbon stuff, Sarah would hang out with my mother. At night she and I would go downtown for dinner and drinks. On the weekend we skied Mount Hood. When it was time for her to return home, I was bereft again. *Dear Sarah, I miss you. I love you.*

She wrote back right away. She missed me, too. She loved me, too.

Then, with the winter rains, there was a slight cooling in her letters. They were less effusive. Or so I thought. Maybe it's just my imagination, I told myself. But I had to know. I phoned her.

It wasn't my imagination. She said she'd given it a lot of thought and she wasn't sure we were right for each other. She wasn't sure I was sophisticated enough for her. "Sophisticated," that was the word she used. Before I could protest, before I could negotiate, she hung up.

I took out a piece of paper and typed her a long letter, begging her to reconsider.

She wrote back right away. No sale.

THE NEW SHIPMENT of shoes arrived from Onitsuka. I could hardly bring myself to care. I spent weeks in a fog. I hid in the basement. I hid in the servants' quarters. I lay on my bed and stared at my blue ribbons.

Though I didn't tell them, my family knew. They didn't ask for details. They didn't need them, or want them.

Except my sister Jeanne. While I was out one day she went into the servants' quarters and into my desk and found Sarah's letters. Later, when I came home and went down to the basement, Jeanne came and found me. She sat on the floor beside me and said she'd read the letters, all of them, carefully, concluding with the final rejection. I looked away. "You're better off without her," Jeanne said.

My eyes filled with tears. I nodded thanks. Not knowing what to say, I asked Jeanne if she'd like to do some part-time work for Blue Ribbon. I was pretty far behind, and I could sure use some help. "Since you're so interested in mail," I said hoarsely, "maybe you'd enjoy doing some secretarial work. Dollar and a half an hour?"

She chuckled.

And thus my sister became the first-ever employee of Blue Ribbon.

1965

I got a letter from that Jeff Johnson fellow at the start of the year. After our chance meeting at Occidental, I'd sent him a pair of Tigers, as a gift, and now he wrote to say that he'd tried them on and gone for a run. He liked them, he said. He liked them a whole lot. Others liked them, too. People kept stopping him and pointing at his feet and asking where they could buy some neat shoes like those.

Johnson had gotten married since I last saw him, he said, and there was already a baby on the way, so he was looking for ways to earn extra cash, apart from his gig as a social worker, and this Tiger shoe seemed to have more upside than Adidas. I wrote him back and offered him a post as a "commissioned salesman." Meaning I'd give him $1.75 for each pair of running shoes he sold, two bucks for each pair of spikes. I was just beginning to put together a crew of part-time sales reps, and that was the standard rate I was offering.

He wrote back right away, accepting the offer.

And then the letters didn't stop. On the contrary, they increased. In length and number. At first they were two pages. Then four. Then eight. At first they came every few days. Then they came faster, and faster, tumbling almost daily through the mail slot like a waterfall, each one with that same return address, P.O. Box 492, Seal Beach, CA 90740, until I wondered what in God's name I'd done in hiring this guy.

I liked his energy, of course. And it was hard to fault his enthusiasm. But I began to worry that he might have too much of each. With the twentieth letter, or the twenty-fifth, I began to worry that the man might be unhinged. I wondered why everything was so breathless. I wondered if he was ever going to run out of things he urgently needed to tell me, or ask me. I wondered if he was ever going to run out of stamps.

Every time a thought crossed Johnson's mind, seemingly, he wrote it down and stuck it into an envelope. He wrote to tell me how many Tigers he'd sold that week. He wrote to tell me how many Tigers he'd sold that day. He wrote to tell me who'd worn Tigers at which high school meet and in what place they'd finished. He wrote to say that he wanted to expand his sales territory beyond California, to include Arizona, and possibly New Mexico. He wrote to suggest that we open a retail store in Los Angeles. He wrote to tell me that he was considering placing ads in running magazines and what did I think? He wrote to inform me that he'd placed those ads in running magazines and the response was good. He wrote to ask why I hadn't answered any of his previous letters. He wrote to plead for encouragement. He wrote to complain that I hadn't responded to his previous plea for encouragement.

I'd always considered myself a conscientious correspondent. (I'd sent countless letters and postcards home during my trip around the world. I'd written faithfully to Sarah.) And I always *meant* to answer Johnson's letters. But before I got around to it there was always another one, waiting. Something about the sheer volume of his correspondence stopped me. Something about his neediness made me not want to encourage him. Many nights I'd sit down at the black Royal typewriter in my basement workshop, curl a piece of paper into the roller, and type, "Dear Jeff." Then I'd draw a blank. I wouldn't know where to begin, which of his fifty questions to start with, so I'd get up, attend to other things, and the next day there'd be yet another letter from Johnson. Or two. Soon I'd be three letters behind, suffering from crippling writer's block.

I asked Jeanne to deal with the Johnson File. Fine, she said.

Within a month she thrust the file at me, exasperated. "You're not paying me enough," she said.

AT SOME POINT I stopped reading Johnson's letters all the way to the bottom. But from skimming them I learned that he was selling Tigers part-time and on weekends, that he'd decided to keep his day job as a social worker for Los Angeles County. I still couldn't fathom it. Johnson just didn't strike me as a people person. In fact he'd always seemed somewhat misanthropic. It was one of the things I'd liked about him.

In April 1965 he wrote to say he'd quit his day job. He'd always hated it, he said, but the last straw had been a distressed woman in the San Fernando Valley. He'd been scheduled to check on her, because she'd threatened to kill herself, but he'd phoned her first to ask "if she really was going to kill herself that day." If so, he didn't want to waste the time and gas money driving all the way out to the valley. The woman, and Johnson's superiors, took a dim view of his approach. They deemed it a sign that Johnson didn't care. Johnson deemed it the same way. He *didn't* care, and in that moment, Johnson wrote me, he understood himself, and his destiny. Social work wasn't it. He wasn't put here on this earth to fix people's problems. He preferred to focus on their feet.

In his heart of hearts Johnson believed that runners are God's chosen, that running, done right, in the correct spirit and with the proper form, is a mystical exercise, no less than meditation or prayer, and thus he felt called to help runners reach their nirvana. I'd been around runners much of my life, but this kind of dewy romanticism was something I'd never encountered. Not even the Yahweh of running, Bowerman, was as pious about the sport as Blue Ribbon's Part-time Employee Number Two.

In fact, in 1965, running wasn't even a sport. It wasn't popular, it wasn't unpopular—it just was. To go out for a three-mile run was something weirdos did, presumably to burn off manic energy. Running for pleasure, running for exercise, running for endorphins, running to live better and longer—these things were unheard of.

People often went out of their way to mock runners. Drivers would slow down and honk their horns. "Get a horse!" they'd yell, throwing a beer or soda at the runner's head. Johnson had been drenched by many a Pepsi. He wanted to change all this. He wanted to help all the oppressed runners of the world, to bring them into the light, enfold them in a community. So maybe he was a social worker after all. He just wanted to socialize exclusively with runners.

Above all, Johnson wanted to make a living doing it, which was next to impossible in 1965. In me, in Blue Ribbon, he thought he saw a way.

I did everything I could to discourage Johnson from thinking like this. At every turn I tried to dampen his enthusiasm for me and my company. Besides not writing back, I never phoned, never visited, never invited him to Oregon. I also never missed an opportunity to tell him the unvarnished truth. In one of my rare replies to his letters I put it flatly: "Though our growth has been good, I owe First National Bank of Oregon $11,000. . . . Cash flow is negative."

He wrote back immediately, asking if he could work for me full-time. "I want to be able to make it on Tiger, and the opportunity would exist for me to do other things as well—running, school, not to mention being my own boss."

I shook my head. I tell the man Blue Ribbon is sinking like the *Titanic*, and he responds by begging for a berth in first class.

Oh well, I thought, if we do go down, misery loves company.

So in the late summer of 1965 I wrote and accepted Johnson's offer to become the first *full-time* employee of Blue Ribbon. We negotiated his salary via the mail. He'd been making $460 a month as a social worker, but he said he could live on $400. I agreed. Reluctantly. It seemed exorbitant, but Johnson was so scattered, so flighty, and Blue Ribbon was so tenuous—one way or another I figured it was temporary.

As ever, the accountant in me saw the risk, the entrepreneur saw the possibility. So I split the difference and kept moving forward.

AND THEN I stopped thinking about Johnson altogether. I had bigger problems at the moment. My banker was upset with me.

After posting eight thousand dollars in sales in my first year, I was projecting sixteen thousand dollars in my second year, and according to my banker this was a very troubling trend.

"A one hundred percent increase in sales is *troubling*?" I asked.

"Your rate of growth is too fast for your equity," he said.

"How can such a small company grow too fast? If a small company grows fast, it *builds up* its equity."

"It's all the same principle, regardless of size," he said. "Growth off your balance sheet is dangerous."

"Life is growth," I said. "Business is growth. You grow or you die."

"That's not how we see it."

"You might as well tell a runner in a race that he's running too fast."

"Apples and oranges."

Your head is full of apples and oranges, I wanted to say.

It was textbook to me. Growing sales, plus profitability, plus unlimited upside, equals quality company. In those days, however, commercial banks were different from investment banks. Their myopic focus was cash balances. They wanted you to never, ever outgrow your cash balance.

Again and again I'd gently try to explain the shoe business to my banker. If I don't keep growing, I'd say, I won't be able to persuade Onitsuka that I'm the best man to distribute their shoes in the West. If I can't persuade Onitsuka that I'm the best, they'll find some other

Marlboro Man to take my place. And that doesn't even take into account the battle with the biggest monster out there, Adidas.

My banker was unmoved. Unlike Athena, he did not admire my eyes of persuasion. "Mr. Knight," he'd say, again and again, "you need to slow down. You don't have enough equity for this kind of growth."

Equity. How I was beginning to loathe this word. My banker used it over and over, until it became a tune I couldn't get out of my head. Equity—I heard it while brushing my teeth in the morning. Equity—I heard it while punching my pillow at night. Equity—I reached the point where I refused to even say it aloud, because it wasn't a real word, it was bureaucratic jargon, a euphemism for cold hard *cash*, of which I had none. Purposely. Any dollar that wasn't nailed down I was plowing directly back into the business. Was that so rash?

To have cash balances sitting around doing nothing made no sense to me. Sure, it would have been the cautious, conservative, prudent thing. But the roadside was littered with cautious, conservative, prudent entrepreneurs. I wanted to keep my foot pressed hard on the gas pedal.

Somehow, in meeting after meeting, I held my tongue. Everything my banker said, I ultimately accepted. Then I'd do exactly as I pleased. I'd place another order with Onitsuka, double the size of the previous order, and show up at the bank all wide-eyed innocence, asking for a letter of credit to cover it. My banker would always be shocked. *You want HOW much?* And I'd always pretend to be shocked that he was shocked. *I thought you'd see the wisdom . . .* I'd wheedle, grovel, negotiate, and eventually he'd approve my loan.

After I'd sold out the shoes, and repaid the borrowing in full, I'd do it all over again. Place a mega order with Onitsuka, double the size of the previous order, then go to the bank in my best suit, an angelic look on my face.

My banker's name was Harry White. Fiftyish, avuncular, with a voice like a handful of gravel in a blender, he didn't seem to want to be a banker, and he particularly didn't want to be *my* banker.

He inherited me by default. My first banker had been Ken Curry, but when my father refused to be my guarantor, Curry phoned him straightaway. "Between us, Bill, if the kid's company goes under—you'll still back him, right?"

"Hell no," my father said.

So Curry decided he wanted no part of this father-son internecine war, and turned me over to White.

White was a vice president at First National, but this title was misleading. He didn't have much power. The bosses were always looking over his shoulder, second-guessing him, and the bossiest of bosses was a man named Bob Wallace. It was Wallace who made life difficult for White, and thereby for me. It was Wallace who fetishized equity and pooh-poohed growth.

Squarely built, with a thuggish face and Nixonian five o'clock shadow, Wallace was ten years my senior, but somehow thought himself the bank's boy wonder. He was also determined to become the bank's next president, and he viewed all bad credit risks as the main roadblock between him and that goal. He didn't like giving credit to anyone, for anything, but with my balance hovering always around zero, he saw me as a disaster waiting to happen. One slow season, one downturn in sales, I'd be out of business, the lobby of Wallace's bank would be filled with my unsold shoes, and the holy grail of bank president would slip from his grasp. Like Sarah atop Mount Fuji, Wallace saw me as a rebel, but he didn't think of this as a compliment. Nor, in the end, come to think of it, had she.

Of course, Wallace didn't always say all this directly to me. It was often conveyed by his middleman, White. White believed in me, and in Blue Ribbon, but he'd tell me all the time, with a sad head shake, that Wallace made the decisions, Wallace signed the checks, and Wallace was no fan of Phil Knight. I thought it was fitting, and telling, and hopeful, that White would use that word—"fan." He was tall, lean, a former athlete who loved to talk sports. No wonder we saw eye to eye. Wallace, on the other hand, looked as if he'd never set foot on a ball field. Unless maybe to repossess the equipment.

What sweet satisfaction it would have been to tell Wallace where he could shove his equity, then storm out and take my business elsewhere. But in 1965 there was no elsewhere. First National Bank was the only game in town and Wallace knew it. Oregon was smaller back then, and it had just two banks, First National and U.S. Bank. The latter had already turned me down. If I got thrown out of the former, I'd be done. (Today you can live in one state and bank in another, no problem, but banking regulations were much tighter in those days.)

Also, there was no such thing as venture capital. An aspiring young entrepreneur had very few places to turn, and those places were all guarded by risk-averse gatekeepers with zero imagination. In other words, bankers. Wallace was the rule, not the exception.

To make everything more difficult, Onitsuka was always late shipping my shoes, which meant less time to sell, which meant less time to make enough money to cover my loan. When I complained, Onitsuka didn't answer. When they did answer, they failed to appreciate my quandary. Time and again I'd send them a frantic telex, inquiring about the whereabouts of the latest shipment, and in response I'd typically get a telex that was maddeningly obtuse. *Little more days*. It was like dialing 911 and hearing someone on the other end yawn.

Given all these problems, given Blue Ribbon's cloudy future, I decided that I'd better get a real job, something safe to fall back on when everything went bust. At the same moment Johnson devoted himself exclusively to Blue Ribbon, I decided to branch out.

By now I'd passed all four parts of the CPA exam. So I mailed my test results and résumé to several local firms, interviewed with three or four, and got hired by Price Waterhouse. Like it or not, I was officially and irrevocably a card-carrying bean counter. My tax returns for that year wouldn't list my occupation as self-employed, or business owner, or entrepreneur. They would identify me as Philip H. Knight, Accountant.

MOST DAYS I didn't mind. For starters, I invested a healthy portion of my paycheck into Blue Ribbon's account at the bank, padding my precious equity, boosting the company's cash balance. Also, unlike Lybrand, the Portland branch of Price Waterhouse was a midsized firm. It had some thirty accountants on staff, compared to Lybrand's four, which made it a better fit for me.

The work suited me better, too. Price Waterhouse boasted a great variety of clients, a mix of interesting start-ups and established companies, all selling everything imaginable—lumber, water, power, food. While auditing these companies, digging into their guts, taking them apart and putting them back together, I was also learning how they survived, or didn't. How they sold things, or didn't. How they got into trouble, how they got out. I took careful notes about what made companies tick, what made them fail.

Again and again I learned that lack of equity was a leading cause of failure.

The accountants worked in teams, generally, and the A Team was headed by Delbert J. Hayes, the best accountant in the office, and by far its most flamboyant character. Six foot two, three hundred pounds, most of it stuffed sausage-like into an exceedingly inexpensive polyester suit, Hayes possessed great talent, great wit, great passion—and great appetites. Nothing gave him more pleasure than laying waste to a hoagie and a bottle of vodka, unless it was doing both while studying a spreadsheet. And he had a comparable hunger for smoke. Rain or shine he needed smoke running through his lungs and nasal passages. He chuffed through at least two packs a day.

I'd met other accountants who knew numbers, who had a way with numbers, but Hayes was to the numbers born. In a column of otherwise unspectacular fours and nines and twos, he could discern the raw elements of Beauty. He looked at numbers the way the poet looks at clouds, the way the geologist looks at rocks. He could draw from them rhapsodic song, demotic truths.

And uncanny predictions. Hayes could use numbers to tell the future.

Day after day I watched Hayes do something I'd never thought possible: He made accounting an art. Which meant he, and I, and all of us, were artists. It was a wonderful thought, an ennobling thought, one that would have never occurred to me.

Intellectually I always knew that numbers were beautiful. On some level I understood that numbers represented a secret code, that behind every row of numbers lay ethereal Platonic forms. My accounting classes had taught me that, sort of. As had sports. Running track gives you a fierce respect for numbers, because you *are* what your numbers say you are, nothing more, nothing less. If I posted a bad time in a race, there might have been reasons—injury, fatigue, broken heart—but no one cared. My numbers, in the end, were all that anyone would remember. I'd lived this reality, but Hayes the artist made me feel it.

Alas, I came to fear that Hayes was the tragic kind of artist, the self-sabotaging, van Gogh kind. He undercut himself at the firm, every day, by dressing badly, slouching badly, behaving badly. He also had an array of phobias—heights, snakes, bugs, confined spaces—which could be off-putting to his bosses and colleagues.

But he was most phobic about diets. Price Waterhouse would have made Hayes a partner, without hesitation, despite all his many vices, but the firm couldn't overlook his weight. It wasn't going to tolerate a three-hundred-pound partner. More than likely it was this unhappy fact that made Hayes eat so much in the first place. Whatever the reason, he ate a lot.

By 1965 he drank as much as he ate, which is saying a lot. And he refused to drink alone. Come quitting time, he'd insist that all his junior accountants join him.

He talked like he drank, nonstop, and some of the other accountants called him Uncle Remus. But I never did. I never rolled my eyes at Hayes's stem-winders. Each story contained some gem of wisdom about business—what made companies work, what the ledgers of a company really *meant*. Thus, many nights, I'd voluntarily, even eagerly, enter some Portland dive and match Hayes round for round, shot for shot. In the morning I'd wake feeling sicker than I had in that hammock in Calcutta, and it would take all my self-discipline to be of any use to Price Waterhouse.

It didn't help that, when I wasn't a foot soldier in Hayes's Army, I was still serving in the Reserves. (A seven-year commitment.) Tuesday nights, from seven to ten, I had to throw a switch in my brain and become First Lieutenant Knight. My unit was composed of longshoremen, and we were often stationed in the warehouse district, a few football fields away from where I picked up my shipments from Onitsuka. Most nights my men and I would load and unload ships, maintain jeeps and trucks. Many nights we'd do PT—physical training. Push-ups, pull-ups, sit-ups, running. I remember one night I led my company on a four-mile run. I needed to sweat out the booze from a Hayes binge, so I set a killing pace, and steadily increased it, grinding myself and the men to dust. After, I overheard one panting soldier tell another: "I was listening real close as Lieutenant Knight counted cadence. I never once heard that man take a deep breath!"

It was perhaps my only triumph of 1965.

SOME TUESDAY NIGHTS in the Reserves were set aside for classroom time. Instructors would talk to us about military strategy, which I found riveting. The instructors would often begin class by dissecting some long-ago, famous battle. But invariably they would drift off topic, onto Vietnam. The conflict was getting hotter. The United States was being drawn toward it, inexorably, as if by a giant magnet. One instructor told us to get our personal lives in order, kiss our wives and girlfriends good-bye. We were going to be "in the shit—real soon."

I had grown to hate that war. Not simply because I felt it was wrong. I also felt it was stupid, wasteful. I hated stupidity. I hated waste. Above all, *that* war, more than other wars, seemed to be run along the same principles as my bank. Fight not to win, but to avoid losing. A surefire losing strategy.

My fellow soldiers felt the same way. Is it any wonder that, the moment we were dismissed, we marched double-time to the nearest bar?

Between the Reserves and Hayes, I wasn't sure my liver was going to see 1966.

NOW AND THEN Hayes would hit the road, visit clients across Oregon, and I frequently found myself part of his traveling medicine show. Of all his junior accountants, I might have been his favorite, but especially when he traveled.

I liked Hayes, a lot, but I was alarmed to discover that when on the road he *really* let his hair down. And as always he expected his cohorts to do the same. It was never enough to just drink with Hayes. He demanded that you match him drop for drop. He counted drinks as carefully as he counted credits and debits. He said often that he believed in teamwork, and if you were on his team, by God you'd better *finish that damn drink*.

Half a century later my stomach rolls when I recall touring with Hayes around Albany, Oregon, doing a job for Wah Chung Exotic Metals. Each night, after crunching the numbers, we'd hit a little dive on the edge of town and close it down. I also recall, dimly, blurred days in Walla Walla, doing a job for Birds Eye, followed by nightcaps at the City Club. Walla Walla was a dry town, but bars got around the law by calling themselves "clubs." Membership in the City Club was one dollar, and Hayes was a member in good standing—until I misbehaved and got us kicked out. I don't remember what I did, but I'm sure it was awful. I'm equally sure I couldn't help myself. By then my blood was 50 percent gin.

I vaguely remember throwing up all over Hayes's car. I vaguely remember him very sweetly and patiently telling me to clean it up. What I remember vividly is that Hayes grew red in the face, righteously indignant on my behalf, even though I was clearly in the wrong, and resigned his membership in the City Club. Such loyalty, such unreasonable and unwarranted fealty—that might have been the moment I fell in love with Hayes. I looked up to the man when he saw something deeper in numbers, but I loved him when he saw something special in me.

On one of those road trips, in one of our boozy late-night conversations, I told Hayes about Blue Ribbon. He saw promise in it. He also saw doom. The numbers, he said, didn't lie. "Starting a new company," he said, "in this economy? And a shoe company? With zero cash balance?" He slouched and shook his big fuzzy head.

On the other hand, he said, I had one thing in my favor. Bowerman. A legend for a partner—that was one asset for which it was impossible to assign a number.

PLUS, MY ASSET was rising in value. Bowerman had gone to Japan for the 1964 Olympics, to support the members of the U.S. track-and-field team he'd coached. (Two of his runners, Bill Dellinger and Harry Jerome, medaled.) And after the Games, Bowerman had switched hats and become an ambassador for Blue Ribbon. He and Mrs. Bowerman—whose Christmas Club account had provided the initial five hundred dollars Bowerman gave me to form our partnership—visited Onitsuka and charmed everyone in the building.

They were given a royal welcome, a VIP tour of the factory, and

Morimoto even introduced them to Mr. Onitsuka. The two old lions, of course, bonded. Both, after all, were built from the same last, shaped by the same war. Both still approached everyday life as a battle. Mr. Onitsuka, however, had the particular tenacity of the defeated, which impressed Bowerman. Mr. Onitsuka told Bowerman about founding his shoe company in the ruins of Japan, when all the big cities were still smoldering from American bombs. He'd built his first lasts, for a line of basketball shoes, by pouring hot wax from Buddhist candles over his own feet. Though the basketball shoes didn't sell, Mr. Onitsuka didn't give up. He simply switched to running shoes, and the rest was shoe history. Every Japanese runner in the 1964 Games, Bowerman told me, was wearing Tigers.

Mr. Onitsuka also told Bowerman that the inspiration for the unique soles on Tigers had come to him while eating sushi. Looking down at his wooden platter, at the underside of an octopus's leg, he thought a similar suction cup might work on the sole of a runner's flat. Bowerman filed that away. Inspiration, he learned, can come from quotidian things. Things you might eat. Or find lying around the house.

Now back in Oregon, Bowerman was happily corresponding with his new friend, Mr. Onitsuka, and with the entire production team at the Onitsuka factory. He was sending them bunches of ideas and modifications of their products. Though all people are the same under the skin, Bowerman had come to believe that all feet are not created equal. Americans have different bodies than Japanese do—longer, heavier—and Americans therefore need different shoes. After dissecting a dozen pairs of Tigers, Bowerman saw how they could be tailored to cater to American customers. To that end, he had a slew of notes, sketches, designs, all of which he was firing off to Japan.

Sadly, he was discovering, as I had, that no matter how well you got along in person with the team at Onitsuka, things were different once you were back on your side of the Pacific. Most of Bowerman's letters went unanswered. When there was an answer, it was cryptic, or curtly dismissive. It pained me at times to think the Japanese were treating Bowerman the way I was treating Johnson.

But Bowerman wasn't me. He didn't take rejection to heart. Like Johnson, when his letters went unanswered, Bowerman simply wrote more. With more underlined words, more exclamation marks.

Nor did he flag in his experiments. He continued to tear apart Tigers, continued to use the young men on his track teams as lab mice. During the autumn track season of 1965, every race had two results for Bowerman. There was the performance of his runners, and there was the performance of their shoes. Bowerman would note how the arches held up, how the soles gripped the cinders, how the toes pinched and the instep flexed. Then he'd airmail his notes and findings to Japan.

Eventually he broke through. Onitsuka made prototypes that conformed to Bowerman's vision of a more American shoe. Soft inner sole, more arch support, heel wedge to reduce stress on the Achilles tendon—they sent the prototype to Bowerman and he went wild for it. He asked for more. He then handed these experimental shoes out to all his runners, who used them to crush the competition.

A little success always went to Bowerman's head, in the best way. Around this time he was also testing sports elixirs, magic potions and powders to give his runners more energy and stamina. When I was on his team he'd talked about the importance of replacing an athlete's salt and electrolytes. He'd forced me and others to choke down a potion he'd invented, a vile goo of mushed bananas, lemonade, tea, honey, and several unnamed ingredients. Now, while tinkering with shoes, he was also monkeying with his sports drink recipe, making it taste worse and work better. It wasn't until years later that I realized Bowerman was trying to invent Gatorade.

In his "free time," he liked to noodle with the surface at Hayward Field. Hayward was hallowed ground, steeped in tradition, but Bowerman didn't believe in letting tradition slow you down. Whenever rain fell, which it did all the time in Eugene, Hayward's cinder lanes turned to Venetian canals. Bowerman thought something rubbery would be easier to dry, sweep, and clean. He also thought something rubbery might be more forgiving on his runners' feet. So he bought a cement mixer, filled it with old shredded tires and assorted chemicals, and spent hours searching for just the right consistency and texture. More than once he made himself violently sick from inhaling the fumes of this witches' brew. Blinding headaches, a pronounced limp, loss of vision—these were a few of the lasting costs of his perfectionism.

Again, it was years before I realized what Bowerman was actually up to. He was trying to invent polyurethane.

I once asked him how he fit everything into a twenty-four-hour day. Coaching, traveling, experimenting, raising a family. He grunted as if to say, "It's nothing." Then he told me, sotto voce, that on top of everything else, he was also writing a book.

"A book?" I said.

"About jogging," he said gruffly.

Bowerman was forever griping that people make the mistake of thinking only elite Olympians are athletes. But everyone's an athlete, he said. If you have a body, you're an athlete. Now he was determined to get this point across to a larger audience. The reading public. "Sounds interesting," I said, but I thought my old coach had popped a screw. Who in heck would want to read a book about jogging?

1966

As I neared the end of my contract with Onitsuka, I checked the mail every day, hoping for a letter that would say they wanted to renew. Or that they didn't. There would be relief in knowing either way. Of course I was also hoping for a letter from Sarah, saying she'd changed her mind. And as always I was braced for a letter from my bank, telling me my business was no longer welcome.

But every day the only letters were from Johnson. Like Bowerman, the man didn't sleep. Ever. I could think of no other explanation for his ceaseless stream of correspondence. Much of which was pointless. Along with gobs of information I didn't need, the typical Johnson letter would include several long parenthetical asides, and some kind of rambling joke.

There might also be a hand-drawn illustration.

There might also be a musical lyric.

Sometimes there was a poem.

Batted out on a manual typewriter that violently Brailled the onionskin pages, many Johnson letters contained some kind of story. Maybe "parable" is a better word. How Johnson had sold this person a pair of Tigers, but down the road said person might be good for X more pairs, and therefore Johnson had a plan . . . How Johnson had chased and badgered the head coach at such-and-such high school, and tried to sell him *six pairs*, but in the end sold him *a baker's dozen* . . . which just went to show . . .

Often Johnson would describe in excruciating detail the latest ad he'd placed or was contemplating placing in the back pages of *Long Distance Log* or *Track & Field News.* Or he'd describe the photograph of a Tiger shoe he'd included with the ad. He'd constructed a make-shift photo studio in his house, and he'd pose the shoes seductively on the sofa, against a black sweater. Never mind that it sounded a bit like shoe porn, I just didn't see the point of placing ads in magazines read exclusively by running nerds. I didn't see the point of advertising, period. But Johnson seemed to be having fun, and he swore the ads worked, so, fine, far be it from me to stop him.

The typical Johnson letter would invariably close with a lament, either sarcastic or pointedly earnest, about my failure to respond to his previous letter. And the one before that, etc. Then there would be a PS, and usually another PS, and sometimes a pagoda of PS's. Then one last plea for encouraging words, which I never sent. I didn't have time for encouraging words. Besides, it wasn't my style.

I look back now and wonder if I was truly being myself, or if I was emulating Bowerman, or my father, or both. Was I adopting their man-of-few-words demeanor? Was I maybe modeling all the men I admired? At the time I was reading everything I could get my hands on about generals, samurai, shoguns, along with biographies of my three main heroes—Churchill, Kennedy, and Tolstoy. I had no love of violence, but I was fascinated by leadership, or lack thereof, under extreme conditions. War is the most extreme of conditions. But business has its warlike parallels. Someone somewhere once said that business is war without bullets, and I tended to agree.

I wasn't that unique. Throughout history men have looked to the warrior for a model of Hemingway's cardinal virtue, pressurized grace. (Hemingway himself wrote most of *A Moveable Feast* while gazing at a statue of Marshal Ney, Napoléon's favorite commander.) One lesson I took from all my home-schooling about heroes was that they didn't say much. None was a blabbermouth. None micromanaged. *Don't tell people how to do things, tell them what to do and let them surprise you with their results.* So I didn't answer Johnson, and I didn't pester him. Having told him what to do, I hoped that he would surprise me.

Maybe with silence.

To Johnson's credit, though he craved more communication, he never let the lack of it discourage him. On the contrary, it motivated him. He was anal, he recognized that I was not, and though he enjoyed complaining (to me, to my sister, to mutual friends), he saw that my managerial style gave him freedom. Left to do as he pleased, he responded with boundless creativity and energy. He worked seven days a week, selling and promoting Blue Ribbon, and when he wasn't selling, he was beaverishly building up his customer data files.

Each new customer got his or her own index card, and each index card contained that customer's personal information, shoe size, and shoe preferences. This database enabled Johnson to keep in touch with all his customers, at all times, and to keep them all feeling special. He sent them Christmas cards. He sent them birthday cards. He sent them notes of congratulation after they completed a big race or marathon. Whenever I got a letter from Johnson I knew it was one of dozens he'd carried down to the mailbox that day. He had hundreds and hundreds of customer-correspondents, all along the spectrum of humanity, from high school track stars to octogenarian weekend joggers. Many, upon pulling yet another Johnson letter from their mailboxes, must have thought the same thing I did: "Where does this guy find the time?"

Unlike me, however, most customers came to depend on Johnson's letters. Most wrote him back. They'd tell him about their lives, their troubles, their injuries, and Johnson would lavishly console, sympathize, and advise. Especially about injuries. Few in the 1960s knew the first thing about running injuries, or sports injuries in general, so Johnson's letters were often filled with information that was impossible to find anywhere else. I worried briefly about liability issues. I also worried that I'd one day get a letter saying Johnson had rented a bus and was driving them all to the doctor.

Some customers freely volunteered their opinion about Tigers, so Johnson began aggregating this customer feedback, using it to create new design sketches. One man, for instance, complained that Tiger flats didn't have enough cushion. He wanted to run the Boston Marathon but didn't think Tigers would last the twenty-six miles. So Johnson hired a local cobbler to graft rubber soles from a pair of shower shoes into a pair of Tiger flats. Voilà. Johnson's Franken-stein flat had space-age, full-length, midsole cushioning. (Today it's standard in all training shoes for runners.) The jerry-rigged Johnson sole was so dynamic, so soft, so new, Johnson's customer posted a personal best in Boston. Johnson forwarded me the results and urged me to pass them along to Tiger. Bowerman had just asked me to do the same with his batch of notes a few weeks earlier. Good grief, I thought, one mad genius at a time.

EVERY NOW AND then I'd make a mental note to warn Johnson about his growing list of pen pals. Blue Ribbon was supposed to confine itself to the thirteen western states, and Full-time Em-ployee Number One was not doing so. Johnson had customers in thirty-seven states, including the entire Eastern Seaboard, which was the heart of Marlboro Country. The Marlboro Man wasn't doing anything with his territory, so Johnson's incursions *seemed* harmless. But we didn't want to rub the man's nose in it.

Still, I never got around to telling Johnson my concerns. Per usual, I didn't tell him anything.

AT THE START of summer I decided my parents' basement was no longer big enough to serve as the headquarters of Blue Ribbon. And the servants' quarters weren't big enough for me. I rented a one-bedroom apartment downtown, in a spiffy new high-rise. The rent was two hundred dollars, which seemed pretty steep, but oh well. I also rented a few essentials—table, chairs, king-sized bed, olive couch—and tried to arrange them stylishly. It didn't look like much, but I didn't care, because my real furniture was shoes. My first-ever bachelor pad was filled from floor to ceiling with shoes.

I toyed with the idea of not giving Johnson my new address. But I did.

Sure enough, my new mailbox began to fill with letters. Return address: P.O. Box 492, Seal Beach, CA 90740.

None of which I answered.

THEN JOHNSON WROTE me two letters I couldn't ignore. First, he said that he, too, was moving. He and his new wife were splitting up. He was planning to stay in Seal Beach, but taking a small bachelor apartment.

Days later he wrote to say he'd been in a car wreck.

It happened in the early morning, somewhere north of San Bernardino. He was on his way to a road race, of course, where he'd intended to both run and sell Tigers. He'd fallen asleep at the wheel, he wrote, and woke to find himself and his 1956 Volkswagen Bug upside down and airborne. He struck the divider, then rolled, then flew out of the car, just before it somersaulted down the embankment. When Johnson's body finally stopped tumbling, he was on his back, looking at the sky, his collarbone, foot, and skull all shattered.

The skull, he said, was actually leaking.

Worse, being newly divorced, he had no one to care for him during his convalescence.

The poor guy was one dead dog from becoming a country-western song.

Despite all these recent calamities, Johnson was of good cheer. He assured me in a series of chirpy follow-up letters that he was managing to meet all his obligations. He was dragging himself around his new apartment, filling orders, shipping shoes, corresponding promptly with all customers. A friend was bringing him his mail, he said, so not to worry, P.O. Box 492 was still fully operational. In closing, he added that because he was now facing alimony, child support, and untold medical bills, he needed to inquire about the long-term prospects of Blue Ribbon. How did I see the future?

I didn't lie . . . exactly. Maybe out of pity, maybe haunted by the image of Johnson, single, lonely, his body wrapped in plaster of Paris, gamely trying to keep himself and my company alive, I sounded an upbeat tone. Blue Ribbon, I said, would probably morph over the years into a generalized sporting goods company. We'd probably have offices on the West Coast. And one day, maybe, in Japan. "Farfetched," I wrote. "But it seems worth shooting for."

This last line was wholly truthful. It *was* worth shooting for. If Blue Ribbon went bust, I'd have no money, and I'd be crushed. But I'd also have some valuable wisdom, which I could apply to the next business. Wisdom seemed an intangible asset, but an asset all the same, one that justified the risk. Starting my own business was the only thing that made life's other risks—marriage, Vegas, alligator wrestling—seem like sure things. But my hope was that when I failed, if I failed, I'd fail quickly, so I'd have enough time, enough years, to implement all the hard-won lessons. I wasn't much for setting goals, but this goal kept flashing through my mind every day, until it became my internal chant: *Fail fast.*

In closing I told Johnson that if he could sell 3,250 pairs of Tigers by the end of June 1966—completely impossible, by my calculations—I would authorize him to open that retail outlet he'd been harassing me about. I even put a PS at the bottom, which I knew he'd devour like a candy treat. I reminded him that he was selling so many shoes, so fast, he might want to speak to an accountant. There are income tax issues to consider, I said.

He fired back a sarcastic thanks for the tax advice. He wouldn't be filing taxes, he said, "because gross income was $1,209 while expenses total $1,245." His leg broken, his heart broken, he told me that he was also flat broke. He signed off: "Please send encouraging words."

I didn't.

SOMEHOW, JOHNSON HIT the magic number. By the end of June he'd sold 3,250 pairs of Tigers. And he'd healed. Thus, he was holding me to my end of the bargain. Before Labor Day he leased a small retail space at 3107 Pico Boulevard, in Santa Monica, and opened our first-ever retail store.

He then set about turning the store into a mecca, a holy of holies for runners. He bought the most comfortable chairs he could find, and afford (yard sales), and he created a beautiful space for runners to hang out and talk. He built shelves and filled them with books that every runner should read, many of them first editions from his own library. He covered the walls with photos of Tiger-shod runners, and laid in a supply of silk-screened T-shirts with *Tiger* across the front, which he handed out to his best customers. He also stuck Tigers to a black lacquered wall and illuminated them with a strip of can lights—very hip. Very mod. In all the world there had never been such a sanctuary for runners, a place that didn't just sell them shoes but celebrated them and their shoes. Johnson, the aspiring cult leader of runners, finally had his church. Services were Monday through Saturday, nine to six.

When he first wrote me about the store, I thought of the temples and shrines I'd seen in Asia, and I was anxious to see how Johnson's compared. But there just wasn't time. Between my hours at Price Waterhouse, my drunken revels with Hayes, my nights and weekends handling the minutiae connected with Blue Ribbon, and my fourteen hours each month soldiering in the Reserves, I was on fumes.

Then Johnson wrote me a fateful letter, and I had no choice. I jumped on a plane.

*　　*　　*

JOHNSON'S CUSTOMER PEN pals now numbered in the hundreds, and one of them, a high school kid on Long Island, had written to Johnson and inadvertently revealed some troubling news. The kid said his track coach had recently been talking about acquiring Tigers from a new source . . . some wrestling coach in Valley Stream or Massapequa or Manhasset.

The Marlboro Man was back. He'd even placed a national ad in an issue of *Track and Field*. While Johnson was busy poaching on the Marlboro Man's turf, the Marlboro Man was poaching our poaching. Johnson had done all this marvelous groundwork, had built up this enormous customer base, had spread the word about Tigers through his doggedness and crude marketing, and now the Marlboro Man was going to swoop in and capitalize?

I'm not sure why I hopped on the next plane to Los Angeles. I could have phoned. Maybe, like Johnson's customers, I needed a sense of community, even if it was a community of just two.

THE FIRST THING we did was go for a long, punishing run on the beach. Then we bought a pizza and brought it back to his apartment, which was your standard Divorced Guy Pad, only more so. Tiny, dark, sparse—it reminded me of some of the no-frills hostels where I'd stayed on my trip around the world.

Of course there were a few distinctly Johnsonian touches. Like shoes everywhere. I thought my apartment was filled with shoes, but Johnson basically lived inside a running shoe. Shoved into every nook and cranny, spread across every surface, were running shoes, and more running shoes, most in some state of deconstruction.

The few nooks and crannies that didn't hold shoes were filled with books, and more books, piled on homemade bookshelves, rough planks laid on cinder blocks. And Johnson didn't read trash. His

collection was mostly thick volumes of philosophy, religion, sociol-
ogy, anthropology, and the classics of Western literature. I thought
I loved to read; Johnson was next level.

What struck me most was the eerie violet light that suffused the
whole place. Its source was a seventy-five-gallon saltwater fish tank.
After clearing a place for me on the sofa, Johnson patted the tank and
explained. Most newly divorced guys like to prowl singles bars, but
Johnson spent his nights prowling under the Seal Beach pier, looking for rare fish. He captured them with something called a "slurp
gun," which he waved under my nose. It looked like a prototype for
the first-ever vacuum cleaner. I asked how it worked. Just stick this
nozzle into shallow water, he said, and suck up the fish into a plastic
tube, then into a small chamber. Then shoot it into your bucket and
schlep it home.

He'd managed to accumulate a wide variety of exotic creatures—
seahorses, opal-eye perch—which he showed me with pride. He
pointed out the jewel of his collection, a baby octopus he'd named
Stretch. "Speaking of which," Johnson said. "Feeding time."

He reached into a paper sack and pulled out a live crab. "Come
on, Stretch," he said, dangling the crab over the tank. The octopus
didn't stir. Johnson lowered the crab, legs wriggling, onto the tank's
sand-strewn floor. Still no reaction from Stretch. "He dead?" I asked.
"Watch," Johnson said.

The crab danced left and right, panicking, seeking cover. There
was none, however. And Stretch knew it. After a few minutes something emerged tentatively from Stretch's undercarriage. An antenna
or tentacle. It unfurled toward the crab and lightly tapped its cara-
pace. Yoo-hoo? "Stretch just injected poison in the crab," Johnson
said, grinning like a proud dad. We watched the crab slowly stop
dancing, stop moving altogether. We watched Stretch gently wrap
his antenna-tentacle around the crab and drag it back to his lair, a
hole he'd dug into the sand beneath a big rock.

It was a morbid puppet show, a dark kabuki play, starring a witless victim and a micro-kraken—was it a sign, a metaphor for our dilemma? One living thing being eaten by another? This was nature, wet in tooth and claw, and I couldn't help wondering if it was also to be the story of Blue Ribbon and the Marlboro Man.

We spent the rest of the evening sitting at Johnson's kitchen table and going over the letter from his Long Island informant. He read it aloud, and then I read it silently, and then we debated what to do.

"Get thee to Japan," Johnson said.

"What?"

"You gotta go," he said. "Tell them about the work we've done. Demand your rights. Kill this Marlboro Man once and for all. Once he starts selling running shoes, once he really gets going, there will be no stopping him. Either we draw a line in the sand, right now, or it's over."

I'd just come back from Japan, I said, and I didn't have the money to go again. I'd poured all my savings into Blue Ribbon, and I couldn't possibly ask Wallace for another loan. The thought nauseated me. Also, I didn't have time. Price Waterhouse allowed two weeks' vacation a year—unless you needed that two weeks for the Reserves, which I did. Then they gave you one extra week. Which I'd already used.

Above all, I told Johnson, "It's no use. The Marlboro Man's relationship with Onitsuka predates mine."

Undaunted, Johnson pulled out his typewriter, the one he'd been using to torture me, and began drafting notes, ideas, lists, which we could then turn into a manifesto for me to deliver to the executives at Onitsuka. While Stretch finished off the crab, we munched our pizza and guzzled beer and plotted late into the night.

BACK IN OREGON the next afternoon, I went straight in to see the office manager at Price Waterhouse. "I've got to have two weeks off," I said, "right now."

He looked up from the papers on his desk and glared at me, and for one hellishly long moment I thought I was going to be fired. Instead, he cleared his throat and mumbled something . . . odd. I couldn't make out every word but he seemed to think . . . from my intensity, my vagueness . . . *I'd gotten someone pregnant.*

I took a step back and started to protest, then shut my mouth. Let the man think what he wants. So long as he gives me the time.

Running a hand through his thinning hair, he finally sighed and said: "Go. Good luck. Hope it all works out."

I PUT THE airfare on my credit card. Twelve months to pay. And unlike my last visit to Japan, this time I wired ahead. I told the executives at Onitsuka that I was coming, and that I wanted a meeting.

They wired back: Come ahead.

But their wire went on to say that I wouldn't be meeting with Morimoto. He was either fired or dead. There was a new export manager, the wire said.

His name was Kitami.

KISHIKAN. JAPANESE FOR déjà vu. Again I found myself boarding a flight for Japan. Again I found myself underlining and memorizing my copy of *How to Do Business with the Japanese*. Again I found myself taking the train to Kobe, checking into the Newport, pacing in my room.

At zero hour I took a cab over to Onitsuka. I expected that we'd go into the old conference room, but no, they'd done some remodeling since my last visit. New conference room, they said. Sleeker, bigger, it had leather chairs instead of the old cloth ones, and a much longer table. More impressive, but less familiar. I felt disoriented, intimidated. It was like prepping for a meet at Oregon State and learning at the last minute that it had been moved to the Los Angeles Memorial Coliseum.

A man walked into the conference room and extended his hand. Kitami. His black shoes were brightly polished, his hair equally polished. Jet black, swept straight back, not a strand out of place. He was a great contrast to Morimoto, who always looked as if he'd dressed blindfolded. I was put off by Kitami's veneer, but suddenly he gave me a warm, ready smile, and encouraged me to sit, relax, tell him why I'd come, and now I got the distinct sense that, despite his slick appearance, he wasn't altogether sure of himself. He was in a brand-new job, after all. He didn't yet have much—equity. The word sprang to mind.

It occurred to me also that I had high value for Kitami. I wasn't a big client, but I wasn't small, either. Location is everything. I was selling shoes in *America*, a market vital to the future of Onitsuka. Maybe, just maybe, Kitami didn't want to lose me just yet. Maybe he wanted to hold on to me until they'd transitioned to the Marlboro Man. I was an asset, I was a credit, for the moment, which meant I might be holding better cards than I thought.

Kitami spoke more English than his predecessors, but with a thicker accent. My ear needed a few minutes to adjust as we chatted about my flight, the weather, sales. All the while other executives were filing in, joining us at the conference table. At last Kitami leaned back. "*Hai* . . ." He waited. "Mr. Onitsuka?" I asked. "Mr. Onitsuka will not be able to join us today," he said.

Damn. I was hoping to draw upon Mr. Onitsuka's fondness for me, not to mention his bond with Bowerman. But no. Alone, without allies, trapped in the unfamiliar conference room, I plunged ahead.

I told Kitami and the other executives that Blue Ribbon had done a remarkable job thus far. We'd sold out every order, while developing a robust customer base, and we expected this solid growth to continue. We had forty-four thousand dollars in sales for 1966, and projected to have eighty-four thousand dollars in 1967. I described our new store in Santa Monica, and laid out plans for other stores—

for a big future. Then I leaned in. "We would very much like to be the exclusive U.S. distributor for Tiger's track-and-field line," I said. "And I think it is very much in Tiger's interest that we become that."

I didn't even mention the Marlboro Man.

I looked around the table. Grim faces. None grimmer than Kitami's. He said in a few terse words that this would not be possible. Onitsuka wanted for its U.S. distributor someone bigger, more established, a firm that could handle the workload. A firm with offices on the East Coast.

"But, but," I spluttered, "Blue Ribbon *does* have offices on the East Coast."

Kitami rocked back in his chair. "Oh?"

"Yes," I said, "we're on the East Coast, the West Coast, and soon we may be in the Midwest. We can handle national distribution, no question." I looked around the table. The grim faces were becoming less grim.

"Well," Kitami said, "this change things."

He assured me that they would give my proposal careful consideration. So. *Hai*. Meeting adjourned.

I walked back to my hotel and spent a second night pacing. First thing the next morning I received a call summoning me back to Onitsuka, where Kitami awarded me exclusive distribution rights for the United States.

He gave me a three-year contract.

I tried to be nonchalant as I signed the papers and placed an order for five thousand more shoes, which would cost twenty thousand dollars I didn't have. Kitami said he'd ship them to my East Coast office, which I also didn't have.

I promised to wire him the exact address.

ON THE FLIGHT home I looked out the window at the clouds above the Pacific Ocean and thought back to sitting atop Mount Fuji. I wondered how Sarah would feel about me now, after this coup. I wondered how the Marlboro Man would feel when he got word from Onitsuka that he was toast.

I stowed away my copy of *How to Do Business with the Japanese*. My carry-on was stuffed with souvenirs. Kimonos for my mother and sisters and Mom Hatfield, a tiny samurai sword to hang above my desk. And my crowning glory—a small Japanese TV. Spoils of war, I thought, smiling. But somewhere over the Pacific the full weight of my "victory" came over me. I imagined the look on Wallace's face when I asked him to cover this gigantic new order. If he said no, *when* he said no, what then?

On the other hand, if he said yes, how was I going to open an office on the East Coast? And how was I going to do it before those shoes arrived? And who was I going to get to run it?

I stared at the curved, glowing horizon. There was only one person on the planet rootless enough, energetic enough, gung-ho enough, crazy enough, to pick up and move to the East Coast, on a moment's notice, and get there before the shoes did.

I wondered how Stretch was going to like the Atlantic Ocean.

1967

I didn't handle it well. Not well at all.
Knowing what his reaction would be, and dreading it, I put off telling Johnson the whole story. I shot him a quick note, saying the meeting with Onitsuka had gone fine, telling him I'd secured national distribution rights. But I left it at that. I think I must have held out hope, in the back of my mind, that I might be able to hire someone else to go east. Or that Wallace would blow the whole plan up.

And in fact I did hire someone else. A former distance runner, of course. But he changed his mind, backed out, just days after agreeing to go. So, frustrated, distracted, mired in a cycle of anxiety and procrastination, I turned to the much simpler problem of finding someone to replace Johnson at the store in Santa Monica. I asked John Bork, a high school track coach in Los Angeles, a friend of a friend. He jumped at the chance. He couldn't have been more eager.

How could I have known he'd be quite so eager? The next morning he appeared at Johnson's store and announced that he was the new boss. "The new—*what*?" Johnson said.

"I've been hired to take over for you when you go back east," Bork said.

"When I go—*where*?" Johnson said, reaching for the phone.

I didn't handle that conversation well, either. I told Johnson that, haha, hey, man, I was *just* about to call you. I said I was sorry he'd heard the news that way, how awkward, and I explained that I'd been forced to lie to Onitsuka and claim we already had an office on the East Coast. Thus, we were in one heck of a jam. The shoes would soon be on the water, an enormous shipment steaming for New York, and no one but Johnson could handle the task of claiming those shoes and setting up an office. The fate of Blue Ribbon rested on his shoulders.

Johnson was flabbergasted. Then furious. Then freaked. All in the space of one minute. So I got on a plane and flew down to visit him at his store.

HE DIDN'T WANT to live on the East Coast, he told me. He loved California. He'd lived in California all his life. He could go running year-round in California, and running, as I knew, was all to Johnson. How was he supposed to go running during those bitter cold winters back east? On and on it went.

All at once his manner changed. We were standing in the middle of his store, his sneaker sanctuary, and in a barely audible mumble he acknowledged that this was a make-or-break moment for Blue Ribbon, in which he was heavily invested, financially, emotionally, spiritually. He acknowledged that there was no one else who could set up an East Coast office. He delivered himself of a long, rambling, semi-internal monologue, saying that the Santa Monica store practically ran itself, so he could train his replacement in one day, and he'd already set up a store in a remote location once, so he could do it again, fast, and we needed it done fast, with the shoes on the water and back-to-school orders about to roll in, and then he looked off and asked the walls or the shoes or the Great Spirit why he shouldn't just shut up and do it, do whatever I asked, and be down-on-his-knees grateful for the damn opportunity, when anyone could see that he was—he searched for the exact words—"a talentless fuck."

I might have said something like, "Oh no you're not. Don't be so hard on yourself." I might have. But I didn't. I kept my mouth shut and waited.

And waited.

"Okay," he said, at last, "I'll go."

"Great. That's great. Terrific. Thank you."

"But *where*?"

"Where what?"

"Do you want me to go?"

"Ah. Yes. Well. Anywhere on the East Coast with a port. Just don't go to Portland, Maine."

"Why?"

"A company based in two different Portlands? That'll confuse the heck out of the Japanese."

We hashed it out some more and finally decided New York and Boston were the most logical places. Especially Boston. "It's where most of our orders are coming from," one of us said.

"Okay," he said. "Boston, here I come."

Then I handed him a bunch of travel brochures for Boston, playing up the fall foliage angle. A little heavy-handed, but I was desperate.

He asked how I happened to have these brochures on me, and I told him I knew he'd make the right decision.

He laughed.

The forgiveness Johnson showed me, the overall good nature he demonstrated, filled me with gratitude, and a new fondness for the man. And perhaps a deeper loyalty. I regretted my treatment of him. All those unanswered letters. There are team players, I thought, and then there are team players, and then there's Johnson.

AND THEN HE threatened to quit.

Via letter, of course. "I think I have been responsible for what success we have had so far," he wrote. "And any success that will be coming in for the next two years at least."

Therefore, he gave me a two-part ultimatum.

1. Make him a full partner in Blue Ribbon.
2. Raise his salary to six hundred dollars a month, plus a third of all profits beyond the first six thousand pairs of shoes sold.

Or else, he said, good-bye.

I phoned Bowerman and told him that Full-time Employee Number One was staging a mutiny. Bowerman listened quietly, considered all the angles, weighed the pros and cons, then rendered his verdict. "Fuck him."

I said I wasn't sure "fucking him" was the best strategy. Maybe there was some middle way of mollifying Johnson, of giving him a stake in the company. But as we talked about it in greater detail, the math just didn't pencil out. Neither Bowerman nor I wanted to surrender any portion of our stake, so Johnson's ultimatum, even if I'd wanted to accept it, was a nonstarter.

I flew to Palo Alto, where Johnson was visiting his parents, and asked for a sit-down. Johnson said he wanted his father, Owen, to join us. The meeting took place at Owen's office, and I was immediately stunned by the similarities between father and son. They looked alike, sounded alike, even had many of the same mannerisms. The similarities ended there, however. From the start Owen was loud, aggressive, and I could see that he'd been the instigator behind this mutiny.

By trade Owen was a salesman. He sold voice recording equipment, like Dictaphones, and he was darned good at it. For him, as with most salesmen, life was one long negotiation, which he relished. In other words, he was my complete opposite. Here we go, I thought. Yet another shootout with a consummate negotiator. When will it end?

Before getting down to brass tacks, Owen first wanted to tell me a story. Salesmen always do. Since I was an accountant, he said, he was reminded of an accountant he'd met recently who had a topless dancer for a client. The story, I believe, revolved around whether the dancer's silicone implants were deductible. At the punch line I laughed, to be polite, then gripped the arms of my chair and waited for Owen to stop laughing and make his opening move.

He began by citing all the things his son had done for Blue Ribbon. He insisted that his son was the main reason Blue Ribbon still existed. I nodded, let him talk himself out, and resisted the urge to make eye contact with Johnson, who sat off to the side. I wondered if they'd rehearsed all this, the way Johnson and I rehearsed my pitch before my last trip to Japan. When Owen finished, when he said that, given the facts, his son obviously should be a full partner in Blue Ribbon, I cleared my throat and conceded that Johnson was a dynamo, that his work had been vital and invaluable. But then I dropped the hammer. "The truth of the matter is, we have forty thousand dollars in sales, and more than that in debt, so there's simply nothing to divvy up here, fellas. We're fighting over slices of a pie that doesn't exist."

Moreover, I told Owen that Bowerman was unwilling to sell any of his stake in Blue Ribbon, and therefore I couldn't sell any of mine. If I did I'd be surrendering majority control of the thing I'd created. That wasn't feasible.

I made my counteroffer. I would give Johnson a fifty-dollar raise.

Owen stared. It was a fierce, tough stare, honed during many intense negotiations. A lot of Dictaphones had moved out the door after that stare. He was waiting for me to bend, to up my offer, but for once in my life I had leverage, because I had nothing left to give. "Take it or leave it" is like four of a kind. Hard to beat.

Finally Owen turned to his son. I think we both knew from the start that Johnson would be the one to settle this, and I saw in Johnson's face that two contrary desires were fighting for his heart. He didn't want to accept my offer. But he didn't want to quit. He loved Blue Ribbon. He needed Blue Ribbon. He saw Blue Ribbon as the one place in the world where he fit, an alternative to the corporate quicksand that had swallowed most of our schoolmates and friends, most of our generation. He'd complained a million times about my lack of communication, but in fact my laissez-faire management style had fostered him, unleashed him. He wasn't likely to find that kind of autonomy anywhere else. After several seconds he reached out his hand. "Deal," he said. "Deal," I said, shaking it.

We sealed our new agreement with a six-mile run. As I remember, I won.

WITH JOHNSON ON the East Coast, and Bork taking over his store, I was awash in employees. And then I got a call from Bowerman asking me to add yet *another*. One of his former track guys—Geoff Hollister.

I took Hollister out for a hamburger, and we got along fine, but he cinched the deal by not even flinching when I reached into my pocket and found I didn't have any money to pay for lunch. So I hired him to go around the state selling Tigers, thereby making him Full-time Employee Number Three.

Soon Bowerman phoned again. He wanted me to hire *another* person. Quadrupling my staff in the span of a few months? Did my old coach think I was General Motors? I might have balked, but then Bowerman said the job candidate's name.

Bob Woodell.

I knew the name, of course. Everyone in Oregon knew the name. Woodell had been a standout on Bowerman's 1965 team. Not quite a star, but a gritty and inspiring competitor. With Oregon defending its second national championship in three years, Woodell had come out of nowhere and won the long jump against vaunted UCLA. I'd been there, I'd watched him do it, and I'd gone away mighty impressed.

The next day there had been a bulletin on TV. An accident at

Oregon's Mother's Day Celebrations. Woodell and twenty of his frat brothers were hoisting a float down to the Millrace, a stream that wound through campus. They were trying to flip it over and someone lost their footing. Then someone lost their hold. Someone else let go. Someone screamed, everyone ran. The float collapsed, trapping Woodell underneath, crushing his first lumbar vertebra. There seemed little hope of his walking again.

Bowerman had held a twilight meet at Hayward Field to raise money for Woodell's medical expenses. Now he faced the task of finding something for Woodell to do. At present, he said, the poor guy was sitting around his parents' house in a wheelchair, staring at the walls. Woodell had made tentative inquiries about being Bowerman's assistant coach, but Bowerman said to me: "I just don't think that's going to work, Buck. Maybe he could do something for Blue Ribbon."

I hung up and dialed Woodell. I nearly said how sorry I was about his accident, but I caught myself. I wasn't sure that was the right thing to say. In my mind I ran through another half dozen things, each of which seemed wrong. I'd never been so at a loss for words, and I'd spent half my life tongue-tied. What does one say to a track star who suddenly can't move his legs? I decided to keep it strictly business. I explained that Bowerman had recommended Woodell and said I might have a job for him with my new shoe company. I suggested we get together for lunch. Sure thing, he said.

We met the next day at a sandwich shop in downtown Beaverton, a suburb north of Portland. Woodell drove there himself; he'd already mastered a special car, a Mercury Cougar with hand controls. In fact, he was early. I was fifteen minutes late.

If not for his wheelchair, I don't know that I'd have recognized Woodell when I first walked in. I'd seen him once in person, and several times on TV, but after his many ordeals and surgeries he was shockingly thinner. He'd lost sixty pounds, and his naturally sharp features were now drawn with a much finer pencil. His hair, however, was still jet black, and still grew in remarkably tight curls.

He looked like a bust or frieze of Hermes I'd seen somewhere in the Greek countryside. His eyes were black, too, and they shone with a steeliness, a shrewdness—maybe a sadness. Not unlike Johnson's. Whatever it was, it was mesmerizing, and endearing. I regretted being late.

Lunch was supposed to be a job interview, but the interview part was a formality, we both knew. Men of Oregon take care of their own. Fortunately, loyalty aside, we hit it off. We made each other laugh, mostly about Bowerman. We reminisced about the many ways he tortured runners, ostensibly to instill toughness, like heating a key on a stove and pressing it against their naked flesh in the sauna. We'd both fallen victim. Before long I felt that I'd have given Woodell a job even if he'd been a stranger. Gladly. He was my kind of people. I wasn't certain what Blue Ribbon was, or if it would ever become a thing at all, but whatever it was or might become, I hoped it would have something of this man's spirit.

I offered him a position opening our second retail store, in Eugene, off the campus, at a monthly salary of four hundred dollars. He didn't negotiate, thank goodness. If he'd asked for four thousand a month, I might have found a way.

"Deal?" I said. "Deal," he said. He reached out, shook my hand. He still had the strong grip of an athlete.

The waitress brought the check and I told Woodell grandly that lunch was on me. I pulled out my wallet and found that it was empty. I asked Blue Ribbon's Full-time Employee Number Four if he could float me. Just till payday.

WHEN HE WASN'T sending me new employees, Bowerman was sending me the results of his latest experiments. In 1966 he'd noticed that the Spring Up's outer sole melted like butter, whereas the midsole remained solid. So he'd urged Onitsuka to take Spring Up's midsole and fuse it with the Limber Up's outer sole, thus creating the ultimate distance training shoe. Now, in 1967, Onitsuka sent us the prototype, and it was astonishing. With its luxurious cushioning and its sleek lines, it looked like the future.

Onitsuka asked what we thought it should be called. Bowerman liked "Aztec," in homage to the 1968 Olympics, which were being held in Mexico City. I liked that, too. Fine, Onitsuka said. The Aztec was born.

And then Adidas threatened to sue. Adidas already had a new shoe named the "Azteca Gold," a track spike they were planning to introduce at the same Olympics. No one had ever heard of it, but that didn't stop Adidas from kicking up a fuss.

Aggravated, I drove up the mountain to Bowerman's house to talk it all over. We sat on the wide porch, looking down at the river. It sparkled that day like a silver shoelace. He took off his ball cap, put it on again, rubbed his face. "Who was that guy who kicked the shit out of the Aztecs?" he asked. "Cortez," I said. He grunted. "Okay. Let's call it the Cortez."

I WAS DEVELOPING an unhealthy contempt for Adidas. Or maybe it was healthy. That one German company had dominated the shoe market for a couple of decades, and they possessed all the arrogance of unchallenged dominance. Of course it's possible that they weren't arrogant at all, that to motivate myself I needed to see them as a monster. In any event, I despised them. I was tired of looking up every day and seeing them far, far ahead. I couldn't bear the thought that it was my fate to do so forever.

The situation put me in mind of Jim Grelle. In high school, Grelle—pronounced *Grella*, or sometimes *Gorilla*—had been the fastest runner in Oregon, and I had been the second-fastest, which meant four years of staring at Grelle's back. Then Grelle and I both went to the University of Oregon, where his tyranny over me continued. By the time I graduated I hoped never again to see Grelle's back. Years later, when Grelle won the 1,500 in Moscow's Lenin Stadium, I was wearing an army uniform, sitting on a couch in the day room at Fort Lewis. I pumped my fist at the screen, proud of my fellow Oregonian, but I also died a little at the memory of the many times he'd bested me. Now I began to see Adidas as a second Grelle. Chasing them, being legally checked by them, irritated me to no end. It also drove me. Hard.

Once again, in my quixotic effort to overtake a superior opponent, I had Bowerman as my coach. Once again he was doing everything he could to put me in position to win. I often drew on the memory of his old prerace pep talks, especially when we were up against our blood rivals Oregon State. I would replay Bowerman's epic speeches, hear him telling us that Oregon State wasn't just any opponent. Beating USC and Cal was important, he said, but beating Oregon State was (pause) *different*. Nearly sixty years later it gives me chills to recall his words, his tone. No one could get your blood going like Bowerman, though he never raised his voice. He knew how to speak in subliminal italics, to slyly insert exclamation marks, like hot keys against the flesh.

For extra inspiration I'd sometimes think back to the first time I saw Bowerman walking around the locker room and handing out new shoes. When he came to me, I wasn't even sure I'd made the team. I was a freshman, still unproven, still developing. But he shoved a new pair of spikes straight into my chest. "Knight," he said. That was all. Just my name. Not a syllable more. I looked down at the shoes. They were Oregon green, with yellow stripes, the most breathtaking things I'd ever seen. I cradled them, and later I carried them back to my room and put them gingerly on the top shelf of my bookcase. I remember that I trained my gooseneck desk lamp on them.

They were Adidas, of course.

By the tail end of 1967 Bowerman was inspiring many people besides me. That book he'd been talking about, that silly book about jogging, was done, and out in bookstores. A slight one hundred pages, *Jogging* preached the gospel of physical exercise to a nation that had seldom heard that sermon before, a nation that was collectively lolling on the couch, and somehow the book caught fire. It sold a million copies, sparked a movement, changed the very meaning of the word "running." Before long, thanks to Bowerman and his book, running was no longer just for weirdos. It was no longer a cult. It was almost—cool?

I was happy for him, but also for Blue Ribbon. His bestseller would surely generate publicity and bump our sales. Then I sat down and read the thing. My stomach dropped. In his discussion of proper equipment, Bowerman gave some commonsense advice, followed by some confounding recommendations. Discussing shin splints, or "buck shins," he said the right shoes were important, but almost any shoes would work. "Probably the shoes you wear for gardening, or working around the house, will do just fine."

What?

As for workout clothes, Bowerman told readers that proper clothing "may help the spirit," but added that people shouldn't get hung up on *brands*.

Maybe he thought this was true for the casual jogger, as opposed to the trained athlete, but by God did he need to say so in print? When we were fighting to establish *a brand*? More to the point, what did this mean about his true opinion of Blue Ribbon—and me? Any shoe would do? If that were true, why in the world were we bothering to sell Tigers? Why were we jackassing around?

Here I was, chasing Adidas, but in a way I was still chasing Bowerman, seeking his approval, and as always it seemed highly unlikely in late 1967 that I'd ever catch either one.

THANKS LARGELY TO Bowerman's Cortez, we closed the year in a blaze, meeting our expectation of revenue: eighty-four thousand dollars. I almost looked forward to my next trip to First National. Finally Wallace would back off, loosen the purse strings. Maybe he'd even concede the value of growth.

In the meantime Blue Ribbon had outgrown my apartment. Maybe it's more accurate to say that it had taken over. The place was now the equal of Johnson's bachelor pad. All it needed was a violet light and a baby octopus. I couldn't put it off any longer, I needed a proper office space, so I rented a large room on the east side of town.

It wasn't much. A plain old workspace with a high ceiling and high windows, several of which were broken or stuck open, meaning the room was a constant, brisk fifty degrees. Right next door was a raucous tavern, the Pink Bucket, and every day at 4:00 p.m., promptly, the jukebox would kick in. The walls were so thin, you could hear the first record drop and feel every thumping note thereafter.

You could almost hear people striking matches, lighting cigarettes, clinking glasses. Cheers. *Salud*. Mud in your eye.

But the rent was cheap. Fifty bucks a month.

When I took Woodell to see it, he allowed it had a certain charm. Woodell needed to like it, because I was transferring him from the Eugene store to this office. He'd shown tremendous skills at the store, a flair for organizing, along with boundless energy, but I could use him better in what I would be calling "the home office." Sure enough, on Day One he came up with a solution to the stuck windows. He brought in one of his old javelins to hook the window latches and push them shut.

We couldn't afford to fix the broken glass in the other windows, so on really cold days we just wore sweaters.

Meanwhile, in the middle of the room I erected a plywood wall, thereby creating warehouse space in the back and retail-office space up front. I was no handyman, and the floor was badly warped, so the wall wasn't close to straight or even. From ten feet away it appeared to undulate. Woodell and I decided that was kind of groovy.

At an office thrift store we bought three battered desks, one for me, one for Woodell, one for "the next person stupid enough to work for us." I also built a corkboard wall, to which I pinned different Tiger models, borrowing some of Johnson's décor ideas in Santa Monica. In a far corner I set up a small sitting area for customers to try on shoes.

One day, at five minutes before 6:00 p.m., a high school kid wandered in. Need some running shoes, he said timidly. Woodell and I looked at each other, looked at the clock. We were beat, but we needed every sale. We talked to the kid about his instep, his stride, his life, and gave him several pairs to try on. He took his time lacing them up, walking around the room, and each pair he declared "not quite right." At 7:00 p.m. he said he'd have to go home and "think about it." He left, and Woodell and I sat amid the mounds of empty boxes and scattered shoes. I looked at him. He looked at me. This is how we're going to build a shoe company?

AS I GRADUALLY moved my inventory out of my apartment, into my new office, the thought crossed my mind that it might make more sense to give up the apartment altogether, just move into the office, since I'd basically be living there anyway. When I wasn't at Price Waterhouse, making the rent, I'd be at Blue Ribbon, and vice versa. I could shower at the gym.

But I told myself that living in your office is the act of a crazy person.

And then I got a letter from Johnson saying he was living in his new office.

He'd chosen to locate our East Coast office in Wellesley, a tony suburb of Boston. Of course he included a hand-drawn map, and a sketch, and more information than I'd ever need about the history and topography and weather patterns of Wellesley. Also, he told me how he'd come to choose it.

At first he'd considered Long Island, New York. Upon his arrival there he'd rendezvoused with the high school kid who'd alerted him to the Marlboro Man's secret machinations. The kid drove Johnson all over, and Johnson saw enough of Long Island to know that this place wasn't his bag. He left the high school kid, headed north on I-95, and when he hit Wellesley, it just spoke to him. He saw people running along quaint country roads, many of them women, many of them Ali MacGraw look-alikes. Ali MacGraw was Johnson's type. He remembered that Ali MacGraw had attended Wellesley College.

Then he learned, or remembered, that the Boston Marathon route ran right through the town. Sold.

He riffled through his card catalog and found the address of a local customer, another high school track star. He drove to the kid's house, knocked at the door, unannounced. The kid wasn't there, but his parents said Johnson was more than welcome to come in and wait. When the kid got home he found his shoe salesman sitting at the dining room table eating dinner with the whole family. The next day, after they went for a run, Johnson got from the kid a list of names—local coaches, potential customers, likely contacts—and a list of what neighborhoods he might like. Within days he'd found and rented a little house behind a funeral parlor. Claiming it in the name of Blue Ribbon, he also made it his home. He wanted me to go halfsies on the two-hundred-dollar rent.

In a PS he said I should buy him furniture also.

I didn't answer.

1968

I was putting in six days a week at Price Waterhouse, spending early mornings and late nights and all weekends and vacations at Blue Ribbon. No friends, no exercise, no social life—and wholly content. My life was out of balance, sure, but I didn't care. In fact, I wanted even more imbalance. Or a different kind of imbalance.

I wanted to dedicate every minute of every day to Blue Ribbon. I'd never been a multitasker, and I didn't see any reason to start now. I wanted to be present, always. I wanted to focus constantly on the one task that really mattered. If my life was to be all work and no play, I wanted my work to be play. I wanted to quit Price Waterhouse. Not that I hated it; it just wasn't me.

I wanted what everyone wants. To be me, full-time.

But it wasn't possible. Blue Ribbon simply couldn't support me. Though the company was on track to double sales for a fifth straight year, it still couldn't justify a salary for its cofounder. So I decided to compromise, find a different day job, one that would pay my bills but require fewer hours, leaving me more time for my passion.

The only job I could think of that fit this criterion was teaching. I applied to Portland State University, and got a job as an assistant professor, at seven hundred dollars a month.

I should have been delighted to quit Price Waterhouse, but I'd learned a lot there, and I was sad about leaving Hayes. No more after-work cocktails, I told him. No more Walla Walla. "I'm going to focus on my shoe thing," I said. Hayes frowned, grumbled something about missing me, or admiring me.

I asked what he was going to do. He said he was going to ride it out at Price Waterhouse. Lose fifty pounds, make partner, that was his plan. I wished him luck.

As part of my formal severing, I had to go in and talk to the boss, a senior partner with the Dickensian name of Curly Leclerc. He was polite, even-handed, smooth, playing a one-act drama he'd played a hundred times—the exit interview. He asked what I was going to do instead of working for one of the finest accounting firms in the world. I said that I'd started my own business and was hoping it might take off, and in the meantime I was going to teach accounting.

He stared. I'd gone off script. Way off. "Why the hell would you do something like that?"

Lastly, the really difficult exit interview. I told my father. He, too, stared. Bad enough I was still jackassing around with shoes, he said, but now . . . *this*. Teaching wasn't respectable. Teaching at Portland State was downright disrespectable. "What am I going to tell my friends?" he asked.

THE UNIVERSITY ASSIGNED me four accounting classes, including Accounting 101. I spent a few hours prepping, reviewing basic concepts, and as fall arrived the balance of my life shifted just as I'd planned. I still didn't have all the time I wanted or needed for Blue Ribbon, but I had more. I was following a path that felt like my path, and though I wasn't sure where it would lead, I was ready to find out.

So I was beaming with hope on that first day of the semester, in early September 1967. My students, however, were not. Slowly they filed into the classroom, each one radiating boredom and hostility. For the next hour they were to be confined in this stifling cage, force-fed some of the driest concepts ever devised, and I was to blame, which made me the target of their resentment. They eyed me, frowned. A few scowled.

I empathized. But I wasn't going to let them rattle me. Standing at the lectern in my black suit and skinny gray tie, I remained calm, for the most part. I was always somewhat restless, somewhat twitchy, and in those days I had several nervous tics—like wrapping rubber bands around my wrist and playing with them, snapping them against my skin. I might have snapped them extra fast, extra hard, as I saw the students slump into the room like prisoners on a chain gang.

Suddenly, sweeping lightly into the classroom and taking a seat in the front row was a striking young woman. She had long golden hair that brushed her shoulders, and matching golden hoop earrings that also brushed her shoulders. I looked at her, and she looked at me. Bright blue eyes set off by dramatic black eyeliner.

I thought of Cleopatra. I thought of Julie Christie. I thought: Jeez, Julie Christie's kid sister has just enrolled in my accounting class.

I wondered how old she was. She couldn't yet be twenty, I guessed, snapping my rubber bands against my wrist, snapping, snapping, and staring, then pretending not to stare. She was hard to look away from. And hard to figure. So young, and yet so worldly. Those earrings—they were strictly hippie, and yet that eye makeup was *très* chic. Who *was* this girl? And how was I going to concentrate on teaching with her in the front row?

I called roll. I can still remember the names. "Mr. Trujillo?"

"Here."

"Mr. Peterson?"

"Here."

"Mr. Jameson?"

"Here."

"Miss Parks?"

"Here," said Julie Christie's kid sister, softly.

I looked up, gave a half smile. She gave a half smile. I penciled a shaky check next to her full name: Penelope Parks. Penelope, like the faithful wife of world-traveling Odysseus.

Present and accounted for.

I DECIDED TO employ the Socratic method. I was emulating the Oregon and Stanford professors whose classes I'd enjoyed most, I guess. And I was still under the spell of all things Greek, still enchanted by my day at the Acropolis. But maybe, by asking questions rather than lecturing, I was also trying to deflect attention from myself, force students to participate. Especially certain pretty students.

"Okay, class," I said, "you buy three virtually identical widgets for one dollar, two dollars, and three dollars, respectively. You sell one for five dollars. What's the *cost* of that sold widget? And what's the gross profit on the sale?"

Several hands went up. None, alas, was Miss Parks's. She was looking down. Shier than the professor, apparently. I was forced to call on Mr. Trujillo, and then Mr. Peterson.

"Okay," I said. "Now, Mr. Trujillo recorded his inventory on a FIFO basis and made a gross profit of four dollars. Mr. Peterson used LIFO and had a gross profit of two dollars. So . . . who has the better business?"

A spirited discussion followed, involving nearly everybody but Miss Parks. I looked at her. And looked. She didn't speak. She didn't look up. Maybe she wasn't shy, I thought. Maybe she just wasn't very bright. How sad if she'd have to drop the class. Or if I'd have to flunk her.

Early on, I drummed into my students the primary principle of all accounting: Assets equal liabilities plus equity. This foundational equation, I said, must always, always be in balance. Accounting is problem-solving, I said, and most problems boil down to some imbalance in this equation. To solve, therefore, get it balanced. I felt a little hypocritical saying this, since my company had an out-of-whack liabilities-to-equity ratio of ninety to ten. More than once I winced to think what Wallace would say if he could sit in on one of my classes.

My students apparently weren't any more capable than I of balancing this equation. Their homework papers were dreadful. That is, with the exception of Miss Parks! She aced the first assignment. With the next and the next she established herself as the top student in the class. And she didn't just get every answer right. Her penmanship was exquisite. Like Japanese calligraphy. A girl that looked like that—*and* whip smart?

She went on to record the highest grade in the class on the midterm. I don't know who was happier, Miss Parks or Mr. Knight.

Not long after I handed back the tests she lingered at my desk, asking if she could have a word. Of course, I said, reaching for my wrist rubber bands, giving them a series of vehement snaps. She asked if I might consider being her adviser. I was taken back. "Oh," I said. "Oh. I'd be honored."

Then I blurted: "How would *you* . . . like . . . a job?"

"A what?"

"I've got this little shoe company . . . uh . . . on the side. And it needs some bookkeeping help."

She was holding her textbooks against her chest. She adjusted them and fluttered her eyelashes. "Oh," she said. "Oh. Well. Okay. That sounds . . . fun."

I offered to pay her two dollars an hour. She nodded. Deal.

DAYS LATER SHE arrived at the office. Woodell and I gave her the third desk. She sat, placed her palms on the desktop, looked around the room. "What do you want me to do?" she asked.

Woodell handed her a list of things—typing, bookkeeping, scheduling, stocking, filing invoices—and told her to pick one or two each day and have at it.

But she didn't pick. She did them all. Quickly, and with ease. Inside a week neither Woodell nor I could remember how we'd ever gotten along without her.

It wasn't just the quality of Miss Parks's work that we found so valuable. It was the blithe spirit in which she did it. From Day One, she was all in. She grasped what we were trying to do, what we were trying to build here. She felt that Blue Ribbon was unique, that it might become something special, and she wanted to do what she could to help. Which proved to be a lot.

She had a remarkable way with people, especially the sales reps we were continuing to hire. Whenever they came into the office, Miss Parks would size them up, fast, and either charm them or put them in their place, depending on what was called for. Though shy, she could be wry, funny, and the sales reps—that is, the ones she liked—often left laughing, looking back over their shoulders, wondering what just hit them.

The impact of Miss Parks was most apparent in Woodell. He was going through a bad time just then. His body was fighting the wheelchair, resisting its life imprisonment. He was plagued by bedsores and other maladies related to sitting motionless, and often he'd be out sick for weeks at a time. But when he was in the office, when he was sitting alongside Miss Parks, she brought the color back to his cheeks. She had a healing effect on him, and seeing this had a bewitching effect on me.

Most days I surprised myself, offering eagerly to run across the street to get lunch for Miss Parks and Woodell. This was the kind of thing we might have asked Miss Parks to do, but day after day I volunteered. Was it chivalry? Devilry? What was happening to me? I didn't recognize myself.

And yet some things never change. My head was so full of debits and credits, and shoes, shoes, shoes, that I rarely got the lunch orders right. Miss Parks never complained. Nor did Woodell. Invariably I'd hand each of them a brown paper bag and they'd exchange a knowing glance. "Can't wait to see what I'm eating for lunch today," Woodell would mutter. Miss Parks would put a hand over her mouth, concealing a smile.

Miss Parks saw my bewitchment, I think. There were several long looks between us, several meaningfully awkward pauses. I recall one burst of particularly nervous laughter, one portentous silence. I remember one long moment of eye contact that kept me awake that night.

Then it happened. On a cold afternoon in late November, when Miss Parks wasn't in the office, I was walking toward the back of the office and noticed her desk drawer open. I stopped to close it and inside I saw . . . a stack of checks? All her paychecks—uncashed.

This wasn't a job to her. This was something else. And so perhaps . . . was I? Maybe?

Maybe.

(Later, I learned Woodell was doing the same thing.)

That Thanksgiving a record cold spell hit Portland. The breeze coming through the holes in the office windows was now a fierce arctic wind. At times the gusts were so strong, papers flew from the desktops, shoelaces on the samples fluttered. The office was intolerable, but we couldn't afford to fix the windows, and we couldn't shut down. So Woodell and I moved to my apartment, and Miss Parks joined us there each afternoon.

One day, after Woodell had gone home, neither Miss Parks nor I said much. At quitting time I walked her out to the elevator. I pressed the down button. We both smiled tensely. I pressed down again. We both stared at the light above the elevator doors. I cleared my throat. "Miss Parks," I said. "Would you like to, uhh . . . maybe go out on Friday night?"

Those Cleopatra eyes. They doubled in size. "Me?"

"I don't see anyone else here," I said.

Ping. The elevator doors slid open.

"Oh," she said, looking down at her feet. "Well. Okay. Okay." She hurried onto the elevator, and as the doors closed she never lifted her gaze from her shoes.

I TOOK HER to the Oregon Zoo. I don't know why. I guess I thought walking around and gazing at animals would be a low-key way of getting to know each other. Also, Burmese pythons, Nigerian goats, African crocodiles, they would give me ample opportunities to impress her with tales of my travels. I felt the need to brag about seeing the pyramids, the Temple of Nike. I also told her about falling ill in Calcutta. I'd never described that scary moment, in detail, to anyone. I didn't know why I was telling Miss Parks, except that Calcutta had been one of the loneliest moments of my life, and I felt very unlonely just then.

I confessed that Blue Ribbon was tenuous. The whole thing might go bust any day, but I still couldn't see myself doing anything else. My little shoe company was a living, breathing thing, I said, which I'd created from nothing. I'd breathed it into life, nurtured it through illness, brought it back several times from the dead, and now I wanted, needed, to see it stand on its own feet and go out into the world. "Does that make sense?" I said.

Mm-hm, she said.

We strolled past the lions and tigers. I told her that I flat-out didn't want to work for someone else. I wanted to build something that was my own, something I could point to and say: I *made* that. It was the only way I saw to make life meaningful.

She nodded. Like basic accounting principles, she grasped it all intuitively, right away.

I asked if she was seeing anyone. She confessed that she was. But the boy—well, she said, he was just a boy. All the boys she dated, she said, were just that—boys. They talked about sports and cars. (I was smart enough not to confess that I loved both.) "But you," she said, "you've seen the world. And now you're putting everything on the line to create this company . . ."

Her voice trailed off. I stood up straighter. We said good-bye to the lions and tigers.

FOR OUR SECOND date we walked over to Jade West, a Chinese restaurant across the street from the office. Over Mongolian beef and garlic chicken she told me her story. She still lived at home, and loved her family very much, but there were challenges. Her father was an admiralty lawyer, which struck me as a good job. Their house certainly sounded bigger and better than the one in which I'd grown up. But five kids, she hinted, was a strain. Money was a constant issue. A certain amount of rationing was standard operating procedure. There was never enough; staples, like toilet paper, were always in low supply. It was a home marked by *insecurity*. She did *not* like insecurity. She preferred security. She said it again. *Security*. That's why she'd been drawn to accounting. It seemed solid, dependable, safe, a line of work she could always rely on.

I asked how she'd happened to choose Portland State. She said she'd started out at Oregon State.

"Oh," I said, as if she'd confessed to doing time in prison.

She laughed. "If it's any consolation, I hated it." In particular, she couldn't abide the school's requirement that every student take at least one class in public speaking. She was far too shy.

"I understand, Miss Parks."

"Call me Penny."

After dinner I drove her home and met her parents. "Mom, Dad, this is Mr. Knight."

"Pleased to meet you," I said, shaking their hands.

We all stared at each other. Then the walls. Then the floor. Lovely weather we're having, isn't it?

"Well," I said, tapping my watch, snapping my rubber bands, "it's late, I'd better be going."

Her mother looked at a clock on the wall. "It's only nine o'clock," she said. "Some hot date."

JUST AFTER OUR second date Penny went with her parents to Hawaii for Christmas. She sent me a postcard, and I took this as a good sign. When she returned, her first day back at the office, I asked her again to dinner. It was early January 1968, a bitterly cold night.

Again we went to Jade West, but this time I met her there, and I was quite late, arriving from my Eagle Scout review board, for which she gave me much grief. "Eagle Scout? You?"

I took this as another good sign. She felt comfortable enough to tease me.

At some point during that third date, I noticed we were both much more at ease. It felt nice. The ease continued, and over the next few weeks deepened. We developed a rapport, a feel for each other, a knack for communicating nonverbally. As only two shy people can. When she was feeling shy, or uncomfortable, I sensed it, and either gave her space or tried to draw her out, depending. When I was spaced out, embroiled in some internal debate with myself about the business, she knew whether to tap me lightly on the shoulder or wait patiently for me to reemerge.

Penny wasn't legally old enough to drink alcohol, but we'd often borrow one of my sisters' driver's licenses and go for cocktails at Trader Vic's downtown. Alcohol and time worked their magic. By February, around my thirtieth birthday, she was spending every minute of her free time at Blue Ribbon, and evenings at my apartment. At some point she stopped calling me Mr. Knight.

INEVITABLY, I BROUGHT her home to meet my family. We all sat around the dining room table, eating Mom's pot roast, washing it down with cold milk, pretending it wasn't awkward. Penny was the second girl I'd ever brought home, and though she didn't have the wild charisma of Sarah, what she had was better. Her charm was real, unrehearsed, and though the Knights seemed to like it, they were still the Knights. My mother said nothing; my sisters tried in vain to be a bridge to my mother and father; my father asked a series of probing, thoughtful questions about Penny's background and up-bringing, which made him sound like a cross between a loan officer and a homicide detective. Penny told me later that the atmosphere was the exact opposite of her house, where dinner was a free-for-all, everyone laughing and talking over one another, dogs barking and TVs blaring in the background. I assured her that no one would have suspected she felt out of her element.

Next she brought me home, and I saw the truth of everything she'd told me. Her house *was* the opposite. Though much grander than Chateau Knight, it was a mess. The carpets were stained from all the animals—a German shepherd, a monkey, a cat, several white rats, an ill-tempered goose. And chaos was the rule. Besides the Parks clan, and their arkful of pets, it was a hangout for all the stray kids in the neighborhood.

I tried my best to be charming, but I couldn't seem to connect with anyone, human or otherwise. Slowly, painstakingly, I made inroads with Penny's mother, Dot. She reminded me of Auntie Mame—zany, madcap, eternally young. In many ways she was a permanent teenager, resisting her role as matriarch. It struck me that she was more like a sis-ter to Penny than a mother, and indeed, soon after dinner, when Penny and I invited her to come get a drink with us, Dot jumped at the chance.

We hit several hot spots and wound up at an after-hours joint on the east side. Penny, after two cocktails, switched to water—but not Dot. Dot kept right on going, and going, and soon she was jumping up to dance with all sorts of strange men. Sailors, and worse. At one point she jabbed a thumb in Penny's direction and said to me, "Let's ditch this wet blanket! She's dead weight!" Penny put both hands over her eyes. I laughed and kicked back. I'd passed the Dot Test.

Dot's seal of approval promised to be an asset some months later, when I wanted to take Penny away for a long weekend. Though Penny had been spending evenings at my apartment, we were still in some ways constrained by propriety. As long as she lived under their roof, Penny felt bound to obey her parents, to abide by their rules and rituals. So I was bound to get her mother's consent before such a big trip.

Wearing a suit and tie, I presented myself at the house. I made nice with the animals, petted the goose, and asked Dot for a word. The two of us sat at the kitchen table, over cups of coffee, and I said that I cared very much for Penny. Dot smiled. I said that I believed Penny cared very much for me. Dot smiled, but less certainly. I said that I wanted to take Penny to Sacramento for the weekend. To the national track-and-field championships.

Dot took a sip of her coffee and puckered her lips. "Hmm . . . no," she said. "No, no, Buck, I don't think so. I don't think we're going to do that."

"Oh," I said. "I'm sorry to hear that."

I went and found Penny in one of the back rooms of the house and told her that her mother said no. Penny put her palms against her cheeks. I told her not to worry, I'd go home, collect my thoughts, and try to think of something.

The next day I returned to the house and again asked Dot for a moment of her time. Again we sat in the kitchen over cups of coffee. "Dot," I said, "I probably didn't do a very good job yesterday of explaining how serious I am about your daughter. You see, Dot, I love Penny. And Penny loves me. And if things continue in this vein, I see us building a life together. So I *really* hope that you'll reconsider your answer of yesterday."

Dot stirred sugar into her coffee, drummed her fingers on the table. She had an odd look on her face, a look of fear, and frustration. She hadn't found herself involved in many negotiations, and she didn't know that the basic rule of negotiation is to know what you want, what you need to walk away with in order to be whole. So she got flummoxed and instantly folded. "Okay," she said. "Okay."

PENNY AND I flew to Sacramento. We were both excited to be on the road, far from parents and curfews, though I suspected Penny might be more excited about getting to use her high school graduation gift—a matching set of pink luggage.

Whatever the reason, nothing could diminish her good mood. It was blazing hot that weekend, more than one hundred degrees, but Penny never once complained, not even about the metal seats in the bleachers, which turned to griddles. She didn't get bored when I explained the nuances of track, the loneliness and craftsmanship of the runner. She was interested. She got it, all of it, right away, as she got everything.

I brought her down to the infield grass, introduced her to the runners I knew, and to Bowerman, who complimented her with great courtliness, saying how pretty she was, asking in complete earnestness what she was doing with a bum like me. We stood with my former coach and watched the day's last races.

That night we stayed at a hotel on the edge of town, in a suite painted and decorated in an unsettling shade of brown. The color of burned toast, we agreed. Sunday morning we spent in the pool, hiding from the sun, sharing the shade beneath the diving board. At some point I raised the subject of our future. I was leaving the next day for a long and vital trip to Japan, to cement my relationship with Onitsuka, I hoped. When I returned, later that summer, we couldn't keep "dating," I told her. Portland State frowned on teacher-student relationships. We'd have to do something to formalize our relationship, to set it above reproach. Meaning, marriage. "Can you handle arranging a wedding by yourself while I'm gone?" I said. "Yes," she said.

There was very little discussion, or suspense, or emotion. There was no negotiation. It all felt like a foregone conclusion. We went inside the burned-toast suite and phoned Penny's house. Dot answered, first ring. I gave her the news, and after a long, strangling pause she said: "You son of a bitch." Click.

Moments later she phoned back. She said she'd reacted impulsively because she'd been planning to spend the summer having fun with Penny, and she'd felt disappointed. Now she said it would be *almost* as much fun to spend the summer planning Penny's wedding.

We phoned my parents next. They sounded pleased, but my sister Jeanne had just gotten married and they were a bit weddinged out.

We hung up, looked at each other, looked at the brown wallpaper, and the brown rug, and both sighed. So this is life.

I kept saying to myself, over and over, I'm engaged, I'm engaged. But it didn't sink in, maybe because we were in a hotel in the middle of a heat wave in exurban Sacramento. Later, when we got home and went to a Zales and picked out an engagement ring with an emerald stone, it started to feel real. The stone and setting cost five hundred dollars—*that* was *very* real. But I never once felt nervous, never asked myself with that typical male remorse, Oh, God, what have I done? The months of dating and getting to know Penny had been the happiest of my life, and now I would have the chance to perpetuate that happiness. That's how I saw it. Basic as Accounting 101. Assets equal liabilities plus equity.

Not until I left for Japan, not until I kissed my fiancée good-bye and promised to write as soon as I got there, did the full reality, with all its dimensions and contours, hit me. I had more than a fiancée, a lover, a friend. I had a partner. In the past I'd told myself Bowerman was my partner, and to some extent Johnson. But this thing with Penny was unique, unprecedented. This alliance was life-altering. It still didn't make me nervous, it just made me more mindful. I'd never before said good-bye to a true partner, and it felt massively different. Imagine that, I thought. The single easiest way to find out how you feel about someone. Say goodbye.

* * *

FOR ONCE, MY former contact at Onitsuka was still my contact. Kitami was still there. He hadn't been replaced. He hadn't been reassigned. On the contrary, his role with the company was more secure, judging by his demeanor. He seemed easier, more self-assured.

He welcomed me like one of the family, said he was delighted with Blue Ribbon's performance, and with our East Coast office, which was thriving under Johnson. "Now let us work on how we can capture the U.S. market," he said.

"I like the sound of that," I said.

In my briefcase I was carrying new shoe designs from both Bowerman and Johnson, including one they'd teamed up on, a shoe we were calling the Boston. It had an innovative full-length midsole cushion. Kitami put the designs on the wall and studied them closely. He held his chin in one hand. He liked them, he said. "Like very very much," he said, slapping me on the back.

We met many times over the course of the next several weeks, and each time I sensed from Kitami an almost brotherly vibe. One afternoon he mentioned that his Export Department was having its annual picnic in a few days. "You come!" he said. "Me?" I said. "Yes, yes," he said, "you are honorary member of Export Department."

The picnic was on Awaji, a tiny island off Kobe. We took a small boat to get there, and when we arrived we saw long tables set up along the beach, each one covered with platters of seafood and bowls of noodles and rice. Beside the tables were tubs filled with cold bottles of soda and beer. Everyone was wearing bathing suits and sunglasses and laughing. People I'd only known in a reserved, corporate setting were being silly and carefree.

Late in the day there were competitions. Team-building exercises like potato sack relays and foot races along the surf. I showed off my speed, and everyone bowed to me as I crossed the finish line first. Everyone agreed that Skinny Gaijin was very fast.

I was picking up the language, slowly. I knew the Japanese word for shoe: *gutzu*. I knew the Japanese word for revenue: *shunyu*. I knew how to ask the time, and directions, and I learned a phrase I used often: *Watakushi domo no kaisha ni tsuite no joh hou des.*

Here is some information about my company.

Toward the end of the picnic I sat on the sand and looked out across the Pacific Ocean. I was living two separate lives, both wonderful, both merging. Back home I was part of a team, me and Woodell and Johnson—and now Penny. Here in Japan I was part of a team, me and Kitami and all the good people of Onitsuka. By nature I was a loner, but since childhood I'd thrived in team sports. My psyche was in true harmony when I had a mix of alone time and team time. Exactly what I had now.

Also, I was doing business with a country I'd come to love. Gone was the initial fear. I connected with the shyness of the Japanese people, with the simplicity of their culture and products and arts. I liked that they tried to add beauty to every part of life, from the tea ceremony to the commode. I liked that the radio announced each day exactly which cherry trees, on which corner, were blossoming, and how much.

My reverie was interrupted when a man named Fujimoto sat beside me. Fiftyish, slouch-shouldered, he had a gloomy air that seemed more than middle-age melancholy. Like a Japanese Charlie Brown. And yet I could see that he was making a concerted effort to extend himself, to be cheerful toward me. He forced a big smile and told me that he loved America, that he longed to live there. I told him that I'd just been thinking how much I loved Japan. "Maybe we should trade places," I said. He smiled ruefully. "Any time."

I complimented his English. He said he'd learned it from the

American GIs. "Funny," I said, "the first things I learned about Japanese culture, I learned from two ex-GIs."

The first words his GIs taught him, he said, were, "Kiss my ass!" We had a good laugh about that.

I asked where he lived and his smile disappeared. "Months ago," he said, "I lose my home. Typhoon Billie." The storm had completely wiped away the Japanese islands of Honshu and Kyushu, along with two thousand houses. "Mine," Fujimoto said, "was one of houses." "I'm very sorry," I said. He nodded, looked at the water. He'd started over, he said. As the Japanese do. The one thing he hadn't been able to replace, unfortunately, was his bicycle. In the 1960s bicycles were exorbitantly expensive in Japan.

Kitami now joined us. I noticed that Fujimoto got up right away and walked off.

I mentioned to Kitami that Fujimoto had learned his English from GIs, and Kitami said with pride that *he'd* learned *his* English all by himself, from a record. I congratulated him, and said I hoped one day to be as fluent in Japanese as he was in English. Then I mentioned that I was getting married soon. I told him a bit about Penny, and he congratulated me and wished me luck. "When is wedding?" he asked. "September," I said. "Ah," he said, "I will be in America one month after, when Mr. Onitsuka and I attend Olympics in Mexico City. We might visit Los Angeles."

He invited me to fly down, have dinner with them. I said I'd be delighted.

The next day I returned to the United States, and one of the first things I did after landing was put fifty dollars in an envelope and airmail it to Fujimoto. On the card I wrote: "For a new bicycle, my friend."

Weeks later an envelope arrived from Fujimoto. My fifty dollars, folded inside a note explaining that he'd asked his superiors if he could keep the money, and they'd said no.

There was a PS: "If you send my house, I can keep."

So I did.

And thus another life-altering partnership was born.

ON SEPTEMBER 13, 1968, Penny and I exchanged our vows before two hundred people at St. Mark's Episcopal Church in downtown Portland, at the same altar where Penny's parents had been married. It was one year, nearly to the day, after Miss Parks had first walked into my classroom. She was again in the front row, of a sort, only this time I was standing beside her. And she was now Mrs. Knight.

Before us stood her uncle, an Episcopal priest from Pasadena, who performed the service. Penny was shaking so much, she couldn't raise her chin to look him, or me, in the eye. I wasn't shaking, because I'd cheated. In my breast pocket I had two miniature airplane bottles of whiskey, stashed from my recent trip to Japan. I nipped one just before, and one just after, the ceremony.

My best man was Cousin Houser. My lawyer, my wingman. The other groomsmen were Penny's two brothers, plus a friend from business school, and Cale, who told me moments before the ceremony, "Second time I've seen you this nervous." We laughed, and reminisced, for the millionth time, about that day at Stanford when I'd given my presentation to my entrepreneurship class. Today, I thought, is similar. Once again I'm telling a roomful of people that something is possible, that something can be successful, when in fact I don't really know. I'm speaking from theory, faith, and bluster, like every groom. And every bride. It would be up to me and Penny to prove the truth of what we said that day.

The reception was at the Garden Club of Portland, where society ladies gathered on summer nights to drink daiquiris and trade gossip. The night was warm. The skies threatened rain, but never opened. I danced with Penny. I danced with Dot. I danced with my mother. Before midnight Penny and I said good-bye to all and jumped into my brand-new car, a racy black Cougar. I sped us to the coast, two hours away, where we planned to spend the weekend at her parents' beach house.

Dot called every half hour.

1969

Suddenly, a whole new cast of characters was wandering in and out of the office. Rising sales enabled me to hire more and more reps. Most were ex-runners, and eccentrics, as only ex-runners can be. But when it came to selling they were all business. Because they were inspired by what we were trying to do, and because they worked solely on commission (two dollars a pair), they were burning up the roads, hitting every high school and college track meet within a thousand-mile radius, and their extraordinary efforts were boosting our numbers even more.

We'd posted $150,000 in sales in 1968, and in 1969 we were on our way to just under $300,000. Though Wallace was still breathing down my neck, hassling me to slow down and moaning about my lack of equity, I decided that Blue Ribbon was doing well enough to justify a salary for its founder. Right before my thirty-first birthday I made the bold move. I quit Portland State and went full-time at my company, paying myself a fairly generous eighteen thousand dollars a year.

Above all, I told myself, the best reason for leaving Portland State was that I'd already gotten more out of the school—Penny—than I'd ever hoped. I got something else, too; I just didn't know it at the time. Nor did I dream how valuable it would prove to be.

*   *   *

IN MY LAST week on campus, walking through the halls, I noticed a group of young women standing around an easel. One of them was daubing at a large canvas, and just as I passed I heard her lamenting that she couldn't afford to take a class on oil painting. I stopped, admired the canvas. "*My* company could use an artist," I said.

"What?" she said.

"My company needs someone to do some advertising. Would you like to make some extra money?"

I still didn't see any bang-for-the-buck in advertising, but I was starting to accept that I could no longer ignore it. The Standard Insurance Company had just run a full-page ad in the *Wall Street Journal*, touting Blue Ribbon as one of the dynamic young companies among its clients. The ad featured a photo of Bowerman and me . . . staring at a shoe. Not as if we were shoe innovators; more as if we'd never seen a shoe before. We looked like morons. It was embarrassing.

In some of our ads the model was none other than Johnson. See Johnson rocking a blue tracksuit. See Johnson waving a javelin. When it came to advertising, our approach was primitive and slapdash. We were making it up as we went along, learning on the fly, and it showed. In one ad—for the Tiger marathon flat, I think—we referred to the new fabric as "swooshfiber." To this day none of us remembers who first came up with the word, or what it meant. But it sounded good.

People were telling me constantly that advertising was important, that advertising was the next wave. I always rolled my eyes. But if icky photos and made-up words—and Johnson, posed seductively on a couch—were slipping into our ads, I needed to start paying more attention. "I'll give you two bucks an hour," I told this starving artist in the hallway at Portland State. "To do what?" she asked. "Design print ads," I said, "do some lettering, logos, maybe a few charts and graphs for presentations."

It didn't sound like much of a gig. But the poor kid was desperate.

She wrote her name on a piece of paper. Carolyn Davidson. And her number. I shoved it in my pocket and forgot all about it.

HIRING SALES REPS and graphic artists showed great optimism, and I didn't consider myself an optimist by nature. Not that I was a pessimist. I generally tried to hover between the two, committing to neither. But as 1969 approached, I found myself staring into space and thinking the future might be bright. After a good night's sleep, after a hearty breakfast, I could see plenty of reason for hope. Aside from our robust and rising sales numbers, Onitsuka would soon be bringing out several exciting new models, including the Obori, which featured a feather-light nylon upper. Also, the Marathon, another nylon, with lines sleek as a Karmann Ghia. These shoes will sell themselves, I told Woodell many times, hanging them on the corkboard.

Also, Bowerman was back from Mexico City, where he'd been an assistant coach on the U.S. Olympic team, meaning he'd played a pivotal role in the U.S. winning more gold medals than any team, from any nation, ever. My partner was more than famous; he was legendary.

I phoned Bowerman, eager to get his overall thoughts on the Games, and particularly on the moment for which they would forever be remembered, the protest of John Carlos and Tommie Smith. Standing on the podium during the playing of "The Star-Spangled Banner," both men had bowed their heads and raised black-gloved fists, a shocking gesture, meant to call attention to racism, poverty, human rights abuses. They were still being condemned for it. But Bowerman, as I fully expected, supported them. Bowerman supported all runners.

Carlos and Smith were shoeless during the protest; they'd conspicuously removed their Pumas and left them on the stands. I told Bowerman I couldn't decide if this had been a good thing or a bad thing for Puma. Was all publicity really good publicity? Was publicity like advertising? A chimera?

Bowerman chuckled and said he wasn't sure.

He told me about the scandalous behavior of Puma and Adidas throughout the Games. The world's two biggest athletic shoe companies—run by two German brothers who despised each other—had chased each other like Keystone Kops around the Olympic Village, jockeying for all the athletes. Huge sums of cash, often stuffed in running shoes or manila envelopes, were passed around. One of Puma's sales reps even got thrown in jail. (There were rumors that Adidas had framed him.) He was married to a female sprinter, and Bowerman joked that he'd only married her to secure her endorsement.

Worse, it didn't stop at mere payouts. Puma had smuggled truckloads of shoes into Mexico City, while Adidas cleverly managed to evade Mexico's stiff import tariffs. I heard through the grapevine they did it by making a nominal number of shoes at a factory in Guadalajara.

Bowerman and I didn't feel morally offended; we felt left out. Blue Ribbon had no money for payouts, and therefore no presence at the Games.

We'd had one meager booth in the Olympic Village, and one guy working it—Bork. I didn't know if Bork had been sitting there reading comic books, or just hadn't been able to compete with the massive presence of Adidas and Puma, but either way his booth generated zero business, zero buzz. No one stopped by.

Actually, one person did stop by. Bill Toomey, a brilliant American decathlete, asked for some Tigers, so he could show the world that he couldn't be bought. But Bork didn't have his size. Nor the right shoes for any of his events.

Plenty of athletes were training in Tigers, Bowerman reported. We just didn't have anybody actually *competing* in them. Part of the reason was quality; Tigers just weren't good enough yet. The main reason, however, was money. We had not a penny for endorsement deals.

"We're not broke," I told Bowerman, "we just don't have any money."

He grunted. "Either way," he said, "wouldn't it be wonderful to be able to *pay* athletes? Legally?"

Lastly, Bowerman told me he'd bumped into Kitami at the Games. He didn't much care for the man. "Doesn't know a damn thing about shoes," Bowerman grumbled. "And he's a little too slick. Little too full of himself."

I was starting to have the same inklings. I'd gotten a sense from Kitami's last few wires and letters that he might not be the man he'd seemed, and that he wasn't the fan of Blue Ribbon he'd appeared to be when I was last in Japan. I had a bad feeling in my bones. Maybe he was getting ready to jack up our prices. I mentioned this to Bowerman, and told him I was taking measures to protect us. Before hanging up I boasted that, though I didn't have enough cash or cachet to pay athletes, I did have enough to buy someone at Onitsuka. I had a man on the inside, I said, a man acting as my eyes and ears and keeping tabs on Kitami.

I sent out a memo saying as much to all Blue Ribbon employees. (By now we had around forty.) Though I'd fallen in love with Japanese culture—I kept my souvenir samurai sword beside my desk—I also warned them that Japanese business practices were thoroughly perplexing. In Japan you couldn't predict what either your competition or your partner might do. I'd given up trying. Instead, I wrote, "I've taken what I think is a big step to keep us informed. I've hired a spy. He works full-time in the Onitsuka Export Department. Without going into a lengthy discussion of why I will just tell you that I feel he is trustworthy.

"This spy may seem somewhat unethical to you, but the spy system is ingrained and completely accepted in Japanese business circles. They actually have schools for industrial spies, much as we have schools for typists and stenographers."

I can't imagine what made me use the word "spy" so wantonly, so boldly, other than the fact that James Bond was all the rage just then. Nor can I understand why, when I was revealing so much, I didn't reveal the spy's name. It was Fujimoto, whose bicycle I'd replaced.

I think I must have known, on some level, that the memo was a mistake, a terribly stupid thing to do. And that I would live to regret it. I *think* I knew. But I often found myself as perplexing as Japanese business practices.

KITAMI AND MR. Onitsuka both attended the Games in Mexico City, and afterward they both flew to Los Angeles. I flew down from Oregon to meet them for dinner at a Japanese restaurant in Santa Monica. I was late, of course, and by the time I arrived they were full of sake. Like schoolboys on holiday: Each was wearing a souvenir sombrero, loudly woohooing.

I tried hard to mirror their festive mood. I matched them shot for shot, helped them finish off several platters of sushi, and generally bonded with them both. At my hotel that night I went to bed thinking, hoping, I'd been paranoid about Kitami.

The next morning we all flew to Portland so they could meet the gang at Blue Ribbon. I realized that in my letters to Onitsuka, not to mention my conversations with them, I might have overplayed the grandeur of our "worldwide headquarters." Sure enough I saw Kitami's face drop as he walked in. I also saw Mr. Onitsuka looking around, bewildered. I hastened to apologize. "It may look small," I said, laughing tightly, "but we do a lot of business out of this room!"

They looked at the broken windows, the javelin window closer, the wavy plywood room divider. They looked at Woodell in his wheelchair. They felt the walls vibrating from the Pink Bucket jukebox. They looked at each other, dubious. I told myself: Whelp, it's all over.

Sensing my embarrassment, Mr. Onitsuka put a reassuring hand on my shoulder. "It is . . . most charming," he said.

On the far wall Woodell had hung a large, handsome map of the United States, and he'd put a red pushpin everywhere we'd sold a pair of Tigers in the last five years. The map was covered with red pushpins. For one merciful moment it diverted attention from our office space. Then Kitami pointed at eastern Montana. "No pins," he said. "Obviously salesman here not doing job."

DAYS WENT SWOOSHING by. I was trying to build a company and a marriage. Penny and I were learning to live together, learning to meld our personalities and idiosyncrasies, though we agreed that she was the one with all the personality and I was the idiosyncratic one. Therefore it was she who had more to learn.

For instance, she was learning that I spent a fair portion of each day lost in my own thoughts, tumbling down mental wormholes, trying to solve some problem or construct some plan. I often didn't hear what she said, and if I did hear I didn't remember it minutes later.

She was learning that I was absentminded, that I would drive to the grocery store and come home empty-handed, without the one item she'd asked me to buy, because all the way there and all the way back I'd been puzzling over the latest bank crisis, or the most recent Onitsuka shipping delay.

She was learning that I misplaced everything, especially the important things, like wallets and keys. Bad enough that I couldn't multitask, but I insisted on trying. I'd often scan the financial pages while eating lunch—and driving. My new black Cougar didn't remain new for long. As the Mr. Magoo of Oregon, I was forever bumping into trees and poles and other people's fenders.

She was learning that I wasn't housebroken. I left the toilet seat up, left my clothes where they fell, left food on the counter. I was effectively helpless. I couldn't cook, or clean, or do even the simplest things for myself, because I'd been spoiled rotten by my mother and sisters. All those years in the servants' quarters, I'd essentially had servants.

She was learning that I didn't like to lose, at anything, that losing for me was a special form of agony. I often flippantly blamed Bowerman, but it went way back. I told her about playing Ping-Pong with my father when I was a boy, and the pain of never being able to beat him. I told her that my father would sometimes laugh when he won, which sent me into a rage. More than once I'd thrown down my paddle and run off crying. I wasn't proud of this behavior, but it was ingrained. It explained me. She didn't really get it until we went bowling. Penny was a very good bowler—she'd taken a bowling class at Oregon State—so I perceived this as a challenge, and I was going to meet the challenge head-on. I was determined to win, and thus everything other than a strike made me glum.

Above all, she was learning that marrying a man with a start-up shoe company meant living on a shoestring budget. And yet she thrived. I could give her only twenty-five dollars a week for groceries, and still she managed to whip up delicious meals. I gave her a credit card with a two-thousand-dollar limit to furnish our entire apartment, and she managed to buy a dinette table, two chairs, a Zenith TV, and a big couch with soft arms, perfect for napping. She also bought me a brown recliner, which she stuck in a corner of the living room. Now, each night, I could lean back at a forty-five-degree angle and spin inside my own head all I wanted. It was more comfortable, and safer, than the Cougar.

I got into the habit every night of phoning my father from my recliner. He'd always be in his recliner, too, and together, recliner to recliner, we'd hash out the latest threat confronting Blue Ribbon. He no longer saw my business as a waste of my time, apparently. Though he didn't say so explicitly, he did seem to find the problems I faced "interesting," and "challenging," which amounted to the same thing.

* * *

IN THE SPRING of 1969 Penny began to complain of feeling poorly in the mornings. Food didn't sit well. By midday she was often a little wobbly around the office. She went to the doctor—the same doctor who'd delivered her—and discovered she was pregnant.

We were both overjoyed. But we also faced a whole new learning curve.

Our cozy apartment was now completely inappropriate. We'd have to buy a house, of course. But could we afford a house? I'd *just* started to pay myself a salary. And in which part of town should we buy? Where were the best schools? And how was I supposed to research real estate prices and schools, plus all the other things that go into buying a house, while running a start-up company? Was it even feasible to run a start-up company while starting a family? Should I go back to accounting, or teaching, or something more stable?

Leaning back in my recliner each night, staring at the ceiling, I tried to settle myself. I told myself: Life is growth. You grow or you die.

WE FOUND A house in Beaverton. Small, only sixteen hundred square feet, but it had an acre of land around it, and a little horse corral, and a pool. There was also a huge pine tree in the front and a Japanese bamboo out back. I loved it. More, I recognized it. When I was growing up my sisters asked me several times what my dream house would look like, and one day they handed me a charcoal pencil and a pad and made me draw it. After Penny and I moved in, my sisters dug out the old charcoal sketch. It was an exact picture of the Beaverton house.

The price was thirty-four thousand dollars, and I popped my shirt buttons to discover that I had 20 percent of that in savings. On the other hand, I'd pledged those savings against my many loans at First National. So I went down to talk to Harry White. I need the savings for a down payment on a house, I said—but I'll pledge the house.

"Okay," he said. "On this one we don't have to consult Wallace."

That night I told Penny that if Blue Ribbon failed we'd lose the house. She put a hand on her stomach and sat down. This was the kind of *insecurity* she'd always vowed to avoid. Okay, she kept saying, okaaaay.

With so much at stake, she felt compelled to keep working for Blue Ribbon, right through her pregnancy. She would sacrifice everything to Blue Ribbon, even her deeply held goal of graduating from college. And when she wasn't physically in the office, she would run a mail order business out of the new house. In 1969 alone, despite morning sickness, swollen ankles, weight gain, and constant fatigue, Penny got out fifteen hundred orders. Some of the orders were nothing more than crude tracings of a human foot, sent in by customers in far-flung places, but Penny didn't care. She dutifully matched the tracing to the correct shoe and filled the order. Every sale counted.

AT THE SAME time that my family outgrew its home, so did my business. One room beside the Pink Bucket could no longer contain us. Also, Woodell and I were tired of shouting to be heard above that jukebox. So each night after work we'd go out for cheeseburgers, then drive around looking at office space.

Logistically, it was a nightmare. Woodell had to drive, because his wheelchair wouldn't fit in my Cougar, and I always felt guilty and uncomfortable, being chauffeured by a man with so many limitations. I also felt crazed with nerves, because many of the offices we looked at were up a flight of stairs. Or several flights. This meant I'd have to wheel Woodell up and down.

At such moments I was reminded, painfully, of his reality. During a typical workday, Woodell was so positive, so energetic, it was easy to forget. But wheeling him, maneuvering him, upstairs, downstairs, I was repeatedly struck by how delicate, how helpless he could be. I'd pray under my breath. *Please don't let me drop him. Please don't let me drop him*. Woodell, hearing me, would tense up, and his tension would make me more nervous. "Relax," I'd say, "I haven't lost a patient yet—haha!"

No matter what happened, he'd never lose his composure. Even at his most vulnerable, with me balancing him precariously at the top of some dark flight of stairs, he'd never lose touch with his essential philosophy: *Don't you dare feel sorry for me. I'm here to kill you.*

(The first time I ever sent him to a trade show, the airline lost his wheelchair. And when they found it, the frame was bent like a pretzel. No problem. In his mutilated chair, Woodell attended the show, ticked off every item on his to-do list, and came home with an ear-to-ear mission-accomplished smile on his face.)

At the end of each night's search for new office space, Woodell and I would always have a big belly laugh about the whole debacle. Most nights we'd wind up at some dive bar, giddy, almost delirious. Before parting we'd often play a game. I'd bring out a stopwatch and we'd see how fast Woodell could fold up his wheelchair and get it and himself into his car. As a former track star, he loved the challenge of a stopwatch, of trying to beat his personal best. (His record was forty-four seconds.) We both cherished those nights, the silliness, the sense of shared mission, and we mutually ranked them among the solid gold memories of our young lives.

Woodell and I were very different, and yet our friendship was based on a selfsame approach to work. Each of us found pleasure, whenever possible, in focusing on one small task. One task, we often said, clears the mind. And each of us recognized that this small task of finding a bigger office meant we were succeeding. We were making a go of this thing called Blue Ribbon, which spoke to a deep desire, in each of us, to win. Or at least not lose.

Though neither of us was much of a talker, we brought out a chatty streak in each other. Those nights we discussed everything, opened up to each other with unusual candor. Woodell told me in detail about his injury. If I was ever tempted to take myself too seriously, Woodell's story always reminded me that things could be worse. And the way he handled himself was a constant, bracing lesson in the virtue, and value, of good spirits.

His injury wasn't typical, he said. And it wasn't total. He still had some feeling, still had hopes of marrying, having a family. He also had hopes of a cure. He was taking an experimental new drug, which had shown promise in paraplegics. Trouble was, it had a garlicky aroma. Some nights on our office-hunting expeditions Woodell would smell like an old-school pizzeria, and I'd let him hear about it.

I asked Woodell if he was—I hesitated, fearing I had no right—*happy*. He gave it some thought. Yes, he said. He was. He loved his work. He loved Blue Ribbon, though he sometimes cringed at the irony. A man who can't walk peddling shoes.

Not sure what to say to this, I said nothing.

Often Penny and I would have Woodell over to the new house for dinner. He was like family, we loved him, but we also knew we were filling a void in his life, a need for company and domestic comforts. So Penny always wanted to cook something special when Woodell came over, and the most special thing she could think of was Cornish game hen, plus a dessert made from brandy and iced milk—she got the recipe from a magazine—which left us all blotto. Though hens and brandy put a serious dent in her twenty-five-dollar grocery budget, Penny simply couldn't economize when it came to Woodell. If I told her that Woodell was coming to dinner, she'd reflexively gush: "I'll get some capons and brandy!" It was more than wanting to be hospitable. She was fattening him up. She was nurturing him. Woodell, I think, spoke to her newly activated maternal streak.

I struggle to remember. I close my eyes and think back, but so many precious moments from those nights are gone forever. Numberless conversations, breathless laughing fits. Declarations, revelations, confidences. They've all fallen into the sofa cushions of time. I remember only that we always sat up half the night, cataloging the past, mapping out the future. I remember that we took turns describing what our little company was, and what it might be, and what it must never be. How I wish, on just one of those nights, I'd had a tape recorder. Or kept a journal, as I did on my trip around the world.

Still, at least I can always call to mind the image of Woodell, seated at the head of our dinette, carefully dressed in his blue jeans, his trademark V-neck sweater over a white T. And always, on his feet, a pair of Tigers, the rubber soles pristine.

By then he'd grown a long beard, and a bushy mustache, both of which I envied. Heck, it was the sixties, I'd have had a beard down to my chin. But I was constantly needing to go to the bank and ask for money. I couldn't look like a bum when I presented myself to Wallace. A clean shave was one of my few concessions to The Man.

WOODELL AND I eventually found a promising office, in Tigard, south of downtown Portland. It wasn't a whole office building—we couldn't afford that—but a corner of one floor. The rest was occupied by the Horace Mann Insurance Company. Inviting, almost plush, it was a dramatic step up, and yet I hesitated. There had been a curious logic in our being next door to a honky-tonk. But an insurance company? With carpeted halls and water coolers and men in tailored suits? The atmosphere was so button-down, so corporate. Our surroundings, I felt, had much to do with our spirit, and our spirit was a big part of our success, and I worried how our spirit might change if we were suddenly sharing space with a bunch of Organization Men and automatons.

I took to my recliner, gave it some thought, and decided a corporate vibe might be asymmetrical, contrary to our core beliefs, but it might also be just the thing with our bank. Maybe when Wallace saw our boring, sterile new office space, he'd treat us with respect.

Also, the office was in Tigard. Selling Tigers out of Tigard—maybe it was meant to be.

Then I thought about Woodell. He said he was happy at Blue Ribbon, but he'd mentioned the irony. Maybe it was more than ironic, sending him out to high schools and colleges to sell Tigers out of his car. Maybe it was torture. And maybe it was a poor use of his talents. What suited Woodell best was bringing order to chaos, problem-solving. One small task.

After he and I went together to sign the Tigard lease, I asked him if he'd like to change jobs, become operations manager for Blue Ribbon. No more sales calls. No more schools. Instead he'd be in charge of dealing with all the things for which I didn't have the time and patience. Like talking to Bork in L.A. Or corresponding with Johnson in Wellesley. Or opening a new office in Miami. Or hiring someone to coordinate all the new sales reps and organize their reports. Or approving expense accounts. Best of all, Woodell would have to oversee the person who monitored company bank accounts. Now, if he didn't cash his own paychecks, he'd have to explain the overage to his boss: himself.

Beaming, Woodell said he liked the sound of that very much. He reached out his hand. Deal, he said.

Still had the grip of an athlete.

PENNY WENT TO the doctor in September 1969. A checkup. The doctor said everything looked fine, but the baby was taking its time. Probably another week, he said.

The rest of that afternoon Penny spent at Blue Ribbon, helping customers. We went home together, ate an early dinner, turned in early. About 4:00 a.m. she jostled me. "I don't feel so good," she said.

I phoned the doctor and told him to meet us at Emanuel Hospital.

In the weeks before Labor Day I'd made several practice trips to the hospital, and it was a good thing, because now, "game time," I was such a wreck that Portland looked to me like Bangkok. Everything was strange, unfamiliar. I drove slowly, to make sure of each turn. Not too slowly, I scolded myself, or you'll have to deliver the baby yourself.

The streets were all empty, the lights were all green. A soft rain was falling. The only sounds in the car were Penny's heavy breaths and the wipers squeaking across the windshield. As I pulled up to the entrance of the emergency room, as I helped Penny into the hospital, she kept saying, "We're probably overreacting, I don't think it's time yet." Still, she was breathing the way I used to breathe in the final lap.

I remember the nurse taking Penny from me, helping her into a wheelchair, rolling her down a hall. I followed along, trying to help. I had a pregnancy kit I'd packed myself, with a stopwatch, the same one I'd used to time Woodell. I now timed Penny's contractions aloud. "Five . . . four . . . three . . ." She stopped panting and turned to me. Through clenched teeth she said, "Stop . . . doing . . . that."

A nurse now helped her out of the wheelchair and onto a gurney and rolled her away. I stumbled back down the hall into something the hospital called "The Bullpen," where expectant fathers were expected to sit and stare into space. I would have been in the delivery room with Penny, but my father had warned me against it. He'd told me that I'd been born bright blue, which scared the daylights out of him, and he therefore cautioned me, "At the decisive moment, be somewhere else."

I sat in a hard plastic chair, eyes closed, doing shoe work in my mind. After an hour I opened my eyes and saw our doctor standing before me. Beads of sweat glistened on his forehead. He was saying something. That is, his lips were moving. But I couldn't hear. *Life's a joy? Here's a toy? Are you Roy?*

He said it again: *It's a boy.*

"A—a—boy? Really?"

"Your wife did a superb job," he was saying, "she did not complain once, and she pushed at all the right times—has she taken many Lamaze classes?"

"Lemans?" I said.

"Pardon?"

"What?"

He led me like an invalid down a long hall and into a small room. There, behind a curtain, was my wife, exhausted, radiant, her face bright red. Her arms were wrapped around a quilted white blanket decorated with blue baby carriages. I pushed back a corner of the blanket to reveal a head the size of a ripe grapefruit, a white stocking cap perched on top. My boy. He looked like a traveler. Which, of course, he was. He'd just begun his own trip around the world.

I leaned down, kissed Penny's cheek. I pushed away her damp hair. "You're a champion," I whispered. She squinted, uncertain. She thought I was talking to the baby.

She handed me my son. I cradled him in my arms. He was so alive, but so delicate, so helpless. The feeling was wondrous, different from all other feelings, though familiar, too. *Please don't let me drop him.*

At Blue Ribbon I spent so much time talking about quality control, about craftsmanship, about delivery—but this, I realized, *this* was the real thing. "We made this," I said to Penny. We. *Made.* This.

She nodded, then lay back. I handed the baby to the nurse and told Penny to sleep. I floated out of the hospital and down to the car. I felt a sudden and overpowering need to see my father, a hunger for my father. I drove to his newspaper, parked several blocks away. I wanted to walk. The rain had stopped. The air was cool and damp. I ducked into a cigar store. I pictured myself handing my father a big fat robusto and saying, "Hiya, Grandpa!"

Coming out of the store, the wooden cigar box under my arm, I bumped straight into Keith Forman, a former runner at Oregon. "Keith!" I cried. "Heya, Buck," he said. I grabbed him by the lapels and shouted, "It's a boy!" He leaned away, confused. He thought I was drunk. There wasn't time to explain. I kept walking.

Forman had been on the famous Oregon team that set the world record in the four-mile relay. As a runner, as an accountant, I always remembered their stunning time: 16:08.9. A star on Bowerman's 1962 national championship team, Forman had also been the fifth American ever to break the four-minute mile. And to think, I told myself, only hours ago I'd thought *those things* made a champion.

FALL. THE WOOLEN skies of November settled in low. I wore heavy sweaters, and sat by the fireplace, and did a sort of self-inventory. I was all stocked up on gratitude. Penny and my new son, whom we'd named Matthew, were healthy. Bork and Woodell and Johnson were happy. Sales continued to rise.

Then came the mail. A letter from Bork. After returning from Mexico City, he was suffering some sort of mental Montezuma's Revenge. He had problems with me, he told me in the letter. He didn't like my management style, he didn't like my vision for the company, he didn't like what I was paying him. He didn't understand why I took weeks to answer his letters, and sometimes didn't answer at all. He had ideas about shoe design, and he didn't like how they were being ignored. After several pages of all this he demanded immediate changes, plus a raise.

My second mutiny. This one, however, was more complicated than Johnson's. I spent several days drafting my reply. I agreed to raise his salary, slightly, and then I pulled rank. I reminded Bork that in any company there could only be one boss, and sadly for him the boss of Blue Ribbon was Buck Knight. I told him if he wasn't happy with me or my management style, he should know that quitting and being fired were both viable options.

As with my "spy memo," I suffered instant writer's remorse. The moment I dropped it in the mail I realized that Bork was a valuable part of the team, that I didn't want to lose him, that I couldn't afford to lose him. I dispatched our new operations manager, Woodell, to Los Angeles, to patch things up.

Woodell took Bork to lunch and tried to explain that I wasn't sleeping much, with a new baby and all. Also, Woodell told him, I was feeling tremendous stress after the visit from Kitami and Mr. Onitsuka. Woodell joked about my unique management style, telling Bork that everyone bitched about it, everyone pulled their hair out about my nonresponses to their memos and letters.

In all Woodell spent a few days with Bork, smoothing his feathers, going over the operation. He discovered that Bork was stressed, too. Though the retail store was thriving, the back room, which had basically become our national warehouse, was in shambles. Boxes everywhere, invoices and papers stacked to the ceiling. Bork couldn't keep pace.

When Woodell returned he gave me the picture. "I think Bork's back in the fold," he said, "but we need to relieve him of that warehouse. We need to transfer all warehouse operations up here." Moreover, he added, we needed to hire Woodell's mother to run it. She'd worked for years in the warehouse at Jantzen, the legendary Oregon outfitter, so it wasn't nepotism, he said. Ma Woodell was perfect for the job.

I wasn't sure I cared. If Woodell was good with it, I was good with it. Plus, the way I saw it: The more Woodells the better.

1970

I had to fly to Japan again, and this time two weeks before Christmas. I didn't like leaving Penny alone with Matthew, especially around the holidays, but it couldn't be avoided. I needed to sign a new deal with Onitsuka. Or not. Kitami was keeping me in suspense. He wouldn't tell me his thoughts about renewing me until I arrived.

YET AGAIN I found myself at a conference table surrounded by Onitsuka executives. This time, Mr. Onitsuka didn't make his trademark late entrance, nor did he absent himself pointedly. He was there from the start, presiding.

He opened the meeting by saying that he intended to renew Blue Ribbon for another three years. I smiled for the first time in weeks. Then I pressed my advantage. I asked for a longer deal. Yes, 1973 seemed light-years away, but it would be here in a blink. I needed more time and security. My bankers needed more. "Five years?" I said.

Mr. Onitsuka smiled. "Three."

He then gave a strange speech. Notwithstanding several years of sluggish worldwide sales, he said, plus some strategic missteps, the outlook was rosy for Onitsuka. Through cost-cutting and reorganization his company had regained its edge. Sales for the upcoming fiscal year were expected to top $22 million, a good portion of which would come from the United States. A recent survey showed that 70 percent of all American runners owned a pair of Tigers.

I knew that. Maybe I'd had a little something to do with that, I wanted to say. That's why I wanted a longer contract.

But Mr. Onitsuka said that one major reason for Onitsuka's solid numbers was . . . Kitami. He looked down the table, bestowed a fatherly smile on Kitami. Therefore, Mr. Onitsuka said, Kitami was being promoted. Henceforth he'd be the company's operations manager. He'd now be Onitsuka's Woodell, though I remember thinking that I wouldn't trade one Woodell for a thousand Kitamis.

With a bow of my head I congratulated Mr. Onitsuka on his company's good fortune. I turned and bowed my head at Kitami, congratulating him on his promotion. But when I raised my head and made eye contact with Kitami I saw in his gaze something cold. Something that stayed with me for days.

We drew up the agreement. It was four or five paragraphs, a flimsy thing. The thought crossed my mind that it should be more substantive, and that it would be nice to have a lawyer vet it. But there wasn't time. We all signed it, then moved on to other topics.

I WAS RELIEVED to have a new contract, but I returned to Oregon feeling troubled, anxious, more so than at any time in the last eight years. Sure, my briefcase held a guarantee that Onitsuka would supply me with shoes for the next three years—but why were they refusing to extend beyond three? More to the point, the extension was misleading. Onitsuka was guaranteeing me a supply, but their supply was chronically, dangerously late. About which they still had a maddeningly blasé attitude. *Little more days.* With Wallace continually acting more like a loan shark than a banker, a little more days could mean disaster.

And when the shipments from Onitsuka did finally arrive? They often contained the wrong number of shoes. Often the wrong sizes.

Sometimes the wrong models. This kind of disarray clogged our warehouse and rankled our sales reps. Before I left Japan Mr. Onitsuka and Kitami assured me that they were building new state-of-the-art factories. Delivery problems would soon be a thing of the past, they said. I was skeptical, but there was nothing I could do. I was at their mercy.

Johnson, meanwhile, was losing his mind. His letters, once mumbly with angst, were becoming shrill with hysteria. The main problem was Bowerman's Cortez, he said. It was simply too popular. We'd gotten people hooked on the thing, turned them into full-blown Cortez addicts, and now we couldn't meet the demand, which created anger and resentment up and down the supply chain.

"God, we are really screwing our customers," Johnson wrote. "Happiness is a boatload of Cortez; reality is a boatload of Bostons with steel wool uppers, tongues made out of old razor blades, sizes 6 to 6½."

He was exaggerating, but not much. It happened all the time. I'd secure a loan from Wallace, then hang fire waiting for Onitsuka to send the shoes, and when the boat finally docked it wouldn't contain any Cortezes. Six weeks later, we'd get too many Cortezes, and by then it was too late.

Why? It couldn't just be Onitsuka's decrepit factories, we all agreed, and sure enough Woodell eventually figured out that Onitsuka was satisfying its local customers in Japan *first*, then worrying about foreign exports. Terribly unfair, but again what could I do? I had no leverage.

Even if Onitsuka's new factories ended all delivery problems, even if every shipment of shoes hit the water right on time, with all the correct quantities of size 10s, and no size 5s, I'd still face problems with Wallace. Bigger orders would require bigger loans, and bigger loans would be harder to pay off, and in 1970 Wallace was telling me that he wasn't interested in playing that game anymore.

I recall one day, sitting in Wallace's office. Both he and White were working me over pretty good. Wallace seemed to be enjoying himself, though White kept giving me looks that said, "Sorry, pal, this is my job." As always I politely took the abuse they dished out, playing the role of meek small business owner. Long on contrition, short on credit. I knew the role backward and forward, but I remember feeling that at any moment I might cut loose a bloodcurdling scream. Here I'd built this dynamic company, from nothing, and by all measures it was a beast—sales doubling every year, like clockwork—and this was the thanks I got? Two bankers treating me like a deadbeat?

White, trying to cool things off, said a few nominal things in support of Blue Ribbon. I watched his words have no effect whatsoever on Wallace. I took a breath, started to speak, then stopped. I didn't trust my voice. I just sat up straighter and hugged myself. This was my new nervous tic, my new habit. Rubber bands were no longer cutting it. Whenever I felt stressed, whenever I wanted to choke someone, I'd wrap my arms good and tight around my torso. That day the habit was more pronounced. I must have looked as if I was practicing some exotic yoga pose I'd learned in Thailand.

At issue was more than the old philosophical disagreement about growth. Blue Ribbon was approaching six hundred thousand dollars in sales, and that day I'd gone in to ask for a loan of $1.2 million, a number that had symbolic meaning for Wallace. It was the first time I'd broken the million-dollar barrier. In his mind this was like the four-minute mile. Very few people were meant to break it. He was weary of this whole thing, he said, weary of me. For the umpteenth time he explained that he lived on cash balances, and for the umpteenth time I suggested ever so politely that if my sales and earnings were going up, up, up, Wallace should be happy to have my business.

Wallace rapped his pen on the table. My credit was maxed out, he said. Officially, irrevocably, immediately. He wasn't authorizing one more cent until I put some cash in my account and left it there.

Meanwhile, henceforth, he'd be imposing strict sales quotas for me to meet. Miss one quota, he said, by even one day, and, well . . . He didn't finish the sentence. His voice trailed off, and I was left to fill the silence with worst-case scenarios.

I turned to White, who gave me a look. *What can I do, pal?*

DAYS LATER WOODELL showed me a telex from Onitsuka. The big spring shipment was ready to hit the water and they wanted twenty thousand dollars. Great, we said. For once they're shipping the shoes on time.

Just one hitch. We didn't have twenty thousand dollars. And it was clear I couldn't go to Wallace. I couldn't ask Wallace for change of a five.

So I telexed Onitsuka and asked them to hold the shoes, please, until we brought in some more revenue from our sales force. "Please don't think we are in financial difficulty," I wrote. It wasn't a lie, per se. As I told Bowerman, we weren't broke, we just had no money. Lots of assets, no cash. We simply needed more time. Now it was my turn to say: *Little more days.*

While awaiting Onitsuka's response, I realized that there was only one way to solve this cash flow problem once and for all. A small public offering. If we could sell 30 percent of Blue Ribbon, at two bucks a share, we could raise three hundred thousand dollars overnight.

The timing for such an offering seemed ideal. In 1970 the first-ever venture capital firms were starting to sprout up. The whole concept of venture capital was being invented before our eyes, though the idea of what constituted a sound investment for venture capitalists wasn't very broad. Most of the new venture capital firms were in Northern California, so they were mainly attracted to high-tech and electronics companies. Silicon Valley, almost exclusively. Since most of those companies had futuristic-sounding names, I formed a holding company for Blue Ribbon and gave it a name designed to attract tech-happy investors: Sports-Tek Inc.

Woodell and I sent out fliers advertising the offering, then sat back and braced for the clamorous response.

Silence.

A month passed.

Deafening silence.

No one phoned. Not one person.

That is, almost no one. We did manage to sell three hundred shares, at one dollar per.

To Woodell and his mother.

Ultimately we withdrew the offering. It was a humiliation, and in its wake I had many heated conversations with myself. I blamed the shaky economy. I blamed Vietnam. But first and foremost I blamed myself. I'd overvalued Blue Ribbon. I'd overvalued my life's work.

More than once, over my first cup of coffee in the morning, or while trying to fall asleep at night, I'd tell myself: Maybe I'm a fool? Maybe this whole damn shoe thing is a fool's errand?

Maybe, I thought.

Maybe.

I SCRAPED TOGETHER the twenty thousand dollars from our receivables, paid off the bank, and took delivery of the order from Onitsuka. Another sigh of relief. Followed by a tightening in the chest. What would I do the next time? And the next?

I needed cash. That summer was unusually warm. Languorous days of golden sunshine, clear blue skies, the world a paradise. It all seemed to mock me and my mood. If 1967 had been the Summer of Love, 1970 was the Summer of Liquidity, and I had none. I spent most of every day thinking about liquidity, talking about liquidity, looking to the heavens and pleading for liquidity. My kingdom for liquidity. An even more loathsome word than "equity."

Eventually I did what I didn't want to do, what I'd vowed never to do. I put the touch on anybody with ears. Friends, family, casual acquaintances. I even went with my hand out to former teammates, guys I'd sweated and trained and raced alongside. Including my former archrival, Grelle.

I'd heard that Grelle had inherited a pile from his grandmother. On top of that, he was involved in all sorts of lucrative business ventures. He worked as a salesman for two grocery store chains, while selling caps and gowns to graduates on the side, and both ventures were said to be humming along. He also owned a great big chunk of land at Lake Arrowhead, someone said, and lived there in a rambling house. The man was born to win. (He was even still running competitively, one year away from becoming the best in the world.)

There was an all-comers road race in Portland that summer, and Penny and I invited a group of people to the house afterward, for a cocktail party. I made sure to invite Grelle, then waited for just the right moment. When everyone was rested, a couple of beers to the good, I asked Grelle for a word in private. I took him into my den and made my pitch short and sweet. New company, cash flow problems, considerable upside, yadda yadda. He was gracious, courteous, and smiled pleasantly. "I'm just not interested, Buck."

With nowhere else to turn, with no other options, I was sitting at my desk one day, staring out the window. Woodell knocked. He rolled into the office, closed the door. He said he and his parents wanted to loan me five thousand dollars, and they wouldn't take no for an answer. They also wouldn't tolerate any mention of interest. In fact they wouldn't even formalize the loan with any sort of papers. He was going to Los Angeles to see Bork, but while he was gone, he said, I should drive to his house and collect the check from his folks.

Days later I did something beyond imagining, something I didn't think myself capable of doing. I drove to Woodell's house and asked for the check.

I knew the Woodells weren't well off. I knew that, with their son's medical bills, they were scuffling more than I. This five thousand dollars was their life savings. I knew that.

But I was wrong. His parents had a little bit more, and they asked if I needed that, too. And I said yes. And they gave me their last three thousand dollars, draining their savings down to zero.

How I wished I could put that check in my desk drawer and not cash it. But I couldn't. I wouldn't.

On my way out the door I stopped. I asked them: "Why are you doing this?"

"Because," Woodell's mother said, "if you can't trust the company your son is working for, then who can you trust?"

PENNY WAS CONTINUING to find creative ways of stretching her twenty-five-dollar grocery allowance, which meant fifty kinds of beef Stroganoff, which meant my weight ballooned. By the middle of 1970 I was around 190, an all-time high. One morning, getting dressed for work, I put on one of my baggier suits and it wasn't baggy. Standing before the mirror I said to my reflection: "Uh-oh."

But it was more than the Stroganoff. Somehow, I'd gotten out of the running habit. Blue Ribbon, marriage, fatherhood—there was never time. Also, I'd felt burned out. Though I'd loved running for Bowerman, I'd hated it, too. The same thing happens to all kinds of college athletes. Years of training and competing at a high level take their toll. You need a rest. But now the rest was over. I needed to get back out there. I didn't want to be the fat, flabby, sedentary head of a running-shoe company.

And if tight suits and the specter of hypocrisy weren't enough incentive, another motivation soon came along.

Shortly after that all-comers race, after Grelle refused me the loan, he and I went for a private run. Four miles in, I saw Grelle looking back at me sadly as I huffed and puffed to keep up. It was one thing to have him refuse me money, it was another to have him give me pity. He knew

I was embarrassed, so he challenged me. "This fall," he said, "let's you and me race—one mile. I'll give you a full minute handicap, and if you beat me I'll pay you a buck for every second of difference in our times."

I trained hard that summer. I got into the habit of running six miles every night after work. In no time I was back in shape, my weight down to 160. And when the day of the big race came—with Woodell on the stopwatch—I took thirty-six dollars from Grelle. (The victory was made all the sweeter the following week when Grelle jumped into an all-comers meet and ran 4:07.) As I drove home that day I felt immensely proud. Keep going, I told myself. Don't stop.

AT ALMOST THE halfway mark of the year—June 15, 1970—I pulled my *Sports Illustrated* from my mailbox and got a shock. On the cover was a Man of Oregon. And not just any Man of Oregon, but perhaps the greatest of all time, greater even than Grelle. His name was Steve Prefontaine, and the photo showed him sprinting up the side of Olympus, aka Bowerman Mountain.

The article inside described Pre as an astonishing, once-a-generation phenom. He'd already made a big splash in high school, setting a national record (8:41) at two miles, but now, in his first year at Oregon, running two miles, he'd beaten Gerry Lindgren, who'd previously been considered unbeatable. And he'd beaten him by 27 seconds. Pre posted 8:40.0, third-fastest time in the nation that year. He'd also run three miles in 13:12.8, which in 1970 was faster than anyone, anywhere, on earth.

Bowerman told the writer from *Sports Illustrated* that Pre was the fastest middle-distance runner alive. I'd never heard such unbridled enthusiasm from my stolid coach. In the days ahead, in other articles I clipped, Bowerman was even more effusive, calling Pre "the best runner I've ever had." Bowerman's assistant, Bill Dellinger, said Pre's secret weapon was his confidence, which was as freakish as his lung capacity. "Usually," Dellinger said, "it takes our guys twelve years to build confidence in themselves, and here's a young man who has the right attitude naturally."

Yes, I thought. Confidence. More than equity, more than liquidity, that's what a man needs.

I wished I had more. I wished I could borrow some. But confidence was cash. You had to have some to get some. And people were loath to give it to you.

Another revelation came that summer via another magazine. Flipping through *Fortune* I spotted a story about my former boss in Hawaii. In the years since I'd worked for Bernie Cornfeld and his Investors Overseas Services, he'd become even richer. He'd abandoned Dreyfus Funds and begun selling shares in his own mutual funds, along with gold mines, real estate, and sundry other things. He'd built an empire, and as all empires eventually do it was now crumbling. I was so startled by news of his downfall that I dazedly turned the page and happened on another article, a fairly dry analysis of Japan's newfound economic power. Twenty-five years after Hiroshima, the article said, Japan was reborn. The world's third-largest economy, it was taking aggressive steps to become even larger, to consolidate its position and extend its reach. Besides simply outthinking and outworking other countries, Japan was adopting ruthless trade policies. The article then sketched the main vehicle for these trade policies, Japan's hyper-aggressive *sosa shoga*.

Trading companies.

It's hard to say exactly what those first Japanese trading companies were. Sometimes they were importers, scouring the globe and acquiring raw materials for companies that didn't have the means to do so. Other times they were exporters, representing those same companies overseas. Sometimes they were private banks, providing all kinds of companies with easy terms of credit. Other times they were an arm of the Japanese government.

I filed away all this information. For a few days. And the next time I went down to First National, the next time Wallace made me

feel like a bum, I walked out and saw the sign for Bank of Tokyo. I'd
seen that sign a hundred times before, of course, but now it meant
something different. Huge pieces of the puzzle fell into place. Dizzy,
I walked directly across the street, straight into the Bank of Tokyo,
and presented myself to the woman at the front desk. I said I owned a
shoe company, which was importing shoes from Japan, and I wanted
to speak with someone about doing a deal. Like the madam of a
brothel, the woman instantly and discreetly led me to a back room.
And left me.

After two minutes a man walked in and sat down very quietly
at the table. He waited. I waited. He continued waiting. Finally I
spoke. "I have a company," I said. "Yes?" he said. "A shoe company,"
I said. "Yes?" he said. I opened my briefcase. "These are my financial
statements. I'm in a terrible bind. I need credit. I just read an article
in *Fortune* about Japanese trading companies, and the article said
these companies are looser with credit—and, well, do you know of
any such companies that you might introduce me to?"

The man smiled. He'd read the same article. He said it just so
happened that Japan's sixth-largest trading company had an office
right above our heads, on the top floor of that building. All the major
Japanese trading companies had offices in Portland, he said, but this
particular one, Nissho Iwai, was the only one in Portland with its
own commodities department. "It's a $100 billion company," the
banker said, eyes widening. "Oh, boy," I said. "Please wait," he said.
He left the room.

Minutes later he returned with an executive from Nissho Iwai.
His name was Cam Murakami. We shook hands and chatted, strictly
hypothetically, about the possibility of Nissho financing my future
imports. I was intrigued. He was quite intrigued. He offered me a
deal on the spot, and extended his hand, but I couldn't shake it. Not
yet. First I had to clear it with Onitsuka.

I sent a wire that day to Kitami, asking if he'd have any objections to my doing side business with Nissho. Days passed. Weeks.

With Onitsuka, silence meant something. No news was bad news, no news was good news—but no news was always some sort of news.

WHILE WAITING TO hear back, I got a troubling call. A shoe distributor on the East Coast said he'd been approached by Onitsuka about becoming its new U.S. distributor. I made him say it again, slower. He did. He said he wasn't trying to make me angry. Nor was he trying to help me out or give me a heads-up. He just wanted to know the status of my deal.

I began to shake. My heart was pounding. Months after signing a new contract with me, Onitsuka was plotting to break it? Had they been spooked when I was late taking delivery of the spring shipment? Had Kitami simply decided he didn't care for me?

My only hope was that this distributor on the East Coast was lying. Or mistaken. Maybe he'd misunderstood Onitsuka. Maybe it was a language thing?

I wrote to Fujimoto. I said I hoped he was still enjoying the bicycle I bought him. (Subtle.) I asked him to find out anything he could.

He wrote back right away. The distributor was telling the truth. Onitsuka was considering a clean break with Blue Ribbon, and Kitami was in touch with several distributors in the United States. There was no firm plan to break my contract, Fujimoto added, but candidates were being vetted and scouted.

I tried to focus on the good. There was no firm plan. This meant there was still hope. I could still restore Onitsuka's faith, change Kitami's mind. I would just need to remind Kitami of what Blue Ribbon was, and who I was. Which would mean inviting him to the United States for a friendly visit.

1971

"Guess who's coming to dinner," Woodell said.

He wheeled into my office and handed me the telex. Kitami had accepted my invitation. He was coming to Portland to spend a few days. Then he was going to make a wider tour of the United States, for reasons he declined to share. "Visiting other potential distributors," I said to Woodell. He nodded.

It was March 1971. We vowed that Kitami was going to have the time of his life, that he would return home feeling love in his heart for America, Oregon, Blue Ribbon—and me. When we were done with him he'd be incapable of doing business with anyone else. And so, we agreed, the visit should close on a high note, with a gala dinner at the home of our prize asset—Bowerman.

IN MOUNTING THIS charm offensive, naturally I enlisted Penny. Together we met Kitami's flight, and together we whisked him straight to the Oregon coast, to her parents' oceanfront cottage, where we'd spent our wedding night.

Kitami had a companion with him, a sort of bag carrier, personal assistant, amanuensis, named Hiraku Iwano. He was just a kid, naïve, innocent, in his early twenties, and Penny had him eating out of her hand before we hit Sunset Highway.

We both slaved to give the two men an idyllic Pacific Northwest weekend. We sat on the porch with them and breathed in the sea air. We took them for long walks on the beach. We fed them world-class salmon and poured them glass after glass of good French wine. We tried to focus most of our attention on Kitami, but both Penny and I found it easier to talk to Iwano, who read books and seemed guileless. Kitami seemed like a man who was importing guile by the boatload.

Monday, bright and early, I drove Kitami back to Portland, to First National Bank. Just as I was determined to charm him on this trip, I thought that he could be helpful in charming Wallace, that he could vouch for Blue Ribbon and make credit easier to get.

White met us in the lobby and walked us into a conference room. I looked around. "Where's Wallace?" I asked. "Ah," White said, "he won't be able to join us today."

What? That was the whole point of visiting the bank. I wanted Wallace to hear Kitami's ringing endorsement. Oh well, I thought— good cop will just have to relay the endorsement to bad cop.

I said a few preliminary words, expressed confidence that Kitami could bolster First National's faith in Blue Ribbon, then turned the floor over to Kitami, who scowled and did the one thing guaranteed to make my life harder. "Why do you not give my friends more *money?*" he said to White.

"W-w-what?" White said.

"Why do you refuse to extend credit to Blue Ribbon?" Kitami said, pounding his fist on the table.

"Well now—" White said.

Kitami cut him off. "What kind of bank is this? I do not understand! Maybe Blue Ribbon would be better off without you!"

White turned white. I tried to jump in. I tried to rephrase what Kitami was saying, tried to blame the language barrier, but the meeting was over. White stormed out, and I stared in astonishment at Kitami, who was wearing an expression that said, Job well done.

*   *   *

I DROVE KITAMI to our new offices in Tigard and showed him around, introduced him to the gang. I was fighting hard to maintain my composure, to remain pleasant, to block out all thoughts about what had just happened. I was afraid that at any second I might lose it. But when I settled Kitami into a chair across from my desk, it was he who lost it—at me. "Blue Ribbon sales are disappointing!" he said. "You should be doing much better."

Stunned, I said that our sales were doubling every year. Not good enough, he snapped. "Should be triple some people say," he said. "What people?" I asked. "Never mind," he said.

He took a folder from his briefcase, flipped it open, read it, snapped it shut. He repeated that he didn't like our numbers, that he didn't think we were doing enough. He opened the folder again, shut it again, shoved it back into his briefcase. I tried to defend myself, but he waved his hand in disgust. Back and forth we went, for quite a while, civil but tense.

After nearly an hour of this he stood and asked to use the men's room. Down the hall, I said.

The moment he was out of sight I jumped from behind my desk. I opened his briefcase and rummaged through and took out what looked like the folder he'd been referring to. I slid it under my desk blotter, then jumped behind my desk and put my elbows on the blotter.

Waiting for Kitami to return, I had the strangest thought. I recalled all the times I'd volunteered with the Boy Scouts, all the times I'd sat on Eagle Scout review boards, handing out merit badges for honor and integrity. Two or three weekends a year I'd question pink-cheeked boys about their probity, their honesty, and now I was stealing documents from another man's briefcase? I was headed down a dark path. No telling where it might lead. Wherever, there was no getting around one immediate consequence of my actions. I'd have to recuse myself from the next review board.

How I longed to study the contents of that folder, and photocopy every scrap of paper in it, and go over it all with Woodell. But

Kitami was soon back. I let him resume scolding me about sluggish numbers, let him talk himself out, and when he stopped I summed up my position. Calmly I said that Blue Ribbon might increase its sales if we could order more shoes, and we might order more shoes if we had more financing, and our bank might give us more financing if we had more security, meaning a longer contract with Onitsuka. Again he waved his hand. "Excuses," he said.

I raised the idea of funding our orders through a Japanese trading company, like Nissho Iwai, as I'd mentioned in my wire months before. "Baah," he said, "trading companies. They send money first— men later. Take over! Work way into your company, then take over."

Translation: Onitsuka was only manufacturing a quarter of its own shoes, subcontracting the other three-quarters. Kitami was afraid that Nissho would find Onitsuka's network of factories, then go right around Onitsuka and become a manufacturer and put Onitsuka out of business.

Kitami stood. He needed to go back to his hotel, he said, have a rest. I said I'd have someone drive him, and I'd meet him for a cocktail later at his hotel bar.

The instant he was gone I went and found Woodell and told him what had happened. I held up the folder. "I stole *this* from his briefcase," I said. "You did *what*?" Woodell said. He started to act appalled, but he was just as curious as I was about the folder's contents. Together we opened it and laid it on his desk and found that it contained, among other things, a list of eighteen athletic shoe distributors across the United States and a schedule of appointments with half of them.

So there it was. In black and white. Some people say. The "some people" damning Blue Ribbon, poisoning Kitami against us, were our competitors. And he was on his way to visit them. Kill one Marlboro Man, twenty more rise up to take his place.

I was outraged, of course. But mostly hurt. For seven years we'd devoted ourselves to Tiger shoes. We'd introduced them to America, we'd reinvented the line. Bowerman and Johnson had shown Onit-suka how to make a better shoe, and their designs were now founda-tional, setting sales records, changing the face of the industry—and this was how we were repaid? "And now," I said to Woodell, "I have to go meet this Judas for cocktails."

First I went for a six-mile run. I don't know when I've run harder, or been less present in my body. With each stride I yelled at the trees, screamed at the cobwebs hanging in the branches. It helped. By the time I'd showered and dressed and driven to meet Kitami at his hotel, I was almost serene. Or maybe I was in shock. What Kitami said during that hour together, what I said—no memory. The next thing I remem-ber is this. The following morning, when Kitami came to the office, Woodell and I ran a sort of shell game. While someone whisked Kit-ami into the coffee room, Woodell blocked the door to my office with his wheelchair and I slid the folder back into the briefcase.

ON THE LAST day of Kitami's visit, hours before the big dinner party, I hurried down to Eugene to confer with Bowerman and his lawyer, Jaqua. I left Penny to drive Kitami down later in the day, thinking: What's the worst that could happen?

Cut to Penny, hair disheveled, dress smeared with grease, pulling up to Bowerman's house. As she stumbled out of the car I thought for a moment that Kitami had attacked her, but she took me aside and explained that they'd had a flat. "That son of a bitch," she whispered, "*stayed in the car—on the highway—and let me fix the tire all by myself!*"

I steered her inside. We both needed something strong to drink.

This wasn't a simple matter, however. Mrs. Bowerman, a devout Christian Scientist, didn't normally allow alcohol in her home. She was making an exception on this special night, but she'd asked me ahead of time to please be sure that everyone behaved and no one overdid it. So, though my wife and I both needed a stiff one, I was forced to make it a small one.

Mrs. Bowerman now gathered us all in the living room. "In honor of our distinguished guests," she announced, "tonight we are serving . . . mai tais!"

Applause.

Kitami and I still had at least one thing in common. We both liked mai tais. Very much. Something about them reminded each of us of Hawaii, that wonderful layover between the West Coast and Japan, where you could unwind before going back into the long workdays. Still, he and I stopped at one that evening. Mindful of Mrs. Bowerman, so did everyone else. Everyone but Bowerman. He'd never been much of a drinker, and he'd certainly never tasted a mai tai before, and we all watched in dread and dismay as the drinks took effect. And then some. Something about that tangy combination of curaçao and lime juice, pineapple and rum, hit Bowerman right on the screws. After two mai tais he was a different person.

As he tried to fix his third mai tai he bellowed, "We're out of ice!" No one answered. So he answered himself. "No problem." He marched out to the garage, to the large meat freezer, and grabbed a bag of frozen blueberries. He tore it open, scattering blueberries everywhere. He then tossed a huge handful of frozen blueberries into his drink. "Tastes better this way," he announced, returning to the living room. Now he walked around the room, slopping handfuls of frozen blueberries into everyone's glass.

Sitting, he began to tell a story, which seemed in highly questionable taste. It built to a crescendo I feared we'd all remember for years to come. That is, if we could understand the crescendo. Bowerman's words, normally so crisp, so precise, were growing squishy around the edges.

Mrs. Bowerman glared at me. But what could I do? I shrugged my shoulders and thought: You married him. And then I thought: Oh, wait, so did I.

Back when the Bowermans attended the 1964 Olympics in Japan, Mrs. Bowerman had fallen in love with nashi pears, which are like small green apples, only sweeter. They don't grow in the United States, so she smuggled a few seeds home in her purse and planted them in her garden. Every few years, she told Kitami, when the nashis bloomed, they refreshed her love of all things Japanese. He seemed quite beguiled by this story. "Och!" Bowerman said, exasperated. "Japples!"

I put a hand over my eyes.

Finally came the moment when I thought the party might spin out of control, when I wondered if we might actually need to call the cops. I looked across the room and spotted Jaqua, sitting beside his wife, glaring at Kitami. I knew that Jaqua had been a fighter pilot in the war, that his wingman, one of his closest friends, had been shot out of the sky by a Japanese Zero. In fact Jaqua and his wife had named their first child after that dead wingman, and I suddenly regretted telling Jaqua about Kitami's Folder of Betrayal. I perceived something bubbling inside Jaqua, and rising to his throat, and I sensed the real possibility that Bowerman's lawyer and best friend and neighbor might stand and march across the room and sock Kitami in the jaw.

The one person who seemed to be having an uncomplicatedly wonderful time was Kitami. Gone was the angry Kitami from the bank. Gone was the scolding Kitami from my office. Talking, laughing, slapping his knee, he was so personable that I wondered what might have happened if I'd given him a mai tai before driving him over to First National.

Late in the evening he spotted something across the room—a guitar. It belonged to one of Bowerman's three sons. Kitami walked over, picked it up, and began to finger the strings. Then strum them. He carried the guitar to a short flight of steps that led from the Bowermans' sunken living room to their dining room and, standing on the top step, started to play. And sing.

All heads turned. Conversation ceased. It was a country-western song, of some sort, but Kitami performed it like a traditional Japanese folk song. He sounded like Buck Owens on a koto harp. Then without any segue he switched to "O Sole Mio." I recall thinking: Is he really singing "O Sole Mio"?

He sang it louder. *O sole mio, sta nfronte a te! O sole, o sole mio, sta nfronte a te!*

A Japanese businessman, strumming a Western guitar, singing an Italian ballad, in the voice of an Irish tenor. It was surreal, then a few miles past surreal, and it didn't stop. I'd never known there were so many verses to "O Sole Mio." I'd never known a roomful of active, restless Oregonians could sit so still and quiet for so long. When he set down the guitar, we all tried not to make eye contact with each other as we gave him a big hand. I clapped and clapped and it all made sense. For Kitami, this trip to the United States—the visit to the bank, the meetings with me, the dinner with the Bowermans—wasn't about Blue Ribbon. Nor was it about Onitsuka. Like everything else, it was all about Kitami.

KITAMI LEFT PORTLAND the next day on his not-so-secret mission, his Give-Blue-Ribbon-the-Brush-Off tour of America. I asked again about his destination, and again he didn't answer. *Yoi tabi de arimas yoh ni*, I said. Safe travels.

I'd recently commissioned Hayes, my old boss from Price Waterhouse, to do some consulting work for Blue Ribbon, and now I huddled with him and tried to decide my next move before Kitami's return. We agreed that the best thing to do was keep the peace, try to convince Kitami not to leave us, not to abandon us. As angry and wounded as I was, I needed to accept that Blue Ribbon would be lost without Onitsuka. I needed, Hayes said, to stick with the devil I knew, and persuade him to stick with the devil *he* knew.

Later that week, when the devil returned, I invited him out to Tigard for one more visit before his flight home. Again I tried to rise above it all. I brought him into the conference room and with Woodell and I on one side of the table, and Kitami and his assistant,

Iwano, on the other, I screwed a big smile onto my face and said that we hoped he'd enjoyed his visit to our country.

He said yet again that he was disappointed in the performance of Blue Ribbon.

This time, however, he said he had a solution.

"Shoot," I said.

"Sell us your company."

He said it so very softly. The thought crossed my mind that some of the hardest things ever said in our lifetimes are said softly.

"Excuse me?" I said.

"Onitsuka Co. Ltd. will buy controlling interest in Blue Ribbon, fifty-one percent. It is best deal for your company. And you. You would be wise to accept."

A takeover. *A hostile freaking takeover.* I looked at the ceiling. You gotta be *kidding*, I thought. Of all the arrogant, underhanded, ungrateful, bullying—

"And if we do not?"

"We will have no choice but to set up superior distributors."

"Superior. Uh-huh. I see. And what about our written agreement?"

He shrugged. So much for agreements.

I couldn't let my mind go to any of those places it was trying to go. I couldn't tell Kitami what I thought of him, or where to stick his offer, because Hayes was right, I *still* needed him. I had no backup, no plan B, no exit strategy. If I was going to save Blue Ribbon, I needed to do it slowly, on my own schedule, so as not to spook customers and retailers. I needed time, and therefore I needed Onitsuka to keep sending me shoes for as long as possible.

"Well," I said, fighting to control my voice, "I have a partner, of course. Coach Bowerman. I'll have to discuss your offer with him."

I was certain Kitami would see through this amateurish stall. But he rose, hitched his pants, and smiled. "Talk it over with Dr. Bowerman. Get back to me."

I wanted to hit him. Instead I shook his hand. He and Iwano walked out.

In the suddenly Kitami-less conference room, Woodell and I stared into the grain of the conference table and let the stillness settle over us.

I SENT MY budget and forecast for the coming year to First National, with my standard credit request. I wanted to send a note of apology, begging forgiveness for the Kitami debacle, but I knew White would roll with it. And besides, Wallace hadn't been there. Days after White got my budget and forecast he told me to come on down, he was ready to talk things over.

I wasn't in the hard little chair across from his desk more than two seconds before he delivered the news. "Phil, I'm afraid First National will not be able to do business any longer with Blue Ribbon. We will issue no more letters of credit on your behalf. We will pay off your last remaining shipments as they come in with what remains in your account—but when that last bill is paid, our relationship will be terminated."

I could see by White's waxy pallor that he was stricken. He'd had no part in this. This was coming from on high. Thus there was no point in arguing. I spread my arms. "What do I do, Harry?"

"Find another bank."

"And if I can't? I'm out of business, right?"

He looked down at his papers, stacked them, fastened them with a paper clip. He told me that the question of Blue Ribbon had deeply divided the bank officers. Some were for us, some were against. Ultimately it was Wallace who'd cast the deciding vote. "I'm sick about this," White said. "So sick that I'm taking a sick day."

I didn't have that option. I staggered out of First National and drove straight to U.S. Bank. I pleaded with them to take me in.

Sorry, they said.

They had no desire to buy First National's secondhand problems.

THREE WEEKS PASSED. The company, my company, born from nothing, and now finishing 1971 with sales of $1.3 million, was on life support. I talked with Hayes. I talked with my father. I talked with every other accountant I knew, one of whom mentioned that Bank of California had a charter allowing it to do business in three western states, including Oregon. Plus, Bank of Cal had a branch in Portland. I hurried over and, indeed, they welcomed me, gave me shelter from the storm. And a small line of credit.

Still, it was only a short-term solution. They were a bank, after all, and banks were, by definition, risk-averse. Regardless of my sales, Bank of California would soon view my zero cash balances with alarm. I needed to start preparing for that rainy day.

My thoughts kept returning to that Japanese trading company. Nissho. Late at night I'd think, "They have $100 billion in sales . . . and they want desperately to help *me*. Why?"

For starters, Nissho did huge volumes on low net margins, and therefore it loved growth companies with big upsides. That was us. In spades. In the eyes of Wallace and First National we'd been a land mine; to Nissho we were a potential gold mine.

So I went back. I met with the man sent from Japan to run the new General Commodities Department, Tom Sumeragi. A graduate of Tokyo University, the Harvard of Japan, Sumeragi looked strikingly like the great film actor Toshiro Mifune, who was famous for his portrayal of Miyamoto Musashi, the epic samurai duelist and author of a timeless manual on combat and inner strength, *The Book of Five Rings*. Sumeragi looked most like the actor when lipping a Lucky Strike. And he lipped them a lot. Twice as much when he drank. Unlike Hayes, however, who drank because he liked the way booze made him feel, Sumeragi drank because he was lonely in America. Almost every evening after work he'd head to the Blue House, a Japanese bar-restaurant, and talk in his native tongue with the *mama-san*, which just made him lonelier.

He told me that Nissho was willing to take a second position to the bank on their loans. That would certainly quell my bankers. He also offered this nugget of information: Nissho had recently dispatched a delegation to Kobe, to investigate financing shoes for us, and to convince Onitsuka to let such a deal go through. But Onitsuka had thrown the Nissho delegation out on their asses. A $25 million company throwing out a $100 billion company? Nissho was embarrassed, and angry. "We can introduce you to many quality sports shoe manufacturers in Japan," Sumeragi said, smiling.

I pondered. I still held out some hope that Onitsuka would come to its senses. And I worried about a paragraph in our written agreement that forbade me from importing other brands of track-and-field shoes. "Maybe down the road," I said.

Sumeragi nodded. All in good time.

REELING FROM ALL this drama, I was deeply tired when I returned home each night. But I'd always get a second wind after my six-mile run, followed by a hot shower and a quick dinner, alone. (Penny and Matthew ate around four.) I'd always try to find time to tell Matthew a bedtime story, and I'd always try to find a bedtime story that would be educational. I invented a character called Matt History, who looked and acted a lot like Matthew Knight, and I inserted him into the center of every yarn. Matt History was there at Valley Forge with George Washington. Matt History was there in Massachusetts with John Adams. Matt History was there when Paul Revere rode through the dark of night on a borrowed horse, warning John Hancock that the British were coming. *Hard on Revere's heels was a precocious young horseman from the suburbs of Portland, Oregon . . .*

Matthew would always laugh, delighted to find himself caught up in these adventures. He'd sit up straighter in bed. He'd beg for more, more.

When Matthew was asleep, Penny and I would talk about the day. She'd often ask what we were going to do if it all went south. I'd say, "I can always fall back on accounting." I did not sound sincere, because I wasn't. I was not delighted to be caught up in these adventures.

Eventually Penny would look away, watch TV, resume her needlepoint, or read, and I'd retreat to my recliner, where I'd administer the nightly self-catechism.

What do you know?

I know Onitsuka can't be trusted.

What else do you know?

I know my relationship with Kitami can't be salvaged.

What does the future hold?

One way or another, Blue Ribbon and Onitsuka are going to break up. I just need to stay together as long as possible while I develop other supply sources, so I can manage the breakup.

What's Step One?

I need to scare off all the other distributors Onitsuka has lined up to replace me. Blast them right out of the water, by firing off letters threatening to sue if they breach my contract.

What's Step Two?

Find my own replacement for Onitsuka.

I flashed on a factory I'd heard about, in Guadalajara, the one where Adidas had manufactured shoes during the 1968 Olympics, allegedly to skirt Mexican tariffs. The shoes were good, as I recalled. So I set up a meeting with the factory managers.

EVEN THOUGH IT was in central Mexico, the factory was called Canada. Right away I asked the managers why. They chose the name, they said, because it sounded foreign, exotic. I laughed. Canada?

Exotic? It was more comic than exotic, not to mention confusing. A factory south of the border named for a country north of the border.

Oh well. I didn't care. After looking the place over, after taking inventory of their present line of shoes, after surveying their leather room, I was impressed. The factory was big, clean, well run. Plus, it was Adidas-endorsed. I told them I'd like to place an order. Three thousand pairs of leather soccer shoes, which I planned to sell as football shoes. The factory owners asked me about the name of my brand. I told them I'd have to get back to them on that.

They handed me the contract. I looked at the dotted line above my name. Pen in hand, I paused. The question was now officially on the table. Was this a violation of my deal with Onitsuka?

Technically, no. My deal said I could import only Onitsuka track and field shoes, no others; it said nothing about importing someone else's *football* shoes. So I knew this contract with Canada wouldn't violate the letter of my Onitsuka deal. But the spirit?

Six months previously I would never have done this. Things were different now. Onitsuka had already broken the spirit of our deal, and my spirit, so I pulled the cap off my pen and signed the contract. I signed the heck out of that Canada contract. Then I went out for Mexican food.

Now about that logo. My new soccer-qua-football shoe would need something to set it apart from the stripes of Adidas and Onitsuka. I recalled that young artist I'd met at Portland State. What was her name? Oh, yes, Carolyn Davidson. She'd been in the office a number of times, doing brochures and ad slicks. When I got back to Oregon I invited her to the office again and told her we needed a logo. "What kind?" she asked. "I don't know," I said. "That gives me a lot to go on," she said. "Something that evokes a sense of motion," I said. "Motion," she said, dubious.

She looked confused. Of course she did, I was babbling. I wasn't sure exactly what I wanted. I wasn't an artist. I showed her the soccer-football shoe and said, unhelpfully: This. We need something for this.

SHOE DOG

She said she'd give it a try.

Motion, she mumbled, leaving my office. Motion.

Two weeks later she came back with a portfolio of rough sketches. They were all variations on a single theme, and the theme seemed to be . . . fat lightning bolts? Chubby check marks? Morbidly obese squiggles? Her designs did evoke motion, of a kind, but also motion sickness. None spoke to me. I singled out a few that held out some promise and asked her to work with those.

Days later—or was it weeks?—Carolyn returned and spread a second series of sketches across the conference table. She also hung a few on the wall. She'd done several dozen more variations on the original theme, but with a freer hand. These were better. Closer.

Woodell and I and a few others looked them over. I remember Johnson being there, too, though why he'd come out from Wellesley, I can't recall. Gradually we inched toward a consensus. We liked . . . *this one* . . . slightly more than the others.

It looks like a wing, one of us said.

It looks like a whoosh of air, another said.

It looks like something a runner might leave in his or her wake.

We all agreed it looked new, fresh, and yet somehow—ancient. Timeless.

For her many hours of work, we gave Carolyn our deepest thanks and a check for thirty-five dollars, then sent her on her way.

After she left we continued to sit and stare at this one logo, which we'd sort of selected, and sort of settled on by default. "Something eye-catching about it," Johnson said. Woodell agreed. I frowned, scratched my cheek. "You guys like it more than I do," I said. "But we're out of time. It'll have to do."

"You don't like it?" Woodell said.

I sighed. "I don't love it. Maybe it will grow on me."

We sent it to Canada.

Now we just needed a name to go with this logo I didn't love.

Over the next few days we kicked around dozens of ideas, until two leading candidates emerged.

Falcon.

And Dimension Six.

I was partial to the latter, because I was the one who came up with it. Woodell and everyone else told me that it was god-awful. It wasn't catchy, they said, and it didn't mean anything.

We took a poll of all our employees. Secretaries, accountants, sales reps, retail clerks, file clerks, warehouse workers—we demanded that each person jump in, make at least one suggestion. Ford had just paid a top-flight consulting firm $2 million to come up with the name of its new Maverick, I announced to everyone. "We haven't got $2 million—but we've got fifty smart people, and we can't do any worse than . . . *Maverick*."

Also, unlike Ford, we had a deadline. Canada was starting production on the shoe that Friday.

Hour after hour was spent arguing and yelling, debating the virtue of this name or that. Someone liked Bork's suggestion, Bengal. Someone else said the only possible name was Condor. I huffed and groused. "Animal names," I said. "*Animal* names! We've considered the name of just about every animal in the forest. *Must* it be an animal?"

Again and again I lobbied for Dimension Six. Again and again I was told by my employees that it was unspeakably bad.

Someone, I forget who, summed up the situation neatly. "All these names . . . suck." I thought it might have been Johnson, but all the documentation says he'd left and gone back to Wellesley by then.

One night, late, we were all tired, running out of patience. If I heard one more animal name I was going to jump out a window. Tomorrow's another day, we said, drifting out of the office, headed out to our cars.

I went home and sat in my recliner. My mind went back and forth, back and forth. Falcon? Bengal? Dimension Six? Something else? Anything else?

* * *

THE DAY OF decision arrived. Canada had already started producing the shoes, and samples were ready to go in Japan, but before anything could be shipped, we needed to choose a name. Also, we had magazine ads slated to run, to coincide with the shipments, and we needed to tell the graphic artists what name to put in the ads. Finally, we needed to file paperwork with the U.S. Patent Office.

Woodell wheeled into my office. "Time's up," he said.

I rubbed my eyes. "I know."

"What's it going to be?"

"I don't know."

My head was splitting. By now the names had all run together into one mind-melting glob. *Falconbengaldimensionsix.*

"There is . . . one more suggestion," Woodell said.

"From who?"

"Johnson phoned first thing this morning," he said. "Apparently a new name came to him in a dream last night."

I rolled my eyes. "A dream?"

"He's serious," Woodell said.

"He's always serious."

"He says he sat bolt upright in bed in the middle of the night and saw the name before him," Woodell said.

"What is it?" I asked, bracing myself.

"Nike."

"Huh?"

"Nike."

"Spell it."

"N-I-K-E," Woodell said.

I wrote it on a yellow legal pad.

The Greek goddess of victory. The Acropolis. The Parthenon. The Temple. I thought back. Briefly. Fleetingly.

PHIL KNIGHT

"We're out of time," I said. "Nike. Falcon. Or Dimension Six."

"Everyone *hates* Dimension Six."

"Everyone but me."

He frowned. "It's your call."

He left me. I made doodles on my pad. I made lists, crossed them out. Tick, tock, tick, tock.

I needed to telex the factory—now.

I hated making decisions in a hurry, and that's all I seemed to do in those days. I looked to the ceiling. I gave myself two more minutes to mull over the different options, then walked down the hall to the telex machine. I sat before it, gave myself three more minutes.

Reluctantly, I punched out the message. *Name of new brand is . . .*

A lot of things were rolling around in my head, consciously, unconsciously. First, Johnson had pointed out that seemingly all iconic brands—Clorox, Kleenex, Xerox—have short names. Two syllables or less. And they always have a strong sound in the name, a letter like "K" or "X," that sticks in the mind. That all made sense. And that all described Nike.

Also, I liked that Nike was the goddess of victory. What's more important, I thought, than victory?

I might have heard, in the far recesses of my mind, Churchill's voice. *You ask, What is our aim? I can answer in one word. It is victory.* I might have recalled the victory medal awarded to all veterans of World War II, a bronze medallion with Athena Nike on the front, breaking a sword in two. I might have. Sometimes I believe that I did. But in the end I don't really know what led me to my decision. Luck? Instinct? Some inner spirit?

Yes.

"What'd you decide?" Woodell asked me at the end of the day. "Nike," I mumbled. "Hm," he said. "Yeah, I know," I said. "Maybe it'll grow on us," he said.

Maybe.

* * *

MY BRAND-NEW RELATIONSHIP with Nissho was promising, but
it was brand new, and who would dare predict how it might evolve?
I'd once felt the relationship with Onitsuka was promising, and look
where that stood. Nissho was infusing me with cash, but I couldn't
let that make me complacent. I needed to develop as many sources
of cash as possible.

Which brought me back to the idea of a public offering. I didn't
think I could withstand the disappointment of a second failed offering, so I plotted with Hayes to ensure that this one would work. We
decided that the first offering hadn't been aggressive enough. We
hadn't sold ourselves. This time we hired a hard-driving salesman.

Also, this time we decided not to sell stocks, but convertible debentures.

If business truly is war without bullets, then debentures are war
bonds. The public loans you money, and in exchange you give them
quasi-stock in your . . . cause. The stock is quasi because debenture holders are strongly encouraged, and incentivized, to hold their
shares for five years. After that, they can convert the shares to common stock or get their money back with interest.

With our new plan, and our gung-ho salesman, we announced in
June 1971 that Blue Ribbon would be offering two hundred thousand shares of debentures, at one dollar per, and this time the shares
sold fast. One of the first to buy was my friend Cale, who didn't
hesitate to cut a check for ten thousand dollars, a princely sum.

"Buck," he said, "I was there at the start, I'll be there at the bitter
end."

CANADA WAS A letdown. The factory's leather football shoe was
pretty, but in cold weather its sole split and cracked. Irony upon
irony—a shoe made in a factory called Canada, which couldn't take

the cold. Then again, maybe it was our fault. Using a soccer shoe for football. Maybe we were asking for it.

The quarterback for Notre Dame wore a pair that season, and it was a thrill to see him trot onto that hallowed gridiron at South Bend in a pair of Nikes. Until those Nikes disintegrated. (Just like the Irish did that year.) Job One, therefore, was finding a factory that could make sturdier, more weather-resistant shoes.

Nissho said they could help. They were only too happy to help. They were beefing up their commodities department, so Sumeragi had a wealth of information about factories around the world. He'd also recently hired a consultant, a bona fide shoe wizard, who'd been a disciple of Jonas Senter.

I'd never heard of Senter, but Sumeragi assured me the man was a genuine, head-to-toe shoe dog. I'd heard this phrase a few times. Shoe dogs were people who devoted themselves wholly to the making, selling, buying, or designing of shoes. Lifers used the phrase cheerfully to describe other lifers, men and women who had toiled so long and hard in the shoe trade, they thought and talked about nothing else. It was an all-consuming mania, a recognizable psychological disorder, to care so much about insoles and outsoles, linings and welts, rivets and vamps. But I understood. The average person takes seventy-five hundred steps a day, 274 million steps over the course of a long life, the equivalent of six times around the globe— shoe dogs, it seemed to me, simply wanted to be part of that journey. Shoes were their way of connecting with humanity. What better way of connecting, shoe dogs thought, than by refining the hinge that joins each person to the world's surface?

I felt an unusual sympathy for such sad cases. I wondered how many I might have met in my travels.

The shoe market just then was flooded with knockoff Adidas, and it was Senter who'd unleashed the flood. He was the knockoff king, apparently. He also knew everything worth knowing about Asia's legitimate shoe trade—factories, importing, exporting. He'd helped set up a shoe division for Mitsubishi, Japan's largest trading company. Nissho couldn't hire Senter himself, for various reasons, so they'd hired Senter's protégé, a man named Sole.

"Really?" I said. "A shoe guy named Sole?"

Before meeting Sole, before going any further with Nissho, I considered if I was walking into another trap. If I partnered with Nissho, I'd soon be into them for a lot of money. If they also became the source of all our footwear, I would then be even more vulnerable to them than I had been to Onitsuka. And if they turned out to be as aggressive as Onitsuka, it would be lights out.

At Bowerman's suggestion I talked it over with Jaqua, and he saw the conundrum. Quite a pickle, he said. He didn't know what to advise. But he knew someone who would. His brother-in-law, Chuck Robinson, was CEO of Marcona Mining, which had joint ventures all over the world. Each of the big eight Japanese trading companies was a partner in at least one of Marcona's mines, so Chuck was arguably the West's leading expert on doing business with these guys.

I finagled a meeting with Chuck at his office in San Francisco and found myself wildly intimidated from the moment I walked in the door. I was agog at his office's size—bigger than my house. And at its view—windows overlooking all of San Francisco Bay, with enormous tankers gliding slowly to and from the world's great ports. And lining the walls were scale models of Marcona's tanker fleet, which supplied coal and other minerals to every corner of the globe. Only a man of enormous power, and brains, could command such a redoubt.

I stammered through my presentation, but Chuck still managed to quickly get the drift. He boiled my complicated situation down to a compelling précis. "If the Japanese trading company understands the rules from the first day," he said, "they will be the best partners you'll ever have."

Reassured, emboldened, I went back to Sumeragi and told him the rules. "No equity in my company. Ever."

He went away and consulted with a few people in his office. Upon returning he said, "No problem. But here's our deal. We take four percent off the top, as a markup on product. And market interest rates on top of that."

I nodded.

Days later Sumeragi sent Sole to meet me. Given the man's reputation, I was expecting some kind of godlike figure with fifteen arms, each one waving a wand made out of shoe trees. But Sole was a plain, ordinary, middle-age businessman, with a New York accent and a sharkskin suit. Not my kind of guy, and I wasn't his kind, either. And yet we had no trouble finding common ground. Shoes, sports—plus an abiding distaste for Kitami. When I mentioned Kitami's name, Sole scoffed. "The man's an ass."

We're going to be fast friends, I thought.

Sole promised to help me beat Kitami, get free of him. "I can solve all your problems," he said. "I know factories." "Factories that can make Nikes?" I asked, handing him my new football shoe. "I can think of five off the top of my head!" he said.

He was adamant. He seemed to have two mental states—adamant and dismissive. I realized that he was selling me, that he wanted my business, but I was willing to be sold, and more than ready to be wanted.

The five factories Sole mentioned were all in Japan. So Sumeragi and I decided to go there and look them over in September 1971. Sole agreed to be our guide.

A WEEK BEFORE we were to leave, Sumeragi phoned. "Mr. Sole has suffered a heart attack," he said. "Oh no," I said. "He's expected to recover," Sumeragi said, "but traveling at this time is impossible. His son, who is very capable, will take his place."

Sumeragi sounded as if he was trying to convince himself, more than me.

I flew alone to Japan, and met Sumeragi and Sole Jr. at Nissho's office in Tokyo. I was taken aback when Sole Jr. stepped forward, hand outstretched. I assumed he'd be young, but he looked like a teenager. I had a hunch he'd be dressed in sharkskin, like his father, and he was. But his suit was three sizes too big. Was it in fact his father's?

And like so many teens, he started every sentence with "I." I think this. I think that. I, I, I.

I shot a glance at Sumeragi. He looked gravely concerned.

THE FIRST OF the factories we wanted to see was outside Hiro-shima. All three of us went there by train, arriving midday. A cool, overcast afternoon. We weren't due at the factory until the next morning, so I felt it important to take the extra time and visit the museum. And I wanted to go by myself. I told Sumeragi and Sole Jr. I would meet them in the hotel lobby the following morning.

Walking through those museum rooms . . . I couldn't take it all in. I couldn't process it. Mannequins dressed in singed clothes. Clumps of scorched, irradiated—jewelry? Cookware? I couldn't tell. Photos that took me to a place far beyond emotion. I stood in horror before a child's liquefied tricycle. I stood, open-mouthed, before the black-ened skeleton of a building, where people had loved and worked and laughed, until. I tried to feel and hear the moment of impact.

I felt sick at heart as I turned a corner and came upon a scorched shoe, under glass, the footprint of its owner still visible.

The next morning, these ghastly images still fresh in my head, I was somber, heavily subdued as I drove with Sumeragi and Sole Jr. into the countryside, and I was almost startled by the good cheer of the factory officials. They were delighted to meet us, to show us their wares. Also, they said forthrightly, they were most eager to do a deal. They'd long been hoping to crack the U.S. market.

I showed them the Cortez, asked how long it might take to pro-duce a sizable order of this shoe.

Six months, they said.

Sole Jr. stepped forward. "You'll do it in *three*," he barked.

I gasped. With the exception of Kitami, I'd always found the Japanese unfailingly polite, even in the heat of disagreement or intense negotiation, and I'd always strived to reciprocate. But in Hiroshima of all places I felt that politeness was that much more essential. Here, if nowhere else on earth, humans should be gentle and kind with one another. Sole Jr. was anything but. The ugliest of Americans.

It got worse. As we made our way across Japan he was brusque, boorish, strutting, swaggering, condescending to everyone we met. He embarrassed me, embarrassed all Americans. Now and then Sumeragi and I exchanged pained looks. We wanted desperately to scold Sole Jr., to leave him—but we needed his father's contacts. We needed this horrid brat to show us where the factories were.

In Kurume, just outside Beppu, in the southern islands, we visited a factory that was part of a vast industrial complex run by the Bridgestone Tire Company. The factory was called Nippon Rubber. It was the biggest shoe factory I'd ever seen, a kind of Shoe Oz, capable of handling any order, no matter how big or complicated. We sat with factory officials in their conference room, just after breakfast, and this time, when Sole Jr. tried to speak, I didn't let him. Each time he opened his mouth I spoke up, cut him off.

I told officials the kind of shoe we wanted, showed them the Cortez. They nodded gravely. I wasn't sure they understood.

After lunch we returned to the conference room and there before me on the table was a brand-new Cortez, Nike side stripe and all, hot off the factory floor. Magic.

I spent the rest of the afternoon describing the shoes I wanted. Tennis, basketball, high top, low top, plus several more models of running shoes. The officials insisted they would have no trouble making any of these designs.

Fine, I said, but before placing an order I'll need to see samples. The factory officials assured me that they could blast out samples and ship them within days to Nissho's offices in Tokyo. We bowed to each other. I went back to Tokyo and waited.

Days and days of crisp fall weather. I walked around the city, drank Sapporo and sake, ate yakitori, and dreamed of shoes. I revisited the Meiji gardens, and sat beneath the ginkgos beside the torii gate. Portal to the sacred.

On Sunday I got a notice at my hotel. The shoes had arrived. I went down to the offices of Nissho, but they were closed. They had trusted me enough to give me a pass, however, so I let myself in, and sat in a big room, amid rows and rows of empty desks, inspecting the samples. I held them to the light, turned them this way and that. I ran my fingers along the soles, along the check or wing or whatever our new side stripe would be called. They were not perfect. The logo on this shoe wasn't quite straight, the midsole on that shoe was a bit too thin. There should be more lift on this other one.

I made notes for the factory officials.

But minor imperfections aside, they were very good.

At last the only thing to do was think up names for the different models. I was panicked. I'd done such a poor job thinking up a name for my new brand—

Dimension Six? Everyone at Blue Ribbon still mocked me. I'd only gone with Nike because I was out of time, and because I'd trusted Johnson's savant-like nature. Now I was on my own, in an empty office building in downtown Tokyo. I'd have to trust myself.

I held up the tennis shoe. I decided to call it . . . the Wimbledon. Well. That was easy.

I held up another tennis shoe. I decided to call it . . . the Forest Hill. After all, that was the setting for the first U.S. Open.

I held up a basketball shoe. I called it the Blazer, after my hometown NBA team.

I held up another basketball shoe. I named it the Bruin, because the best college basketball team of all time was John Wooden's Bruins. Not too creative, but.

Now the running shoes. Cortez, of course. And Marathon. And Obori. And Boston and Finland. I was feeling it. I was in the zone. I started dancing around the room. I heard a secret music. I held up a running shoe. I named it the Wet-Flyte. Boom, I said.

To this day I don't know where that name came from.

It took a half hour to name them all. I felt like Coleridge, writing "Kubla Khan" in an opium daze. I then mailed my names off to the factory.

It was dark as I walked out of the office building, into the crowded Tokyo street. A feeling came over me, unlike anything I'd ever experienced. I felt spent, but proud. I felt drained, but exhilarated. I felt everything I ever hoped to feel after a day's work. I felt like an artist, a *creator*. I looked back over my shoulder, took one last look at Nissho's offices. Under my breath I said, "We made this."

I'D BEEN IN Japan three weeks, longer than I expected, which posed two problems. The world was large, but the shoe world was small, and if Onitsuka got wind that I was in their "neighborhood," and didn't stop by, they'd know I was up to something. It wouldn't take much for them to find out, or figure out, that I was lining up their replacement. So I needed to go down to Kobe, make an appearance at Onitsuka's offices. But extending my trip, being gone from home another week, was unacceptable. Penny and I had never been apart that long.

I phoned her and asked her to fly over and join me for this last leg.

Penny jumped at the chance. She'd never seen Asia, and this might be her last chance before we were out of business and out of money. It might also be her last chance to use that matching pink luggage. And Dot was available for babysitting.

The flight was long, though, and Penny didn't like planes. When I went to the Tokyo airport to meet her, I knew I'd be collecting a fragile woman. I forgot, however, how intimidating Haneda Airport could be. It was a solid mass of bodies and baggage. I couldn't move, couldn't find Penny. Suddenly she appeared at the sliding glass doors of customs. She was trying to push forward, trying to get through. There were too many people—and armed police—on every side of her. She was trapped.

The doors slid open, the crowd surged forward, and Penny fell into my arms. I'd never seen her so exhausted, not even after she gave birth to Matthew. I asked if the plane had a flat tire and she'd gotten out to change it. *Joke? Kitami? Remember?* She didn't laugh. She said the plane hit turbulence two hours outside Tokyo and the flight was a roller coaster.

She was wearing her best lime-green suit, now badly wrinkled and stained, and she was the same shade of lime-green. She needed a hot shower, and a long rest, and some fresh clothes. I told her we had a suite waiting at the wonderful Imperial Hotel, designed by Frank Lloyd Wright.

A half hour later, when we pulled up to the hotel, she said she was going to use the ladies' room while I checked us in. I hurried to the front desk, got our room keys, and sat on one of the lobby sofas to wait.

Ten minutes.

Fifteen minutes.

I went to the door of the ladies' room and cracked it open. "Penny?"

"I'm frozen," she said.

"What?"

"I'm on the floor of the ladies' room . . . and I am frozen."

I went in and found her on the cold tiles, lying on her side, ladies stepping over and around her. She was having a panic attack. And severe leg cramps. The long flight, the chaos at the airport, the months of stress about Kitami—it was too much for her. I spoke calmly, told her everything would be fine, and gradually she unclenched. I helped her to her feet, guided her upstairs, and asked the hotel to send up a masseuse.

As she lay on the bed, a cold washcloth on her forehead, I was worried, but a little bit grateful. I'd been on the edge of panic for weeks. Months. The sight of Penny in this state gave me a shot of adrenaline. One of us had to keep it together, for the sake of Matthew. This time it would have to be me.

THE NEXT MORNING I phoned Onitsuka and told them my wife and I were in Japan. Come on down, they said. Within an hour we were on the train for Kobe.

Everyone came out to meet us, including Kitami and Fujimoto and Mr. Onitsuka. What brings you to Japan? I told them we were vacationing. Spur-of-the-moment thing. "Very good, very good," Mr. Onitsuka said. He made a big fuss over Penny, and we sat down to a hastily arranged tea ceremony. For a moment, amid all the small talk, all the laughter and pleasantries, it was possible to forget that we were on the edge of war.

Mr. Onitsuka even offered a car and driver to take Penny and me around and show us Kobe. I accepted. Then Kitami invited us to dinner that night. Again I reluctantly said yes.

Fujimoto came along, which added an extra layer of complexity. I looked around the table and thought: my bride, my enemy, my spy. Some life. Though the tone was friendly, cordial, I could feel the tangled subtext of every remark. It was like a loose wire buzzing and sparking in the background. I kept waiting for Kitami to come out with it, press me for an answer to his offer to buy Blue Ribbon. Oddly, he never brought it up.

Around nine o'clock he said he needed to be getting home. Fujimoto said he'd stay and have a nightcap with us. The moment Kitami was gone, Fujimoto told us everything he knew of the plan to cut off Blue Ribbon. It wasn't much more than I'd gleaned from the folder in Kitami's briefcase. Still, it was nice to sit with an ally, so we had several nightcaps, and a few laughs, until Fujimoto looked at his watch and let out a scream. "Oh no! It is after eleven. The train stop running!"

"Ah, no problem," I said. "Come stay with us."

"We have a big tatami in our room," Penny said. "You can sleep on that."

Fujimoto accepted, with many bows. He thanked me yet again for the bicycle.

An hour later, there we were, in one small room, pretending there was nothing out of the ordinary about the three of us bedding down together.

At sunrise I heard Fujimoto get up, cough, and stretch. He went to the bathroom, ran the water, brushed his teeth. Then he put on his clothes from the night before and slipped out. I fell back asleep but a short while later Penny went to the bathroom and when she came back to bed she was—laughing? I rolled over. Nope, she was crying. She looked as if she was on the verge of another panic attack. "He used . . . ," she rasped. "What?" I said. She buried her head in the pillows. "He used . . . my toothbrush."

AS SOON AS I got back to Oregon I invited Bowerman up to Portland to meet with me and Woodell, talk about the state of the business.

It seemed like any old meeting.

At some point, in the course of conversation, Woodell and I pointed out that the outer sole of the training shoe hadn't changed in fifty years. The tread was still just waves or grooves across the bottom of the foot. The Cortez and Boston were breakthroughs in cushioning and nylon, revolutionary in upper construction, but there hadn't been a single innovation in outer soles since before the Great Depression. Bowerman nodded. He made a note. He didn't seem all that interested.

As I recall, once we'd covered all the new business on the agenda, Bowerman told us that a wealthy alum had just donated a million dollars to Oregon, earmarked for a new track—the world's finest.

His voice rising, Bowerman described the surface he'd created with that windfall. It was polyurethane, the same spongy surface that was to be used in Munich in the 1972 Olympics, where Bowerman was on tap to be head coach of the track team.

He was pleased. And yet, he said, he was far from satisfied. His runners still weren't getting the full benefit of this new surface. Their shoes still weren't gripping it right.

On the two-hour drive back to Eugene, Bowerman mulled what Woodell and I had said, and mulled his problem with the new track, and these two problems simmered and congealed in his thoughts.

The following Sunday, sitting over breakfast with his wife, Bowerman's gaze drifted to her waffle iron. He noted the waffle iron's gridded pattern. It conformed with a certain pattern in his mind's eye, a pattern he'd been seeing, or seeking, for months, if not years. He asked Mrs. Bowerman if he could borrow it.

He had a vat of urethane in his garage, left over from the installation of the track. He carried the waffle iron out to the garage, filled it with urethane, heated it up—and promptly ruined it. The urethane sealed it shut, because Bowerman hadn't added a chemical releasing agent. He didn't know from chemical releasing agents.

Another person would have quit right then. But Bowerman's brain also didn't have a releasing agent. He bought another waffle iron, and this time filled it with plaster, and when the plaster hardened the jaws of the waffle iron opened, no problem. He took the resulting mold to the Oregon Rubber Company, and paid them to pour liquid rubber into it.

Another failure. The rubber mold was too rigid, too brittle. It broke right away.

But Bowerman felt he was getting closer.

He gave up the waffle iron altogether. Instead he took a sheet of stainless steel and punched it with holes, creating a waffle-like surface, and brought this back to the rubber company. The mold they made from that steel sheet was pliable, workable, and Bowerman now had two foot-sized squares of hard rubber nubs, which he brought home and sewed to the sole of a pair of running shoes. He gave these to one of his runners. The runner laced them on and ran like a rabbit.

Bowerman phoned me, excited, and told me about his experiment. He wanted me to send a sample of his waffle-soled shoes to one of my new factories. Of course, I said. I'd send it right away—to Nippon Rubber.

I look back over the decades and see him toiling in his workshop, Mrs. Bowerman carefully helping, and I get goosebumps. He was Edison in Menlo Park, Da Vinci in Florence, Tesla in Wardenclyffe. Divinely inspired. I wonder if he knew, if he had any clue, that he was the Daedalus of sneakers, that he was making history, remaking an industry, transforming the way athletes would run and stop and jump for generations. I wonder if he could conceive in that moment all that he'd done. All that would follow.

I know I couldn't.

1972

Everything depended on Chicago. Our every thought, our every conversation at the start of 1972, began and ended with Chicago, because Chicago was the site of the National Sporting Goods Association Show.

Chicago was important every year. The sporting goods show was where sales reps from across the nation got their first look at all the new athletic products, from all the different companies, and voted up or down, via the sizes of their orders. But this 1972 show was going to be more than important. It was going to be our Super Bowl and our Olympics and our Bar Mitzvah, because it was where we'd decided to introduce the world to Nike. If sales reps liked our new shoe, we'd live to see another year. If not, we wouldn't be back for the 1973 show.

Onitsuka, meanwhile, was eyeing Chicago, too. Days before the start of the show, without a word to me, Onitsuka gave the Japanese press an announcement trumpeting their "acquisition" of Blue Ribbon. The announcement set off shock waves everywhere, but especially at Nissho. Sumeragi wrote me, asking, in essence, "What the—?"

In my impassioned two-page reply I told him that I had nothing to do with Onitsuka's announcement. I assured him that Onitsuka was trying to bully us into selling, but they were our past, and Nissho, like Nike, was our future. In closing I confessed to Sumeragi that I hadn't yet mentioned any of this to Onitsuka, so mum's the word. "I ask that you keep the above information in strict confidence for obvious reasons. In order to maintain our present distribution system for future Nike sales, it's important that we have about one or two more months of shipments from Onitsuka, and if these shipments were cut off it would be very harmful."

I felt like a married man caught in a tawdry love triangle. I was assuring my lover, Nissho, that it was only a matter of time before I divorced my spouse, Onitsuka. Meanwhile, I was encouraging Onitsuka to think of me as a loving and devoted husband. "I do not like this way of doing business," I wrote Sumeragi, "but I feel it was thrust upon us by a company with the worst possible intentions." *We'll be together soon, darling. Just have patience.*

Right before we all left for Chicago, a wire came from Kitami. He'd thought up a name for "our" new company. The Tiger Shoe Company. He wanted me to unveil it in Chicago. I wired back that the name was beautiful, lyrical, sheer poetry—but alas it was too late to unveil anything at the show. All the signs and promotional literature had been printed already.

ON DAY ONE of the show I walked into the convention center and found Johnson and Woodell already busy arranging our booth. They'd stacked the new Tigers in neat rows, and now they were stacking the new Nikes in pyramids of orange shoe boxes. In those days shoe boxes were either white or blue, period, but I'd wanted something that would stand out, that would pop on the shelves of sporting goods stores. So I'd asked Nippon Rubber for boxes of bright neon orange, figuring it was the boldest color in the rainbow. Johnson and Woodell loved the orange, and loved the lowercase "nike," lettered in white on the side of the box. But as they opened the boxes and examined the shoes themselves, both men were shaken up.

These shoes, the first wave produced by Nippon Rubber, didn't have the quality of Tigers, nor of the samples we'd seen earlier. The leather was shiny, and not in a good way. The Wet-Flyte looked literally wet, as if covered with cheap paint or lacquer that hadn't dried. The upper was coated with polyurethane, but apparently Nippon was no more proficient than Bowerman at working with that tricky, mercurial substance. The logo on the side, Carolyn's wing-whoosh thingamajig, which we'd taken to calling a swoosh, was crooked.

I sat down and put my head in my hands. I looked at our orange pyramids. My mind went to the pyramids of Giza. Only ten years before I'd been there, riding a camel like Lawrence of Arabia across the sands, free as a man could be. Now I was in Chicago, saddled with debt, head of a teetering shoe company, rolling out a new brand with shoddy workmanship and crooked swooshes. All is vanity.

I gazed around the convention center, at the thousands of sales reps swarming the booths, the *other* booths. I heard them oohing and aahing at all the other shoes being introduced for the first time. I was that boy at the science fair who didn't work hard enough on his project, who didn't start until the night before. The other kids had built erupting volcanoes, and lightning machines, and all I had was a mobile of the solar system made with mothballs stuck to my mother's coat hangers.

Darn it, this was no time to be introducing flawed shoes. Worse, we had to push these flawed shoes on people who weren't our kind of people. They were *salesmen*. They talked like salesmen, walked like salesmen, and they dressed like salesmen—tight polyester shirts, Sansabelt slacks. They were extroverts, we were introverts. They didn't get us, we didn't get them, and yet our future depended on them. And now we'd have to persuade them somehow that this Nike thing was worth their time and trust—and money.

I was on the verge of losing it, right on the verge. Then I saw that Johnson and Woodell were already losing it, and I realized that I couldn't afford to. Like Penny, they beat me to the panic attack punch. "Look," I said, "fellas, this is the worst the shoes will ever be. They'll get better. So if we can just sell these . . . we'll be on our way."

Each gave a resigned shake of the head. *What choice do we have?*

We looked out, and here they came, a mob of salesmen, walking like zombies toward our booth. They picked up the Nikes, held them to the light. They touched the swoosh. One said to another, "The hell is this?" "Hell if I know," said the other.

They started to barrage us with questions. *Hey—what IS this?*

That's a Nike.

The hell's a Nike?

It's the Greek goddess of victory.

Greek what now?

Goddess of vic—

And what's THIS?

That's a swoosh.

The hell's a swoosh?

The answer flew out of me: It's the sound of someone going past you.

They liked that. Oh, they liked it a whole lot.

They gave us business. They actually *placed orders* with us. By the end of the day we'd exceeded our grandest expectations. We were one of the smash hits of the show. At least, that's how I saw it.

Johnson, as usual, wasn't happy. Ever the perfectionist. "The irregularities of this whole situation," he said, left him dumbfounded. That was his phrase, *the irregularities of this whole situation*. I begged him to take his dumbfoundedness and irregularity elsewhere, leave well enough alone. But he just couldn't. He walked over and buttonholed one of his biggest accounts and demanded to know what was going on. "Whaddya mean?" the man said. "I mean," Johnson said, "we show up with this new Nike, and it's totally untested, and frankly it's not even all that good—and you guys are buying it. What gives?"

The man laughed. "We've been doing business with you Blue Ribbon guys for years," he said, "and we know that you guys tell the truth. Everyone else bullshits, you guys always shoot straight. So if you say this new shoe, this Nike, is worth a shot, we believe."

Johnson came back to the booth, scratching his head. "Telling the truth," he said. "Who knew?"

Woodell laughed. Johnson laughed. I laughed and tried not to think about my many half truths and untruths with Onitsuka.

GOOD NEWS TRAVELS fast. Bad news travels faster than Grelle and Prefontaine. On a rocket. Two weeks after Chicago, Kitami walked into my office. No advance notice. No heads-up. And he cut right to the car chase. "What is this, this . . . thing," he demanded, "this . . . NEE-kay?"

I made my face blank. "Nike? Oh. It's nothing. It's a sideline we've developed, to hedge our bets, in case Onitsuka does as threatened and yanks the rug out from under us."

The answer disarmed him. As it should have. I'd rehearsed it for weeks. It was so reasonable and logical that Kitami didn't know how to respond. He'd come spoiling for a fight, and I'd countered his bull rush with a rope-a-dope.

He demanded to know who made the new shoes. I told him they were made by different factories in Japan. He demanded to know how many Nikes we'd ordered. A few thousand, I said.

He gave an "Ooh." I wasn't sure what that meant.

I didn't mention that two members of my scrappy home-town Portland Trail Blazers had just worn Nikes during a rout of the New York Knicks, 133–86. The *Oregonian* had recently run a photo of Geoff Petrie driving past a Knick (Phil Jackson, by name), and visible on Petrie's shoes was a swoosh. (We'd just made a deal with a couple of other Blazers to supply them with shoes, too.) Good thing the *Oregonian* didn't have a wide circulation in Kobe.

Kitami asked if the new Nike was in stores. Of course not, I lied. Or fibbed. He asked when I was going to sign his papers and sell him my company. I told him my partner still hadn't decided.

End of meeting. He buttoned and unbuttoned the coat of his suit and said he had other business in California. But he'd be back. He marched out of my office and I immediately reached for the phone. I dialed our retail store in Los Angeles. Bork answered. "John, our old friend Kitami is coming to town! I'm sure he'll come by your store! Hide the Nikes!"

"Huh?"

"He knows about Nike, but I told him it isn't in stores!"

"What you're asking of me," Bork said, "I don't know."

He sounded frightened. And irritated. He didn't want to do anything dishonest, he said. "I'm asking you to stash a few pairs of shoes," I cried, then slammed down the phone.

Sure enough, Kitami showed up that afternoon. He confronted Bork, badgered him with questions, shook him down like a cop with a shaky witness. Bork played dumb—or so he told me later.

Kitami asked to use the bathroom. A ploy, of course. He knew the bathroom was somewhere in the back, and he needed an excuse to snoop back there. Bork didn't see the ploy, or didn't care to. Moments later Kitami was standing in the stockroom, under a bare lightbulb, glowering at hundreds of orange shoe boxes. Nike, Nike, everywhere, and not a drop to drink.

Bork phoned me after Kitami left. "Jig's up," he said. "What happened?" I asked. "Kitami forced his way into the stockroom—it's over, Phil."

I hung up, slumped in my chair. "Well," I said, out loud, to no one, "I guess we're going to find out if we can exist without Tiger."

We found out something else, too.

Soon after that day, Bork quit. Actually, I don't remember if he quit or Woodell fired him. Either way, not long after *that*, we heard Bork had a new job.

Working for Kitami.

I SPENT DAYS and days staring into space, gazing out windows, waiting for Kitami to play his next card. I also watched a lot of TV. The nation, the world, was agog at the sudden opening of relations between the United States and China. President Nixon was in Beijing, shaking hands with Mao Zedong, an event nearly on a par with the moon landing. I never thought I'd see it in my lifetime, a U.S. president in the Forbidden City, touching the Great Wall. I thought of my time in Hong Kong. I'd been so close to China, and yet so far. I thought I'd never have another chance. But now I thought, One day? Maybe?

Maybe.

At last Kitami made his move. He returned to Oregon and asked for a meeting, at which he requested that Bowerman be present. To make that easier for Bowerman, I suggested Jaqua's office down in Eugene as the site.

When the day came, as we were all filing into the conference room, Jaqua grabbed my arm and whispered, "Whatever he says, you say nothing." I nodded.

On one side of the conference table were Jaqua, Bowerman, and I. On the other side were Kitami and his lawyer, a local guy, who didn't look like he wanted to be there. Plus, Iwano was back. I thought he might have half-smiled at me, before remembering that this wasn't a social call.

Jaqua's conference room was bigger than ours in Tigard, but that day it felt like a dollhouse. Kitami had asked for the meeting, so he kicked it off. And he didn't beat around the bonsai tree. He handed Jaqua a letter. Effective immediately, our contract with Onitsuka was null and void. He looked at me, then back to Jaqua. "Very very regret," he said.

Furthermore, insult to injury, he was billing us $17,000, which he claimed we owed for shoes delivered. To be exact, he demanded $16,637.13.

Jaqua pushed the letter aside and said that if Kitami dared to pursue this reckless course, if he insisted on cutting us off, we'd sue.

"You cause this," Kitami said. Blue Ribbon had breached its contract with Onitsuka by making Nike shoes, he said, and he was at a loss to understand why we'd ruined such a profitable relationship, why we'd launched this, this, this—*Nike*. That was more than I could bear. "I'll tell you why—" I blurted. Jaqua turned on me and shouted: "Shut up, Buck!"

Jaqua then told Kitami that he hoped something could still be worked out. A lawsuit would be highly damaging to both companies. Peace was prosperity. But Kitami was in no mood for peace. He stood, motioned to his lawyer and Iwano to follow. When he got to the door, he stopped. His face changed. He was about to say something conciliatory. He was preparing to offer an olive branch. I felt myself softening toward him. "Onitsuka," he said, "like to continue use Mr. Bowerman . . . as consultant."

I pulled on my ear. Surely I hadn't heard him correctly. Bowerman shook his head and turned to Jaqua, who said that Bowerman would henceforth consider Kitami a competitor, aka a sworn enemy, and would help him in no way whatsoever.

Kitami nodded. He asked if someone could please drive him and Iwano to the airport.

I TOLD JOHNSON to get on a plane. "What plane?" he said. "The *next* plane," I said.

He arrived the following morning. We went for a run, during which neither of us said anything. Then we drove to the office and gathered everyone into the conference room. There were about thirty people there. I expected to be nervous. They expected me to be nervous. On any different day, under any other circumstances, I would have been. For some reason, however, I felt weirdly at peace.

I laid out the situation we faced. "We've come, folks, to a crossroads. Yesterday, our main supplier, Onitsuka, cut us off."

I let that sink in. I watched everyone's jaw drop.

"We've threatened to sue them for damages," I said, "and of course they've threatened to file a lawsuit of their own. Breach of contract. If they sue us first, in Japan, we'll have no choice but to sue them here in America, and sue fast. We're not going to win a lawsuit in Japan, so we'll have to beat them to the courthouse, get a quick verdict here, to pressure them into withdrawing.

"Meanwhile, until it all sorts out, we're completely on our own. We're set adrift. We have this new line, Nike, which the reps in Chicago seemed to like. But, well, frankly, that's all we've got. And as we know, there are big problems with the quality. It's not what we hoped. Communications with Nippon Rubber are good, and Nissho is there at the factory at least once a week, trying to get it all fixed, but we don't know how soon they can do it. It better be soon, though, because we have no time and suddenly no margin for error."

I looked down the table. Everyone was sinking, slumping forward. I looked at Johnson. He was staring at the papers before him, and there was something in his handsome face, some quality I'd never seen there before. Surrender. Like everyone else in the room, he was giving up. The nation's economy was in the tank, a recession was under way. Gas lines, political gridlock, rising unemployment, Nixon being Nixon—Vietnam. It seemed like the end times. Everyone in the room had already been worrying about how they were going to make the rent, pay the light bill. Now this.

I cleared my throat. "So . . . in other words," I said. I cleared my throat again, pushed aside my yellow legal pad. "What I'm trying to say is, we've got them right where we want them."

Johnson lifted his eyes. Everyone around the table lifted their eyes. They sat up straighter.

"This is—the moment," I said. "This is the moment we've been waiting for. Our moment. No more selling someone else's brand. No more working for someone else. Onitsuka has been holding us down for years. Their late deliveries, their mixed-up orders, their refusal to hear and implement our design ideas—who among us isn't sick of dealing with all that? It's time we faced facts: If we're going to succeed, or fail, we should do so on our own terms, with our own ideas—our own *brand*. We posted two million in sales last year . . . none of which had anything to do with Onitsuka. That number was a testament to our ingenuity and hard work. Let's not look at this as a crisis. Let's look at this as our liberation. Our Independence Day.

"Yes, it's going to be rough. I won't lie to you. We're definitely going to war, people. But we know the terrain. We know our way around Japan now. And that's one reason I feel in my heart this is a war we can win. And if we win it, when we win it, I see great things for us on the other side of victory. We are still alive, people. We are still. Alive."

As I stopped speaking I could see a wave of relief swirl around the table like a cool breeze. Everyone felt it. It was as real as the wind that used to swirl around the office next to the Pink Bucket. There were nods, murmurs, nervous chuckles. We spent the next hour brainstorming about how to proceed, how to hire contract factories, how to play them against one another for the best quality and price. And how were we going to fix these new Nikes? Anyone?

We adjourned with a jovial, jittery, elated feeling.

Johnson said he wanted to buy me a cup of coffee. "Your finest hour," he said.

"Ach," I said. "Thanks." But I reminded him: I just told the truth. As he had in Chicago. Telling the truth, I said. Who knew?

* * *

JOHNSON WENT BACK to Wellesley for the time being, and we turned our attention to the Olympic track-and-field trials, which in 1972 were being held, for the first time ever, in our backyard: Eugene. We needed to own those trials, so we sent an advance team down to give shoes to any competitor willing to take them, and we set up a staging area in our store, which was now being ably run by Hollister. As the trials opened we descended on Eugene and set up a silk-screen machine in the back of the store. We cranked out scores of Nike T-shirts, which Penny handed out like Halloween candy.

With all that work, how could we not break through? And, indeed, Dave Davis, a shot-putter from USC, dropped by the store the first day to complain that he wasn't getting free stuff from either Adidas or Puma, so he'd gladly take our shoes and wear them. And then he finished fourth. Hooray! Better yet, he didn't just wear our shoes, he waltzed around in one of Penny's T-shirts, his name stenciled on the back. (The trouble was, Dave wasn't the ideal model. He had a bit of a gut. And our T-shirts weren't big enough. Which accentuated his gut. We made a note. Buy smaller athletes, or make bigger shirts.)

We also had a couple of semifinalists wear our spikes, including an employee, Jim Gorman, who competed in the 1,500. I told Gorman he was taking corporate loyalty too far. Our spikes weren't that great. But he insisted that he was in "all the way." And then in the marathon we had Nike-shod runners finish fourth, fifth, sixth, and seventh. None made the team, but still. Not too shabby.

The main event of the trials, of course, would come on the final day, a duel between Prefontaine and the great Olympian George Young. By then Prefontaine was universally known as Pre, and he was far more than a phenom; he was an outright superstar. He was the biggest thing to hit the world of American track and field since Jesse Owens. Sportswriters frequently compared him to James Dean, and Mick Jagger, and *Runner's World* said the most apt comparison might be Muhammad Ali. He was that kind of swaggery, transformative figure.

To my thinking, however, these and all other comparisons fell short. Pre was unlike any athlete this country had ever seen, though it was hard to say exactly why. I'd spent a lot of time studying him, admiring him, puzzling about his appeal. I'd asked myself, time and again, what it was about Pre that triggered such visceral responses from so many people, including myself. I never did come up with a totally satisfactory answer.

It was more than his talent—there were other talented runners. And it was more than his swagger—there were plenty of swaggering runners.

Some said it was his look. Pre was so fluid, so poetic, with that flowing mop of hair. And he had the broadest, deepest chest imaginable, set on slender legs that were all muscle and never stopped churning.

Also, most runners are introverts, but Pre was an obvious, joyous extrovert. It was never simply running for him. He was always putting on a show, always conscious of the spotlight.

Sometimes I thought the secret to Pre's appeal was his passion. He didn't care if he died crossing the finish line, so long as he crossed first. No matter what Bowerman told him, no matter what his body told him, Pre refused to slow down, ease off. He pushed himself to the brink and beyond. This was often a counterproductive strategy, and sometimes it was plainly stupid, and occasionally it was suicidal. But it was always uplifting for the crowd. No matter the sport—no matter the human endeavor, really—total effort will win people's hearts.

Of course, all Oregonians loved Pre because he was "ours." He was born in our midst, raised in our rainy forests, and we'd cheered him since he was a pup. We'd watched him break the national two-mile record as an eighteen-year-old, and we were with him, step by step, through each glorious NCAA championship. Every Oregonian felt emotionally invested in his career.

And at Blue Ribbon, of course, we were preparing to put our money where our emotions were. We understood that Pre couldn't switch shoes right before the trials. He was used to his Adidas. But in time, we were certain, he'd be a Nike athlete, and perhaps the paradigmatic Nike athlete.

With these thoughts in mind, walking down Agate Street toward Hayward Field, I wasn't surprised to find the place shaking, rocking, trembling with cheers—the Coliseum in Rome could not have been louder when the gladiators and lions were turned loose. We found our seats just in time to see Pre doing his warm-ups. Every move he made caused a new ripple of excitement. Every time he jogged down one side of the oval, or up the other, the fans along his route stood and went wild. Half of them were wearing T-shirts that read: LEGEND.

All of a sudden we heard a chorus of deep, guttural boos. Gerry Lindgren, arguably the world's best distance runner at the time, appeared on the track—wearing a T-shirt that read: STOP PRE. Lindgren had beaten Pre when he was a senior and Pre a freshman, and he wanted everyone, especially Pre, to remember. But when Pre saw Lindgren, and saw the shirt, he just shook his head. And grinned. No pressure. Only more incentive.

The runners took their marks. An unearthly silence fell. Then, bang. The starting gun sounded like a Napoléon cannon.

Pre took the lead right away. Young tucked in right behind him. In no time they pulled well ahead of the field and it became a two-man affair. (Lindgren was far behind, a nonfactor.) Each man's strategy was clear. Young meant to stay with Pre until the final lap, then use his superior sprint to go by and win. Pre, meanwhile, intended to set such a fast pace at the outset that by the time they got to that final lap, Young's legs would be gone.

For eleven laps they ran a half stride apart. With the crowd now roaring, frothing, shrieking, the two men entered the final lap. It felt like a boxing match. It felt like a joust. It felt like a bullfight, and we were down to that moment of truth—death hanging in the air. Pre reached down, found another level—we saw him do it. He opened up a yard lead, then two, then five. We saw Young grimacing and we knew that he could not, would not, catch Pre. I told myself, Don't forget this. Do not forget. I told myself there was much to be learned from such a display of passion, whether you were running a mile or a company.

As they crossed the tape we all looked up at the clock and saw that both men had broken the American record. Pre had broken it by a shade more. But he wasn't done. He spotted someone waving a STOP PRE T-shirt and he went over and snatched it and whipped it in circles above his head, like a scalp. What followed was one of the greatest ovations I've ever heard, and I've spent my life in stadiums.

I'd never witnessed anything quite like that race. And yet I didn't just witness it. I took part in it. Days later I felt sore in my hams and quads. This, I decided, *this* is what sports are, what they can do. Like books, sports give people a sense of having lived other lives, of taking part in other people's victories. And defeats. When sports are at their best, the spirit of the fan merges with the spirit of the athlete, and in that convergence, in that transference, is the oneness that the mystics talk about.

Walking back down Agate Street I knew that race was part of me, would forever be part of me, and I vowed it would also be part of Blue Ribbon. In our coming battles, with Onitsuka, with whomever, we'd be like Pre. We'd compete as if our lives depended on it.

Because they did.

NEXT, WITH SAUCER eyes, we looked to the Olympics. Not only was our man Bowerman going to be the head coach of the track team, but our homeboy Pre was going to be the star. After his performance at the trials? Who could doubt it?

Certainly not Pre. "Sure there will be a lot of pressure," he told *Sports Illustrated*. "And a lot of us will be facing more experienced competitors, and maybe we don't have any right to win. But all I know is if I go out and bust my gut until I black out and somebody still beats me, and if I have made that guy reach down and use everything he has and then more, why then it just proves that on that day he's a better man than I."

Right before Pre and Bowerman left for Germany, I filed for a patent on Bowerman's waffle shoe. Application no. 284,736 described the "improved sole having integral polygon shaped studs . . . of square, rectangular or triangle cross section . . . [and] a plurality of flat sides which provide gripping edges that give greatly improved traction."

A proud moment for both of us.

A golden moment of my life.

Sales of Nike were steady, my son was healthy, I was able to pay my mortgage on time. All things considered, I was in a damned fine mood that August.

And then it began. In the second week of the Olympic Games, a squad of eight masked gunmen scaled a back wall of the Olympic village and kidnapped eleven Israeli athletes. In our Tigard office we set up a TV and no one did a lick of work. We watched and watched, day after day, saying little, often holding our hands over our mouths. When the terrible denouement came, when the news broke that all the athletes were dead, their bodies strewn on a blood-spattered tarmac at the airport, it recalled the deaths of both Kennedys, and of Dr. King, and of the students at Kent State University, and of all the tens of thousands of boys in Vietnam. Ours was a difficult, death-drenched age, and at least once every day you were forced to ask yourself: What's the point?

When Bowerman returned I drove straight down to Eugene to see him. He looked as though he hadn't slept in a decade. He told me that he and Pre had been within a hair of the attack. In the first minutes, as the terrorists took control of the building, many Israeli athletes were able to flee, slipping out side doors, jumping out windows. One made his way to the next building over, where Bowerman and Pre were staying. Bowerman heard a knock, opened the door of his room, and found this man, a race walker, shivering with fear, babbling about masked gunmen. Bowerman pulled the man inside and phoned the U.S. consul. "Send the marines!" he shouted into the phone.

They did. Marines quickly secured the building where Bowerman and the U.S. team were staying.

For this "overreaction," Bowerman was severely reprimanded by Olympic officials. He'd exceeded his authority, they said. In the heat of the crisis they made time to summon Bowerman to their headquarters. Thank goodness Jesse Owens, the hero of the last German Olympics, the man who "beat" Hitler, went with Bowerman and voiced his support for Bowerman's actions. That forced the bureaucrats to back off.

Bowerman and I sat and stared at the river for a long while, saying little. Then, his voice scratchy, Bowerman told me that those 1972 Olympics marked the low point of his life. I'd never heard him say a thing like that, and I'd never seen him look like that. Defeated.

I couldn't believe it.

The cowards never started and the weak died along the way—that leaves us.

Soon after that day Bowerman announced that he was retiring from coaching.

A GRIM TIME. Skies were grayer than usual, and low. There was no fall. We just woke up and winter was upon us. The trees went overnight from full to bare. Rain fell without stop.

At last, a needed boon. We got word that a few hours north, in Seattle, at the Rainier International Classic, a fiery Romanian tennis player was destroying every opponent in his path, and doing it in a brand-new pair of Nike Match Points. The Romanian was Ilie Nastase, aka "Nasty," and every time he hit his patented overhead smash, every time he went up on his toes and stroked another unreturnable serve, the world was seeing our swoosh.

We'd known for some time that athlete endorsements were important. If we were going to compete with Adidas—not to mention Puma and Gola, and Diadora and Head, and Wilson and Spalding, and Karhu and Etonic and New Balance and all the other brands popping up in the 1970s—we'd need top athletes wearing and talking up our brand. But we still didn't have money to pay top athletes. (We had less money than ever before.) Nor did we know the first thing about getting to them, persuading them that our shoe was good, that it would soon be better, that they should endorse us at a discounted price. Now here was a top athlete *already* wearing Nike, and winning in it. How hard could it be to sign him?

I found the number for Nastase's agent. I phoned and offered him a deal. I said I'd give him $5,000—I gagged as I said it—if his boy would wear our stuff. He countered with $15,000. How I *hated* negotiating.

We settled on $10,000. I felt that I was being robbed.

Nastase was playing a tourney that weekend in Omaha, the agent said. He suggested I fly out with the papers.

I met Nasty and his wife, Dominique, a stunning woman, that Friday night, at a steakhouse in downtown Omaha. After I got him to sign on the dotted line, after I locked the papers in my briefcase, we ordered a celebratory dinner. A bottle of wine, another bottle of wine. At some point, for some reason, I started speaking with a Romanian accent, and for some reason Nasty started calling *me* Nasty, and for no reason I could think of his supermodel wife started making goo-goo eyes at everyone, including me, and by night's end, stumbling up to my room, I felt like a tennis champion, and a tycoon, and a kingmaker. I lay in bed and stared at the contract. Ten thousand dollars, I said aloud. Ten. Thousand. Dollars.

It was a fortune. But Nike had a celebrity athlete endorser.

I closed my eyes, to stop the room from spinning. Then I opened them, because I didn't want the room to stop spinning.

Take that, Kitami, I said to the ceiling, to all of Omaha. Take *that*.

BACK THEN, THE historic football rivalry between my University of Oregon Ducks and the dreaded Oregon State Beavers was lop-sided, at best. My Ducks usually lost. And they usually lost by a lot. And they often lost with a lot on the line. Example: In 1957, with the two teams vying for the conference crown, Oregon's Jim Shanley was going in for the winning touchdown when he fumbled on the one-yard line. Oregon lost 10–7.

In 1972, my Ducks had lost to the Beavers eight straight times, sending me, eight straight times, into a sour funk. But now, in this topsy-turvy year, my Ducks were going to wear Nikes. Hollister had persuaded Oregon's head coach, Dick Enright, to don our new waffle-soled shoes for the Big Game, the Civil War.

The setting was their place, down in Corvallis. Scattered rain had been falling all morning, and it was coming down in sheets by game time. Penny and I stood in the stands, shivering inside our sopping ponchos, peering into the raindrops as the opening kickoff spun into the air. On the first play from scrimmage, Oregon's burly quarterback, a sharpshooter named Dan Fouts, handed the ball to Donny Reynolds, who made one cut on his Nike waffles and . . . *took it to the house*. Ducks 7, Nike 7, Beavers 0.

Fouts, closing out a brilliant college career, was out of his mind that night. He passed for three hundred yards, including a sixty-yard touchdown bomb that landed like a feather in his receiver's hands. The rout was soon on. At the final gun *my* Ducks were on top of the Bucktooths, 30–3. I always called them *my* Ducks, but now they really were. They were in my shoes. Every step they took, every cut they made, was partly mine. It's one thing to watch a sporting event and put yourself in the players' shoes. Every fan does that. It's another thing when the athletes are actually in your shoes.

I laughed as we walked to the car. I laughed like a maniac. I laughed all the way back to Portland. This, I kept telling Penny, *this* is how 1972 needed to end. With a victory. Any victory would have been healing, but this, oh boy—this.

1973

Like his coach, Pre just wasn't himself after the 1972 Olympics. He was haunted and enraged by the terrorist attacks. And by his performance. He felt he'd let everyone down. He'd finished fourth.

No shame in being the world's fourth-best at your distance, we told him. But Pre knew he was better than that. And he knew he'd have done better if he hadn't been so stubborn. He showed no patience, no guile. He could have slipped behind the front runner, coasted in his wake, stolen silver. That, however, would have gone against Pre's religion. So he'd run all out, as always, holding nothing back, and in the final hundred yards he tired. Worse, the man he considered his archrival, Lasse Viren, of Finland, once more took the gold.

We tried to lift Pre's spirits. We assured him that Oregon still loved him. City officials in Eugene were even planning to name a street after him. "Great," Pre said, "what're they gonna call it— *Fourth* Street?" He locked himself in his metal trailer on the banks of the Willamette and he didn't come out for weeks.

In time, after pacing a lot, after playing with his German shepherd puppy, Lobo, and after large quantities of cold beer, Pre emerged. One day I heard that he'd been seen again around town, at dawn, doing his daily ten miles, Lobo trotting at his heels.

It took a full six months, but the fire in Pre's belly came back. In his final races for Oregon he shone. He won the NCAA three-mile for a fourth straight year, posting a gaudy 13:05.3. He also went to

Scandinavia and crushed the field in the 5,000, setting an American record: 13:22.4. Better yet, he did it in Nikes. Bowerman finally had him wearing our shoes. (Months into his retirement, Bowerman was still coaching Pre, still polishing the final designs for the waffle shoe, which was about to go on sale to the general public. He'd never been busier.) And our shoes were finally worthy of Pre. It was a perfect symbiotic match. He was generating thousands of dollars of publicity, making our brand a symbol of rebellion and iconoclasm—and we were helping his recovery.

Pre began to talk warily with Bowerman about the 1976 Olympics in Montreal. He told Bowerman, and a few close friends, that he wanted redemption. He was determined to capture that gold medal that eluded him in Munich.

Several scary stumbling blocks stood in his path, however. Vietnam, for one. Pre, whose life, like mine, like everyone's, was governed by numbers, drew a horrible number in the draft lottery. He was going to be drafted, there was little doubt, as soon as he graduated. In a year's time he'd be sitting in some fetid jungle, taking heavy machine-gun fire. He might have his legs, his godlike legs, blown out from under him.

Also, there was Bowerman. Pre and the coach were clashing constantly, two headstrong guys with different ideas about training methods and running styles. Bowerman took the long view: a distance runner peaks in his late twenties. He therefore wanted Pre to rest, preserve himself for certain select races. Save something, Bowerman kept pleading. But of course Pre refused. I'm all-out, all the time, he said. In their relationship I saw a mirror of my relationship with banks. Pre didn't see the sense in going slow—ever. Go fast or die. I couldn't fault him. I was on his side. Even against our coach.

Above all, however, Pre was broke. The know-nothings and oligarchs who governed American amateur athletics at that time decreed that Olympic athletes couldn't collect endorsement money, or government money, which meant our finest runners and swimmers and boxers were reduced to paupers. To stay alive Pre sometimes tended bar in Eugene, and sometimes he ran in Europe, taking illicit cash from race promoters. Of course those extra races were starting to cause issues. His body—in particular his back—was breaking down.

At Blue Ribbon we worried about Pre. We talked about him often, formally and informally, around the office. Eventually we came up with a plan. To keep him from injuring himself, to avoid the shame of him going around with a begging bowl, we hired him. In 1973 we gave him a "job," a modest salary of five thousand dollars a year, and access to a beach condo Cale owned in Los Angeles. We also gave him a business card that said *National Director of Public Affairs*. People often narrowed their eyes and asked me what that meant. I narrowed my eyes right back. "It means he can run fast," I said.

It also meant he was our second celebrity athlete endorser.

The first thing Pre did with his windfall was go out and buy himself a butterscotch MG. He drove it everywhere—fast. It looked like my old MG. I remember feeling enormously, vicariously proud. I remember thinking: We bought that. I remember thinking Pre was the living, breathing embodiment of what we were trying to create. Whenever people saw Pre going at his breakneck pace—on a track, in his MG—I wanted them to see Nike. And when they bought a pair of Nikes, I wanted them to see Pre.

I felt this strongly about Pre even though I'd only had a few conversations with the man. And you could hardly call them conversations. Whenever I saw him at a track, or around the Blue Ribbon offices, I became mute. I tried to con myself; more than once I told myself that Pre was just a kid from Coos Bay, a short, shaggy-haired jock with a porn star mustache. But I knew better. And a few minutes in his presence would prove it. A few minutes was all I could take.

The world's most famous Oregonian at the time was Ken Kesey, whose blockbuster novel, *One Flew Over the Cuckoo's Nest*, appeared in 1962, the exact moment I left on my trip around the world. I knew

Kesey at the University of Oregon. He wrestled, and I ran track, and on rainy days we'd do indoor workouts at the same facility. When his first novel came out I was stunned by how good it was, especially since the plays he'd written in school had been dreck. Suddenly he was a literary lion, the toast of New York, and yet I never felt star-struck in his presence, as I did in Pre's. In 1973 I decided that Pre was every bit the artist that Kesey was, and more. Pre said as much himself. "A race is a work of art," he told a reporter, "that people can look at and be affected in as many ways as they're capable of understanding."

Each time Pre came into the office, I noted, I wasn't alone in my swooning. Everyone became mute. Everyone became shy. Men, women, it didn't matter, everyone turned into Buck Knight. Even Penny Knight. If I was the first to make Penny care about track and field, Pre was the one who made her a real fan.

Hollister was the exception to this rule. He and Pre had an easy way around each other. They were like brothers. I never once saw Hollister act any differently with Pre than he did with, say, me. So it made sense to have Hollister, the Pre Whisperer, bring Pre in, help us get to know him, and vice versa. We arranged a lunch in the conference room.

When the day came, it wasn't wise, but it was typical of Wood-ell and me—we chose *that* moment to tell Hollister that we were tweaking his duties. In fact, we told him the second his butt hit the chair in the conference room. The change would affect how he got paid. Not how much, just how. Before we could fully explain, he threw down his napkin and stormed out. Now we had nobody to help us break the ice with Pre. We all stared silently into our sandwiches.

Pre spoke first. "Is Geoff coming back?"

"I don't think so," I said.

Long pause.

"In that case," Pre said, "can I eat his sandwich?"

We all laughed, and Pre seemed suddenly mortal, and the luncheon ultimately proved invaluable.

Shortly after that day, we soothed Hollister, and tweaked his duties again. From now on, we said, you're Pre's full-time liaison. You're in charge of handling Pre, taking Pre out on the road, introducing Pre to the fans. In fact, we told Hollister, take the boy on a cross-country tour. Hit all the track meets, state fairs, high schools, and colleges you can. Go everywhere, and nowhere. Do everything, and nothing.

Sometimes Pre would conduct a running clinic, answering questions about training and injuries. Sometimes he'd just sign autographs and pose for photos. No matter what he did, no matter where Hollister took him, worshipful crowds would appear around their bright blue Volkswagen bus.

Though Pre's job title was intentionally imprecise, his role was real, and his belief in Nike was authentic as well. He wore Nike T-shirts everywhere he went, and he allowed his foot to be Bowerman's last for all shoe experiments. Pre preached Nike as gospel, and brought thousands of new people into our revival tent. He urged everyone to give this groovy new brand a try—even his competitors. He'd often send a pair of Nike flats or spikes to a fellow runner with a note: Try these. You'll love them.

Among those most inspired by Pre was Johnson. While continuing to build up our East Coast operation, Johnson had spent much of 1972 slaving on something that he christened the Pre Montreal, a shoe that would be an homage to Pre, and to the upcoming Olympics, and to the American Bicentennial. With a blue suede toe, a red nylon back, and a white swoosh, it was our jazziest shoe yet, and also our best spike. We knew that we were going to live or die based on quality, and thus far our quality on spikes had been spotty. Johnson was going to fix that with this design.

But he was going to do it in Oregon, I decided, not Boston.

I'd been giving a lot of thought to Johnson, for months. He was turning into a truly fine designer, and we needed to take full advantage of his talent. The East Coast was running smoothly, but it now involved too much administration for him. The whole thing needed reorganizing, streamlining, and that wasn't the best use of Johnson's time or creativity. That was a job tailor-made for someone like . . . Woodell.

Night after night, during my six-mile run, I'd wrestle with this situation. I had two guys in the wrong jobs, on the wrong coasts, and neither one was going to like the obvious solution. Each guy loved where he lived. And each irritated the other, though they both denied it. When I'd promoted Woodell to operations manager, I'd also bequeathed him Johnson. I'd put him in charge of overseeing Johnson, answering Johnson's letters, and Woodell made the mistake of reading them thoroughly and trying to keep up. Consequently the two had developed a chippy, deeply sarcastic rapport.

For instance. Woodell wheeled into my office one day and said, "This is depressing. Jeff complains *constantly* about inventory, expense reimbursements, lack of communications. He says he's working his butt off while we're lolling around. He doesn't listen to any reason, including that our sales are doubling every year."

Woodell told me he wanted to take a different approach to Johnson.

By all means, I said. Have at it.

So he wrote Johnson a long letter "admitting" that we'd all been colluding against him, trying to make him unhappy. He wrote, "I'm sure you realize we don't work quite as hard out here as you do; with only three hours in the working day it is hard to get everything done. Still, I make time to place you in all sorts of embarrassing situations with customers and the business community. Whenever you need money desperately to pay bills, I send only a tiny fraction of what you need so that you'll have to deal with bill collectors and lawsuits. I take the destruction of your reputation as a personal compliment."

And so on.

Johnson answered back: "Finally someone out there understands me."

What I was getting ready to propose wasn't going to help.

I approached Johnson first. I chose my moment carefully—a trip we made to Japan, to visit Nippon Rubber and discuss the Pre Montreal. Over dinner I laid it all out for him. We were in a ferocious battle, a siege. Day by day, we were doing everything we could to keep the troops fed and the enemy at bay. For the sake of victory, for the sake of survival, everything else needed to be sacrificed, subordinated. "And so, at this crucial moment in the evolution of Blue Ribbon, in the rollout of Nike . . . I'm sorry, but, well . . . you two dummies need to switch cities."

He groaned. Of course. It was Santa Monica all over again.

But slowly, agonizingly, he came around.

As did Woodell.

Around the close of 1972 each man handed his house keys to the other, and now in early 1973 they switched places. Talk about team players. It was an enormous sacrifice, and I was deeply grateful. But in keeping with my personality, and Blue Ribbon tradition, I expressed no gratitude. I spoke not a word of thanks or praise. In fact, in several office memos I referred to the switch as "Operation Dummy Reversal."

IN THE LATE spring of 1973 I met with our recent investors, the debenture holders, for a second time. The first time they'd loved me. How could they not? Sales were booming, celebrity athletes were promoting our shoes. Sure, we'd lost Onitsuka, and we were facing a legal fight down the road, but we were on the right track.

This time, however, it was my duty to inform the investors that, one year after launching Nike, for the first time in Blue Ribbon history . . . we'd lost money.

The meeting took place at the Valley River Inn in Eugene. It was thirty men and women crammed into the conference room, with me at the head of a long conference table. I wore a dark suit and tried to project an air of confidence as I delivered the bad news. I gave them the same speech I'd given Blue Ribbon employees a year before. *We've got them right where we want them.* But this group wasn't buying any pep talks. These were widows and widowers, retirees and pensioners. Also, the previous year I'd been flanked by Jaqua and Bowerman; this year both men were busy.

I was alone.

Half an hour into my pitch, with thirty horrified faces staring at me, I suggested we break for lunch. The previous year I'd handed out Blue Ribbon's financial statements before lunch. This year I decided to wait until after. It didn't help. Even on a full stomach, *with* a chocolate chip cookie, the numbers looked bad. Despite $3.2 million in sales, we showed a net loss of $57,000.

Several clusters of investors now began private conversations while I was trying to talk. They were pointing at this troubling number—$57,000—and repeating it, over and over. At some point I mentioned that Anne Caris, a young runner, had just made the cover of *Sports Illustrated* wearing Nikes. *We're breaking through, people!* No one heard. No one cared. They cared only about the bottom line. Not even *the* bottom line, but *their* bottom line.

I came to the end of my presentation. I asked if anyone had a question. Thirty hands went up. "I'm very disappointed in this," said one older man, rising to his feet. "Any more questions?" Twenty-nine hands went up. Another man called out, "I'm not *happy*."

I said I sympathized. My sympathy only served to annoy them.

They had every right. They'd put their confidence in Bowerman and me, and we'd failed. We never could have anticipated Tiger's betrayal, but nonetheless, these people were hurting, I saw it in their faces, and I needed to take responsibility. To make it right. I decided it was only fair to offer them a concession.

Their stock had a conversion rate, which went up every year. In the first year the rate was $1.00 a share, in the second year it was $1.50, and so on. In light of all this bad news, I told them, I'll keep the conversion rate the same for the full five years you own your stock.

They were placated, mildly. But I left Eugene that day knowing they had a low opinion of me, and Nike. I also left thinking I'd never, ever, *ever* take this company public. If thirty people could cause this kind of acid stomach, I couldn't imagine being answerable to thousands of stockholders.

We were better off financing through Nissho and the bank.

THAT IS, IF there was anything to finance. As feared, Onitsuka had filed suit against us in Japan. So now we had to file quickly against them in the United States, for breach of contract and trademark infringement.

I put the case in the hands of Cousin Houser. It wasn't a tough call. There was the trust factor, of course. Kinship, blood, so on. Also, there was the confidence factor. Though he was only two years older, Cousin Houser seemed vastly more mature. He carried himself with remarkable assurance. Especially before a judge and jury. His father had been a salesman, and a good one, and Cousin Houser learned from him how to sell his client.

Better yet, he was a tenacious competitor. When we were kids Cousin Houser and I used to play vicious, marathon games of badminton in his backyard. One summer we played exactly 116 games. Why 116? Because Cousin Houser beat me 115 straight times. I refused to quit until I'd won. And he had no trouble understanding my position.

But the main reason I chose Cousin Houser was poverty. I had no money for legal fees, and Cousin Houser talked his firm into taking my case on contingency.

Much of 1973 was spent in Cousin Houser's office, reading documents, reviewing memos, cringing at my own words and actions. My memo about hiring a spy—the court would take a dim view of this, Cousin Houser warned. And my "borrowing" Kitami's folder from his briefcase? How could a judge view that as anything but theft? MacArthur came to mind. *You are remembered for the rules you break.*

I contemplated hiding these painful facts from the court. In the end, however, there was only one thing to do. Play it straight. It was the smart thing, the right thing. I'd simply have to hope the court would see the stealing of Kitami's folder as a kind of self-defense.

When I wasn't with Cousin Houser, studying the case, I was being studied. In other words, deposed. For all my belief that business was war without bullets, I'd never felt the full fury of conference-room combat until I found myself at a table surrounded by five lawyers. They tried everything to get me to say I'd violated my contract with Onitsuka. They tried trick questions, hostile questions, squirrelly questions, loaded questions. When questions didn't work, they twisted my answers. A deposition is strenuous for anyone, but for a shy person it's an ordeal. Badgered, baited, harassed, mocked, I was a shell of myself by the end. My condition was worsened by the sense that I hadn't done very well—a sense Cousin Houser reluctantly confirmed.

At the close of those difficult days, it was my nightly six-mile run that saved my life. And then it was my brief time with Matthew and Penny that preserved my sanity. I'd always try to find the time and energy to tell Matthew his bedtime story. *Thomas Jefferson was toiling to write the Declaration of Independence, you see, struggling to find the words, when little Matt History brought him a new quill pen and the words seemed to magically flow . . .*

Matthew almost always laughed at my bedtime stories. He had a liquid laugh, which I loved to hear, because at other times he could be moody, sullen. Cause for concern. He'd been very late learning to talk, and now he was showing a worrisome rebellious streak. I blamed myself. If I were home more, I told myself, he'd be less rebellious.

Bowerman spent quite a bit of time with Matthew, and he told me not to worry. I like his spirit, he said. The world needs more rebels.

That spring, Penny and I had the added worry of how our little rebel would handle a sibling. She was pregnant again. Secretly, I wondered more about how *we* were going to handle it. By the end of 1973, I thought, it's very possible I'll have two kids and no job.

AFTER TURNING OUT the light next to Matthew's bed, I'd usually go and sit in the living room with Penny. We'd talk about the day. Which meant the looming trial. Growing up, Penny had watched several of her father's trials, and it gave her an avid fondness for courtroom drama. She never missed a legal show on TV. *Perry Mason* was her favorite, and I sometimes called her Della Street, after Mason's intrepid secretary. I kidded her about her enthusiasm, but I also fed off it.

The final act of every evening was my phone call to my father. Time for my own bedtime story. By then he'd left the newspaper, and in his retirement he had loads of time to research old cases and precedents, to spin out arguments that might be useful to Cousin Houser. His involvement, plus his sense of fair play, plus his bedrock belief in the rightness of Blue Ribbon's cause, was restorative.

It was always the same. My father would ask about Matthew and Penny, and then I'd ask about Mom, and then he'd tell me what he'd found in the law books. I'd take careful notes on a yellow legal pad. Before signing off he'd always say that he liked our chances. *We're going to win, Buck.* That magical pronoun, "we"—he'd always use it, and it would always make me feel better. It's possible that we were never closer, maybe because our relationship had been reduced to its primal essence. He was my dad, I was his son, and I was in the fight of my life.

Looking back, I see that something else was going on. My trial was providing my father with a healthier outlet for his inner chaos. My legal troubles, my nightly phone calls, were keeping him on high alert, and at home. There were fewer late nights at the bar of the club.

"I'm bringing someone else onto the team," Cousin Houser told me one day. "Young lawyer. Rob Strasser. You'll like him."

He was fresh out of UC Berkeley School of Law, Cousin Houser said, and he didn't know a damn thing. Yet. But Cousin Houser had an instinct about the kid. Thought he showed tremendous promise. Plus, Strasser had a personality that was sure to mesh with our company. "The moment Strasser read our brief," Cousin Houser told me, "he saw this case as a holy crusade."

Well, I liked the sound of that. So the next time I was at Cousin Houser's firm I walked down the hall and poked my head into the office of this Strasser fellow. He wasn't there. The office was pitch-dark. Shades drawn, lights off. I turned to leave. Then I heard . . . Hello? I turned back. Somewhere within the darkness, behind a big walnut desk, a shape moved. The shape grew, a mountain rising from a dark sea.

It slid toward me. Now I saw the rough contours of a man. Six-three, 280 pounds, with an extra helping of shoulders. And fire-log arms. This was one part Sasquatch, one part Snuffleupagus, though somehow light on his feet. He minced toward me and thrust one of his fire logs in my direction. I reached, we shook.

Now I could make out the face—brick red, covered by a full strawberry-blond beard—and glazed with sweat. (Hence the darkness. He required dimly lit, cool spaces. He also couldn't bear wearing a suit.) Everything about this man was different from me, from everyone I knew, and yet I felt a strange, instant kinship.

He said that he was thrilled to be working on my case. Honored. He believed that Blue Ribbon had been the victim of a terrible injustice. Kinship became love. "Yes," I said. "Yes, we have."

DAYS LATER STRASSER came out to Tigard for a meeting. Penny was in the office at the time and when Strasser glimpsed her walking down a hall his eyes bulged. He tugged on his beard. "My God!" he said. "Was that Penny Parks?!"

"She's Penny Knight now," I said.

"She dated my best friend!"

"Small world."

"Smaller when you're my size."

Over the coming days and weeks Strasser and I discovered more and more ways our lives and psyches intersected. He was a native Oregonian, and proud of it, in that typical, truculent way. He'd grown up with a bug about Seattle, and San Francisco, and all the nearby places that outsiders saw as our betters. His geographical inferiority complex was exacerbated by his ungainly size, and homeliness. He'd always feared that he wouldn't find his place in the world, that he was doomed to be an outcast. I got that. He compensated, at times, by being loud, and profane, but mostly he kept his mouth shut and downplayed his intelligence, rather than risk alienating people. I got that, too.

Intelligence like Strasser's, however, couldn't be hidden for long. He was one of the greatest thinkers I ever met. Debater, negotiator, talker, seeker—his mind was always whirring, trying to understand. And to conquer. He saw life as a battle and found confirmation for this view in books. Like me, he read compulsively about war.

Also, like me, he lived and died with the local teams. Especially the Ducks. We had a huge laugh over the fact that Oregon's basketball coach that year was Dick Harter, while the football coach was still Dick Enright. The popular cheer at Oregon State games was:

"If you can't get your Dick Enright, get your Dick Harter!" After we stopped laughing, Strasser started up again. I was amazed by the pitch of his laughter. High, giggly, twee, it was startling from a man his size.

More than anything else we bonded over fathers. Strasser was the son of a successful businessman, and he, too, feared that he'd never live up to his old man's expectations. His father, however, was an exceptionally hard case. Strasser told me many stories. One stayed with me. When Strasser was seventeen his parents went away for the weekend, and Strasser seized the moment to throw a party. It turned into a riot. Neighbors called the police, and just as the patrol cars arrived, so did Strasser's parents. They'd come home early from their trip. Strasser told me that his father looked around—house in shambles, son in handcuffs—and coldly told the cops, "Take him away."

I asked Strasser early on how he gauged our chances against Onitsuka. He said we were going to win. He said it straight out, no hesitation, as if I'd asked him what he'd had for breakfast. He said it the way a sports fan would talk about "next year," with uncompromising faith. He said it the way my father said it every night, and there and then I decided that Strasser was one of the chosen, one of the brethren. Like Johnson and Woodell and Hayes. Like Bowerman and Hollister and Pre. He was Blue Ribbon, through and through.

WHEN I WASN'T obsessing about the trial, I was fixated on sales. Every day I'd get a telex from our warehouses with a "pair count," meaning the exact number of pairs shipped that day to all customers—schools, retailers, coaches, individual mail-order clients. On general accounting principles, a pair shipped was a pair sold, so the daily pair count determined my mood, my digestion, my blood pressure, because it largely determined the fate of Blue Ribbon. If we didn't "sell through," sell all the shoes in our most recent order, and quickly convert that product into cash, we'd be in big trouble. The daily pair count told me if we were on our way to selling through.

"So," I'd say to Woodell on a typical morning, "Massachusetts is good, Eugene looks good—what happened in Memphis?"

"Ice storm," he might say. Or: "Truck broke down."

He had a superb talent for underplaying the bad, and underplaying the good, for simply being in the moment. For instance, after the dummy reversal, Woodell occupied an office that was hardly deluxe. It sat on the top floor of an old shoe factory, and a water tower directly overhead was caked with a century's worth of pigeon poop. Plus, the ceiling beams were gapped, and the building shook every time the die cutters stamped out the uppers. In other words, throughout the day a steady rain of pigeon poop would fall on Woodell's hair, shoulders, desktop. But Woodell would simply dust himself off, casually clear his desk with the side of his hand, and continue with his work.

He also kept a piece of company stationery carefully draped over his coffee cup at all times, to ensure it was only cream in his joe.

I tried often to copy Woodell's Zen monk demeanor. Most days, however, it was beyond me. I boiled with frustration, knowing that our pair count could have been so much higher if not for our constant problems with supply. People were crying out for our shoes, but we just couldn't get them out on time. We'd traded Onitsuka's capricious delays for a new set of delays, caused by demand. The factories and Nissho were doing their jobs, we were now getting what we ordered, on time and intact, but the booming marketplace created new pressures, making it harder and harder to correctly allocate what we got.

Supply and demand is *always* the root problem in business. It's been true since Phoenician traders raced to bring Rome the coveted purple dye that colored the clothing of royals and rich people; there was never enough purple to go around. It's hard enough to invent and manufacture and market a product, but then the logistics, the mechanics, the hydraulics of getting it to the people who want it, when they want it—this is how companies die, how ulcers are born.

In 1973 the supply-and-demand problems facing the running-shoe industry were unusually knotty, seemingly insoluble. The whole world was suddenly demanding running shoes, and the supply wasn't simply inconsistent, it was slowing to a sputter. There were never enough shoes in the pipeline.

We had many smart people working on the problem, but no one could figure out how to significantly boost supply without taking on huge inventory risks. There was *some* consolation in the fact that Adidas and Puma were having the same problems—but not much. *Our* problems could tip us into bankruptcy. We were leveraged to the hilt, and like most people who live from paycheck to paycheck, we were walking the edge of a precipice. When a shipment of shoes was late, our pair count plummeted. When our pair count plummeted, we weren't able to generate enough revenue to repay Nissho and the Bank of California on time. When we couldn't repay Nissho and the Bank of California on time, we couldn't borrow more. When we couldn't borrow more we were late placing our next order.

Round and round it went.

Then came the last thing we needed. A dockworkers' strike. Our man went down to Boston Harbor to pick up a shipment of shoes and found it locked tight. He could see it through the locked fence: boxes and boxes of what the world was clamoring for. And no way to get at it.

We scrambled and arranged for Nippon to send a new shipment—110,000 pairs, on a chartered 707. We split the cost of jet fuel with them. *Anything* was preferable to not bringing product to market on time.

Our sales for 1973 rose 50 percent, to $4.8 million, a number that staggered me the first time I saw it on a piece of paper. Wasn't it only yesterday that we'd done $8,000? And yet there was no celebration. Between our legal troubles and our supply woes, we might be out of business any minute. Late at night I'd sit with Penny and she'd ask, for the umpteenth time, what we were going to do if Blue Ribbon went under. What was the plan? And for the umpteenth time I'd reassure her with optimistic words that I didn't wholly believe.

Then, that fall, I had an idea. Why not go to all of our biggest retailers and tell them that if they'd sign ironclad commitments, if they'd give us large and nonrefundable orders, six months in advance, we'd give them hefty discounts, up to 7 percent? This way we'd have longer lead times, and fewer shipments, and more *certainty*, and therefore a better chance of keeping cash balances in the bank. Also, we could use these long-term commitments from heavyweights like Nordstrom, Kinney, Athlete's Foot, United Sporting Goods, and others, to squeeze more credit out of Nissho and the Bank of California. Especially Nissho.

The retailers were skeptical, of course. But I begged. And when that didn't work I made bold predictions. I told them that this program, which we were calling "Futures," was *the future*, for us and everyone else, so they'd better get on board. Sooner rather than later.

I was persuasive because I was desperate. *If we could just take the lid off our annual growth limits.* But retailers continued to resist. Over and over we heard: "You newbies at Nike don't understand the shoe industry. This new idea will never fly."

My bargaining position was suddenly improved when we rolled out several eye-popping new shoes, which customers were sure to demand. The Bruin was already popular, with its outsoles and uppers cooked together to give a more stable ride. Now we debuted an enhanced version, with bright green suede uppers. (Paul Silas of the Boston Celtics had agreed to wear a pair.) Plus, two new Cortezes, a Leather and a Nylon, both of which figured to be our bestselling shoes yet.

At last, a few retailers signed on. The program started to gain traction. Before long, the stragglers and holdouts were desperate to be included.

SEPTEMBER 13, 1973. My fifth wedding anniversary. Once again Penny woke me in the middle of the night to say she wasn't feeling well. But this time, on the drive to the hospital, I had more on my mind than just the baby. Futures program. Pair count. Pending trial. So of course I got lost.

I circled back, retraced my steps. My brow beginning to bead with sweat, I turned down a street and saw the hospital up ahead. Thank goodness.

Once again they wheeled Penny away, and once again I waited, and wilted, in the bullpen. This time I tried to do some paperwork, and when the doctor came and found me, and told me I had another son, I thought: Two sons. A pair of sons.

The ultimate pair count.

I went to Penny's room and met my new boy, whom we named Travis. Then I did a bad thing.

Smiling, Penny said the doctors told her she could go home after two days, instead of the three they'd required after Matthew. Whoa, I said, hold on there, the insurance is willing to pay for another day in the hospital—what's your hurry? Might as well kick back, relax. Take advantage.

She lowered her head, cocked an eyebrow. "Who's playing and where is it?" she said.

"Oregon," I whispered. "Arizona State."

She sighed. "Okay," she said. "Okay, Phil. Go."

1974

I sat in the federal courthouse in downtown Portland, at a little wooden table, alongside Strasser and Cousin Houser, staring at the high ceiling. I tried to take deep breaths. I tried not to look to my left, at the opposing table, at the five raptor-eyed lawyers representing Onitsuka and four other distributors, all of whom wanted to see me ruined.

It was April 14, 1974.

We'd tried one last time to avoid this nightmare. In the moments before the trial began we'd offered to settle. We'd told Onitsuka: Pay us eight hundred thousand dollars in damages, withdraw your suit in Japan, we'll withdraw ours, and we'll all walk away. I didn't think there was much chance of acceptance, but Cousin Houser thought it worth a try.

Onitsuka rejected the offer instantly. And made no counter. They were out for blood.

Now the bailiff shouted, "Court is in session!" The judge swooped into the courtroom and banged his gavel and my heart jumped. This is it, I told myself.

The head lawyer for Onitsuka's side, Wayne Hilliard, gave his opening statement first. He was a man who enjoyed his work, who knew he was good at it. "These men . . . have *unclean* hands!" he cried, pointing at our table. "Unclean . . . *hands*," he repeated. This was a standard legal term, but Hilliard made it sound lurid,

237

almost pornographic. (Everything Hilliard said sounded somewhat sinister to me, because he was short and had a pointy nose and looked like the Penguin.) Blue Ribbon "conned" Onitsuka into this partnership, he bellowed. Phil Knight went to Japan in 1962 and pretended there was a company called Blue Ribbon, and thereafter he employed subterfuge, theft, spies, whatever necessary, to perpetuate this con.

By the time Hilliard was done, by the time he'd taken his seat next to his four fellow lawyers, I was ready to find in favor of Onitsuka. I looked into my lap and asked myself, How could you have done all those terrible things to those poor Japanese businessmen?

Cousin Houser stood. Right away it was clear that he didn't have Hilliard's fire. It just wasn't in his nature. Cousin Houser was organized, prepared, but he wasn't fiery. At first I was disappointed. Then I looked more closely at Cousin Houser, and listened to what he was saying, and thought about his life. As a boy he'd suffered a severe speech impediment. Every "r" and "l" had been a hurdle. Even into his teens he'd sounded like a cartoon character. Now, though he retained slight traces of the impediment, he'd largely overcome it, and as he addressed the packed courtroom that day, I was filled with admiration, and filial loyalty. What a journey he'd made. We'd made. I was proud of him, proud he was on our side.

Moreover, he'd taken our case on contingency because he'd thought it would come to trial in months. Two years later he hadn't seen a dime. And his costs were astronomical. My photocopying bill alone was in the tens of thousands. Now and then Cousin Houser mentioned that he was under intense pressure from his partners to kick us to the curb. At one point he'd even asked Jaqua to take over the case. (No thanks, Jaqua said.) Fire or no, Cousin Houser was a true hero. He finished speaking, seated himself at our table, and looked at me and Strasser. I patted his back. Game on.

*　*　*

AS THE PLAINTIFFS, we presented our case first, and the first witness we called was the founder and president of Blue Ribbon, Philip H. Knight. Walking to the stand I felt as if it must be some other Philip Knight being called, some other Philip Knight now raising his hand, swearing to tell the truth, in a case marked by so much deceit and rancor. I was floating above my body, watching the scene unfold far below.

I told myself as I settled deep into the creaky wooden chair in the witness stand and straightened my necktie, This is the most important account you'll ever give of yourself. *Don't blow it.*

And then I blew it. I was every bit as bad as I'd been in the depositions. I was even a little worse.

Cousin Houser tried to help me, to lead me. He struck an encouraging tone, gave me a friendly smile with each question, but my mind was going in multiple directions. I couldn't concentrate. I hadn't slept the night before, hadn't eaten that morning, and I was running on adrenaline, but the adrenaline wasn't giving me extra energy or clarity. It was only clouding my brain. I found myself entertaining strange, almost hallucinatory thoughts, like how much Cousin Houser resembled me. He was about my age, about my height, with many of my same features. I'd never noticed the family resemblance until now. What a Kafkaesque twist, I thought, being interrogated by yourself.

By the end of his questioning, I had made a slight recovery. The adrenaline was gone and I was starting to make sense. But now it was the other side's turn to have a go at me.

Hilliard drilled down, down. He was relentless and I was soon reeling. I hemmed, hawed, couched every other word in strange qualifiers. I sounded shady, shifty, even to myself. When I talked about going through Kitami's briefcase, when I tried to explain that Mr. Fujimoto wasn't *really* a corporate spy, I saw the courtroom spectators, and the judge, look skeptical. Even I was skeptical. Several times I looked into the distance and squinted and thought, Did I *really* do that?

I scanned the courtroom, looking for help, and saw nothing but hostile faces. The most hostile was Bork's. He was sitting right behind the Onitsuka table, glaring. Now and then he'd lean into the Onitsuka lawyers, whispering, handing them notes. Traitor, I thought. Benedict Arnold. Prompted by Bork, presumably, Hilliard came at me from new angles, with new questions, and I lost track of the plot. I often had no idea what I was saying.

The judge, at one point, scolded me for not making sense, for being overly complicated. "Just answer the questions concisely," he said. "How concisely?" I said. "Twenty words or less," he said.

Hilliard asked his next question.

I ran a hand over my face. "There's no way I can answer that question in twenty words or less," I said.

The judge required lawyers on both sides to stay behind their tables while questioning witnesses, and to this day I think that ten yards of buffer might have saved me. I think if Hilliard had been able to get closer, he might have cracked me, might have reduced me to tears.

Toward the end of his two-day cross I was numb. I'd hit bottom. The only place to go was up. I could see Hilliard decide that he'd better let me go before I started to rise and make a comeback. As I slid off the stand I gave myself a grade of D minus. Cousin Houser and Strasser didn't disagree.

THE JUDGE IN our case was the Honorable James Burns, a noto-rious figure in Oregon jurisprudence. He had a long, dour face, and pale gray eyes that looked out from beneath two protruding black eyebrows. Each eye had its own little thatch roof. Maybe it was be-cause factories were so much on my mind in those days, but I often thought Judge Burns looked as if he'd been built in some far-off factory that manufactured hanging judges. And I thought he knew it, too. And took pride in it. He called himself, in all seriousness, James the Just. In his operatic basso he'd announce, "You are now in the courtroom of James the Just!"

Heaven have mercy on anyone who, thinking James the Just was being a bit dramatic, dared to laugh.

Portland was still a small town—minuscule, really—and we'd heard through the grapevine that someone had recently bumped into James the Just at his men's club. The judge was having a martini, moaning about our case. "Dreadful case," he was saying to the bartender and anyone who'd listen, "perfectly dreadful." So we knew he didn't want to be there any more than we did, and he often took out his unhappiness on us, berating us over small points of order and decorum.

Still, despite my horrid performance on the stand, Cousin Houser and Strasser and I had a sense that James the Just was inclining toward our side. Something about his demeanor: He was slightly less ogreish to us. On a hunch, therefore, Cousin Houser told the opposing counsel that, if they were still considering our original settlement, forget it, the offer was no longer on the table.

That same day, James the Just called a halt to the trial and admonished both sides. He was perturbed, he said, by all he was reading about this case in the local newspapers. He was damned if he was going to preside over a media circus. He ordered us to cease and desist discussing the case outside the courthouse.

We nodded. Yes, Your Honor.

Johnson sat behind our table, often sending notes to Cousin Houser, and always reading a novel during sidebars and breaks. After court adjourned each day, he'd unwind by taking a stroll around downtown, visiting different sporting goods stores, checking on our sales. (He also did this every time he found himself in a new city.)

Early on he reported back that Nikes were selling like crazy, thanks to Bowerman's waffle trainer. The shoe had just hit the market, and it was sold out everywhere, meaning we were outpacing Onitsuka, even Puma. The shoe was such a hit that we could envision, for the first time, one day approaching Adidas's sales numbers.

Johnson got to talking with one store manager, an old friend, who knew the trial was under way. "How's it going?" the store manager said. "Going well," Johnson said. "So well, in fact, we withdrew our settlement offer."

First thing the next morning, as we gathered in the courtroom, each of us sipping our coffee, we noticed an unfamiliar face at the defense table. There were the five lawyers . . . and one new guy? Johnson turned, saw, and went white. "Oh . . . shit," he said. In a frantic whisper he told us that the new guy was the store manager . . . *with whom he'd inadvertently discussed the trial.*

Now Cousin Houser and Strasser went white.

The three of us looked at each other, and looked at Johnson, and in unison we turned and looked at James the Just. He was banging his gavel and clearly about to explode.

He stopped banging. Silence filled the courtroom. Now he started yelling. He spent a full twenty minutes tearing into us. One day after his gag order, he said, *one day,* someone on Team Blue Ribbon had walked into a local store and run his mouth. We stared straight ahead, like naughty children, wondering if we were about to be a mistrial. But as the judge wound down his tirade, I thought I detected the tiniest twinkle in his eye. Maybe, I thought, just maybe, James the Just is more performer than ogre.

Johnson redeemed himself with his testimony. Articulate, dazzlingly anal about the tiniest details, he described the Boston and the Cortez better than anyone else in the world could, including me. Hilliard tried and tried to break him, and couldn't. What a pleasure it was to watch Hilliard bang his head against that cement-like Johnson unflappability. Stretch versus the crab was less of a mismatch.

Next we called Bowerman to the stand. I had high hopes for my old coach, but he just wasn't himself that day. It was the first time

I ever saw him flustered, even a bit intimidated, and the reasons quickly became obvious. He hadn't prepared. Out of contempt for Onitsuka, and disdain for the whole sordid business, he'd decided to wing it. I was saddened. Cousin Houser was annoyed. Bowerman's testimony could have put us over the top.

Ah well. We consoled ourselves with the knowledge that at least he hadn't done anything to hurt us.

Next Cousin Houser read into the record the deposition of Iwano, the young assistant who'd accompanied Kitami on his two trips to the United States. Happily, Iwano proved to be as guileless, as pure of heart, as he'd first seemed to me and Penny. He'd told the truth, the whole truth, and it flatly contradicted Kitami. Iwano testified that there was a firm, fixed plan in place to break our contract, to abandon us, to replace us, and that Kitami had discussed it openly many times.

We then called a noted orthopedist, an expert on the impact of running shoes on feet, joints, and the spine, who explained the differences among the many brands and models on the market, and described how the Cortez and Boston differed from anything Onitsuka ever made. Essentially, he said, the Cortez was the first shoe ever that took pressure off the Achilles. Revolutionary, he said. Game-changing. While testifying, he spread out dozens of shoes, and pulled them apart, and tossed them around, which agitated James the Just. Apparently the judge was OCD. He liked his courtroom neat, always. Repeatedly he asked our orthopedist to stop making a mess, to keep the shoes in orderly pairs, and repeatedly our orthopedist ignored him. I started to hyperventilate, thinking James the Just was going to find our expert witness in contempt.

Lastly we called Woodell. I watched him wheel his chair slowly to the stand. It was the first time I'd ever seen him in a coat and tie. He'd recently met a woman, and gotten married, and now, when he told me that he was happy, I believed him. I took a moment to enjoy how far he'd come since we'd first met at that Beaverton sandwich shop. Then I immediately felt awful, because I was the cause of his being dragged through this muck. He looked more nervous up there than I'd been, more intimidated than Bowerman. James the Just asked him to spell his name and Woodell paused as if he couldn't remember. "Um . . . W, double o, double d, . . ." Suddenly, he started to giggle. His name didn't have a double d. But some ladies had double Ds. Oh boy. Now he was really laughing. Nerves, of course. But James the Just thought Woodell was mocking the proceedings. He reminded Woodell that he was in the courtroom of James the Just. Which only made Woodell giggle more.

I put a hand over my eyes.

WHEN ONITSUKA PRESENTED their case, they called as their first witness Mr. Onitsuka. He didn't testify long. He said that he'd known nothing about my conflict with Kitami, nor about Kitami's plans to stab us in the back. Kitami interviewing other distributors? "I never informed," Mr. Onitsuka said. Kitami planning to cut us out? "I not know."

Next up was Kitami. As he walked to the stand the Onitsuka lawyers rose and told the judge they would need a translator. I cupped my ear. A *what*? Kitami spoke perfect English. I recalled him boasting about learning his English from a record. I turned to Cousin Houser, my eyes bulging, but he only extended his hands, palms facing the floor. Easy.

In two days on the stand Kitami lied, again and again, through his translator, through his teeth. He insisted that he'd never planned to break our contract. He'd only decided to do so when he discovered we'd done so by making Nikes. Yes, he said, he'd been in touch with other distributors before we manufactured the first Nike, but he was just doing market research. Yes, he said, there was some discussion of Onitsuka's buying Blue Ribbon, but the idea *was initiated by Phil Knight*.

After Hilliard and Cousin Houser had given their closing arguments, I turned and thanked many of the spectators for coming. Then

Cousin Houser and Strasser and I went to a bar around the corner and loosened our neckties and drank several ice-cold beers. And several more. We discussed different ways it might have gone, different things we might have done. Oh, the things we might have done, we said.

And then we all went back to work.

IT WAS WEEKS later. Early morning. Cousin Houser phoned me at the office. "James the Just is going to rule at eleven o'clock," he said.

I raced to the courthouse and met him and Strasser at our old table. Oddly, the courtroom was empty. No spectators. No opposing counsel, except Hilliard. His fellow lawyers had been unable to get here on such short notice.

James the Just came barging through the side door and ascended the bench. He shuffled some papers and began speaking in a low monotone, as if to himself. He said favorable things about both sides. I shook my head. How could he have favorable things to say about Onitsuka? Bad sign. Bad, bad, bad. If only Bowerman had been more prepared. If only I hadn't melted under pressure. If only the ortho-pedist had kept his shoes in order!

The judge looked down at us, his protruding eyebrows longer and shaggier than when the trial began. He would not rule on the matter of the contract between Onitsuka and Blue Ribbon, he said.

I slumped forward.

Instead he would rule solely on the issue of trademarks. It seemed clear to him that this was a case of he-said, he-said. "We have here two conflicting stories," he said, "and it's the opinion of this court that Blue Ribbon's is the more convincing."

Blue Ribbon has been more truthful, he said, not only through-out the dispute, as evidenced by documents, but in this courtroom. "Truthfulness," he said, "is ultimately all I have to go on, to gauge this case."

He noted Iwano's testimony. Compelling, the judge said. It would seem Kitami had lied. He then noted Kitami's use of a translator: During the course of Mr. Kitami's testimony, on more than one occasion, he interrupted the translator to correct him. Each time Mr. Kitami corrected him in perfect English.

Pause. James the Just looked through his papers. So, he declared, it's therefore my ruling that Blue Ribbon will retain all rights to the names Boston and Cortez. Further, he said, there are clearly damages here. Loss of business. Misappropriation of trademark. The question is, how to assign a dollar figure for those damages. The normal course is to name a special master to determine what the damages are. This I will do in the coming days.

He slammed down his gavel. I turned to Cousin Houser and Strasser.

We won?

Oh my . . . *we won.*

I shook hands with Cousin Houser and Strasser, then clapped their shoulders, then hugged them both. I allowed myself one delicious sidelong look at Hilliard. But to my disappointment he had no reaction. He was staring straight ahead, perfectly still. It had never really been his fight. He was just a mercenary. Coolly, he shut his briefcase, clicked the locks, and without a glance in our direction he stood and strolled out of the courtroom.

WE WENT STRAIGHT to the London Grill at the Benson Hotel, not far from the courthouse. We each ordered a double and toasted James the Just. And Iwano. And ourselves. Then I phoned Penny from the pay phone. "We won!" I cried, not caring that they could hear me in all the rooms of the hotel. "Can you believe it—we won!"

I called my father and yelled the same thing.

Both Penny and my father asked *what* we'd won. I couldn't tell them. We still didn't know, I said. One dollar? One million? That was tomorrow's problem. Today was about relishing victory.

Back in the bar Cousin Houser and Strasser and I had one more stiff one. Then I phoned the office to find out the daily pair count.

A WEEK LATER we got a settlement offer: four hundred thousand dollars. Onitsuka knew full well that a special master might come up with any kind of number, so they were seeking to move preemptively, contain their losses. But four hundred thousand dollars seemed low to me. We haggled for several days. Hilliard wouldn't budge.

We all wanted to be done with this, forever. Especially Cousin Houser's overlords, who now authorized him to take the money, of which he'd get half, the largest payment in the history of his firm. Sweet vindication.

I asked him what he was going to do with all that loot. I forget what he said. With ours, Blue Ribbon would simply leverage Bank of California into greater borrowing. More shoes on the water.

THE FORMAL SIGNING was scheduled to take place in San Francisco, at the offices of a blue-chip firm, one of many on Onitsuka's side. The office was on the top floor of a high-rise downtown, and our party arrived that day in a loud, raucous mood. We were four—me, Cousin Houser, Strasser, and Cale, who said he wanted to be present for all the big moments in Blue Ribbon history. Present at the Creation, he said, and present now for the Liberation.

Maybe Strasser and I had read too many war books, but on the way to San Francisco we talked about famous surrenders through history. Appomattox. Yorktown. Reims. It was always so dramatic, we agreed. The opposing generals meeting in a train car or abandoned farmhouse, or on the deck of an aircraft carrier. One side contrite, the other stern but gracious. Then the fountain pens scratching across the "surrender instrument." We talked about MacArthur accepting the Japanese surrender on the USS *Missouri*, giving the speech of a lifetime. We were getting carried away, to be sure, but our sense of history, and martial triumph, was underscored by the date. It was July 4.

A clerk led us into a conference room crammed full of attorneys. Our mood abruptly changed. Mine did, anyway. At the center of the room was Kitami. A surprise.

I don't know why I was surprised to see him. He needed to sign the papers, cut the check. He reached out his hand. A bigger surprise. I shook it.

We all took seats around the table. Before each of us stood a stack of twenty documents, and each document had dozens of dotted lines. We signed until our fingers tingled. It took at least an hour. The mood was tense, the silence profound, except for one moment. I recall that Strasser let forth with a huge sneeze. Like an elephant. And I also recall that he was begrudgingly wearing a brand-new navy-blue suit, which he'd had tailored by his mother-in-law, who put all the extra material into the breast pocket. Strasser, affirming his status as the world's foremost antisartorialist, now reached into his pocket and pulled out a long string of extra gabardine and used it to blow his nose.

At last a clerk collected all the documents, and we all capped our pens, and Hilliard instructed Kitami to hand over the check.

Kitami looked up, dazed. "I have no check."

What did I see in his face at that moment? Was it spite? Was it defeat? I don't know. I looked away, scanned the faces around the conference table. They were easier to read. The lawyers were in total shock. A man comes to a settlement conference without a check?

No one spoke. Now Kitami looked ashamed; he knew he'd erred. "I will mail check when I return to Japan," he said.

Hilliard was gruff. "See that it's mailed as soon as possible," he told his client.

I picked up my briefcase and followed Cousin Houser and Strasser out of the conference room. Behind me came Kitami and the other lawyers. We all stood and waited for the elevator. When the doors opened we all crowded on, shoulder to shoulder, Strasser himself taking up half the car. No one spoke as we dropped to the street. No one breathed. Awkward doesn't begin to describe it. Surely, I thought, Washington and Cornwallis weren't forced to ride the same horse away from Yorktown.

STRASSER CAME TO the office some days after the verdict, to wind things down, to say good-bye. We steered him into the conference room and everyone gathered around and gave him a thunderous ovation. His eyes were teary as he raised a hand and acknowledged our cheers and thanks.

"Speech!" someone yelled.

"I've made so many close friends here," he said, choking up. "I'm going to miss you all. And I'm going to miss working on this case. Working on the side of *right*."

Applause.

"I'm going to miss defending this wonderful company."

Woodell and Hayes and I looked at each other. One of us said: "So why don't you come work here?"

Strasser turned red and laughed. That laugh—I was struck again by the incongruous falsetto. He waved his hand, pshaw, as if we were kidding.

We weren't kidding. A short while later I invited Strasser to lunch at the Stockpot in Beaverton. I brought along Hayes, who by now was working full-time for Blue Ribbon, and we made a hard pitch. Of all the pitches in my life, this might have been the most carefully prepared and rehearsed, because I wanted Strasser, and I knew there would be pushback. He had before him a clear path to the very top of Cousin Houser's firm, or any other firm he might choose. Without much effort he could become partner, secure a life of means, privilege, prestige. That was the known, and we were offering him The Unknown. So Hayes and I spent days role-playing, polishing our arguments and counterarguments, anticipating what objections Strasser might raise.

I opened by telling Strasser that it was all a foregone conclusion, really. "You're one of us," I said. *One of us.* He knew what those words meant. We were the kind of people who simply couldn't put up with corporate nonsense. We were the kind of people who wanted our work to be play. But meaningful play. We were trying to slay Goliath, and though Strasser was bigger than two Goliaths, at heart he was an utter David. We were trying to create a brand, I said, but also a culture. We were fighting against conformity, against boringness, against drudgery. More than a product, we were trying to sell an idea—a spirit. I don't know if I ever fully understood who we were and what we were doing until I heard myself saying it all that day to Strasser.

He kept nodding. He never stopped eating, but he kept nodding. He agreed with me. He said he'd gone directly from our battle royal with Onitsuka to working on several humdrum insurance cases, and every morning he'd wanted to slit his wrists with a paper clip. "I miss Blue Ribbon," he said. "I miss the clarity. I miss that feeling, every day, of getting a win. So I thank you for your offer."

Still, he wasn't saying yes. "What's up?" I said.

"I need . . . to ask . . . my dad," he said.

I looked at Hayes. We both guffawed. "Your dad!" Hayes said.

The same dad who'd told the cops to haul Strasser away? I shook my head. The one argument Hayes and I hadn't prepared for. The eternal pull of the old man.

"Okay," I said. "Talk to your father. Get back to us."

Days later, with his old man's blessing, Strasser agreed to become the first-ever in-house counsel for Blue Ribbon.

WE HAD ABOUT two weeks to relax and enjoy our legal victory. Then we looked up and saw a new threat looming on the horizon.

The yen. It was fluctuating wildly, and if it continued to do so it would spell certain doom.

Before 1972 the yen-to-dollar rate had been pegged, constant, unvarying. One dollar was always worth 360 yen, and vice versa. You could count on that rate, every day, as sure as you could count on the sun rising. President Nixon, however, felt the yen was undervalued. He feared America was "sending all its gold to Japan," so he cut the yen loose, let it float, and now the yen-to-dollar rate was like the weather. Every day different. Consequently, no one doing business in Japan could possibly plan for tomorrow. The head of Sony famously complained: "It's like playing golf and your handicap changes on every hole."

At the same time, Japanese labor costs were on the rise. Combined with a fluctuating yen, this made life treacherous for any company doing the bulk of its production in Japan. No longer could I envision a future in which most of our shoes were made there. We needed new factories, in new countries, fast.

To me, Taiwan seemed the next logical step. Taiwanese officials, sensing Japan's collapse, were rapidly mobilizing to fill the coming void. They were building factories at warp speed. And yet the factories weren't yet capable of handling our workload. Plus, their quality control was poor. Until Taiwan was ready, we'd need to find a bridge, something to hold us over.

I considered Puerto Rico. We were already making some shoes there. Alas, they weren't very good. Also, Johnson had been down there to scout factories, in 1973, and he'd reported that they weren't much better than the dilapidated ones he saw all over New England. So we talked about some sort of hybrid solution: taking raw materials from Puerto Rico and sending them to New England for lasting and bottoming.

Toward the end of 1974, that impossibly long year, this became our plan. And I was well prepared to implement it. I'd done my homework. I'd been making trips to the East Coast, to lay the groundwork, to look at various factories we might lease. I'd gone twice—first with Cale, then with Johnson.

The first time, the clerk at the rental car company declined my credit card. Then confiscated it. When Cale tried to smooth it over, offering up his credit card, the clerk said he wouldn't accept Cale's card, either, because Cale was with me. Guilt by association.

Talk about your deadbeats. I couldn't bring myself to look Cale in the eye. Here we were, a dozen years out of Stanford, and while he was an eminently successful businessman, I was still struggling to keep my head above water. He'd known I was struggling, but now he knew exactly how much. I was mortified. He was always there at the big moments, the triumphant moments, but this humiliating little moment, I feared, would define me in his eyes.

Then, when we got to the factory, the owner laughed in my face. He said he wouldn't consider doing business with some fly-by-night company he'd never heard of—*let alone from Oregon*.

On the second trip I met up with Johnson in Boston. I picked him up at *Footwear News*, where he'd been scouting potential suppliers, and together we drove to Exeter, New Hampshire, to see an ancient, shuttered factory. Built around the time of the American Revolution, the factory was a ruin. It had once housed the Exeter Boot and Shoe Company, but now it housed rats. As we pried open the doors and swatted away cobwebs the size of fishing nets, all sorts of creatures scurried past our feet and flew past our ears. Worse, there were gaping holes in the floor; one wrong step could mean a trip to the earth's core.

The owner led us up to the third floor, which was usable. He said he could rent us this floor, with an option to buy the whole place. He also said we'd need help getting the factory properly cleaned and staffed, and he gave us the name of a local guy who could help. Bill Giampietro.

We met Giampietro the next day at an Exeter tavern. Within minutes I could see this was our man. A true shoe dog. He was fifty, thereabouts, but his hair had no gray. It seemed painted with black polish. He had a thick Boston accent, and besides shoes the only subject he ever broached was his beloved wife and kids. He was first-generation American—his parents came from Italy, where his father (of course) had been a cobbler. He had the serene expression and callused hands of a craftsman, and he proudly wore the standard uniform: stained pants, stained denim shirt, rolled up to the stained elbows. He said he'd never done anything in his life but cobble, and never wanted to. "Ask anyone," he said, "they'll tell you." Everyone in New England called him Geppetto, he added, because everyone thought (and still thinks) Pinocchio's father was a cobbler. (He was actually a carpenter.)

We each ordered a steak and a beer, and then I removed a pair of Cortezes from my briefcase. "Can you equip the Exeter factory to turn out these babies?" I asked. He took the shoes, examined them, pulled them apart, yanked out their tongues. He peered into them like a doctor. "No fucking problem," he said, dropping them on the table.

The cost? He did the math in his head. Renting and fixing up the Exeter factory, plus workers, materials, sundries—he guessed $250,000.

Let's do it, I said.

Later, while Johnson and I were on a run, he asked me how we were going to pay a quarter of a million dollars for a factory when we could barely pay for Giampietro's steak. I told him calmly—in fact with the calm of a madman—that I was going to have Nissho pay for it. "Why on earth is Nissho going to give you money to run a factory?" he asked. "Simple," I said, "I'm not going to tell them."

I stopped running, put my hands on my knees, and told Johnson, furthermore, that I was going to need *him* to run that factory.

His mouth opened, then shut. Just one year ago I'd asked him to move across the country to Oregon. Now I wanted him to move back east again? To work in close proximity to Giampietro? And Woodell? With whom he had a very . . . complicated . . . rapport?

"Craziest thing I've ever heard," he said. "Never mind the inconvenience, never mind the insanity of schlepping all the way back to the East Coast, what do I know about running a factory? I'd be in completely over my head."

I laughed. I laughed and laughed. "Over your head?" I said. "Over your *head*! We're *all* in over our heads! *Way* over!"

He moaned. He sounded like a car trying to start on a cold morning.

I waited. Just give it a second, I thought.

He denied, fumed, bargained, got depressed, then accepted. The Five Stages of Jeff. At last he let out a long sigh and said he knew this was a big job, and, like me, he didn't trust anyone else to handle it. He said he knew that, when it came to Blue Ribbon, each of us was willing to do whatever was necessary to win, and if "whatever was necessary" fell outside our area of expertise, hey, as Giampietro would say, "No fucking problem." He didn't know anything about running a factory, but he was willing to try. To learn.

Fear of failure, I thought, will never be our downfall as a company. Not that any of us thought we *wouldn't* fail; in fact we had every expectation that we *would*. But when we did fail, we had faith that we'd do it fast, learn from it, and be better for it.

Johnson frowned, nodded. Okay, he said. Deal.

And so, as we entered the final days of 1974, Johnson was firmly ensconced in Exeter, and often, late at night, thinking of him back there, I'd smile and say under my breath: Godspeed, old friend.

You're Giampietro's problem now.

OUR CONTACT AT the Bank of California, a man named Perry Holland, was very much like Harry White at First National. Agreeable, friendly, loyal, but absolutely feckless, because he had rigid loan limits that were always well below our requests. And his bosses, like White's, were always pressing us to slow down.

We responded in 1974 by mashing the accelerator. We were on pace for $8 million in sales, and nothing, but nothing, was going to stop us from hitting that number. In defiance of the bank, we made deals with more stores, and opened several stores of our own—and continued to sign celebrity athlete endorsers we couldn't afford.

At the same time Pre was smashing American records in Nikes, the best tennis player in the world was smashing rackets in them. His name was Jimmy Connors, and his biggest fan was Jeff Johnson. Connors, Johnson told me, was the tennis version of Pre. Rebellious. Iconoclastic. He urged me to reach out to Connors, sign him to an endorsement deal, fast. Thus, in the summer of 1974 I phoned Connors's agent and made my pitch. We'd signed Nastase for ten thousand dollars, I said, and we were willing to offer his boy half that.

The agent jumped at the deal.

Before Connors could sign the papers, however, he left the country for Wimbledon. Then, against all odds, he *won* Wimbledon. In our shoes. Next, he came home and shocked the world by *winning* the U.S. Open. I was giddy. I phoned the agent and asked if Connors had signed those papers yet. We wanted to get started promoting him. "What papers?" the agent said.

"Uh, the papers. We had a deal, remember?"

"Yeah, I don't remember any deal. We've already got a deal three times better than your deal, which I don't remember."

Disappointing, we all agreed. But oh well.

Besides, we all said, we've still got Pre.

We'll always have Pre.

1975

Pay Nissho first. This was my morning chant, my nightly prayer, my number one priority. And it was my daily instruction to the man who played the Sundance Kid to my Butch Cassidy—Hayes. Before paying back the bank, I said, before paying back anyone . . . *pay Nissho.*

It wasn't so much a strategy as a necessity. Nissho was like equity. Our line of credit at the bank was $1 million, but we had another million in credit with Nissho, which willingly took second position, which made the bank feel more secure. All of this would unspool, however, if Nissho weren't there. Ergo, we needed to keep Nissho happy. Always, always, pay Nissho first.

It wasn't easy, however, this paying Nissho first. It wasn't easy paying anyone. We were undergoing an explosion in assets, and inventory, which put enormous strains on our cash reserves. With any growth company, this is the typical problem. But we were growing faster than the typical growth company, faster than any growth company I knew of. Our problems were unprecedented. Or so it seemed.

I was also partly to blame, of course. I refused to even consider ordering *less inventory*. Grow or die, that's what I believed, no matter the situation. Why cut your order from $3 million down to $2 million if you believed in your bones that the demand out there was for $5 million? So I was forever pushing my conservative bankers to the brink, forcing them into a game of chicken. I'd order a number of shoes that seemed to them absurd, a number we'd need to stretch to pay for, and I'd always just barely pay for them, in the nick of time, and then just barely pay our other monthly bills, at the last minute, always doing just enough, and no more, to prevent the bankers from booting us. And then, at the end of the month, I'd empty our accounts to pay Nissho and start from zero again.

To most observers this would've seemed a brazenly reckless, dangerous way of doing business, but I believed the demand for our shoes was always greater than our annual sales. Besides, eight of every ten orders were solid gold, guaranteed, thanks to our Futures program. Full speed ahead.

Others might have argued that we didn't need to fear Nissho. The company was our ally, after all. We were making them money, how mad could they get? Also, I had a strong personal relationship with Sumeragi.

But suddenly in 1975 Sumeragi was no longer running things. Our account had grown too big for him; our credit was no longer his call alone. We were now overseen by the West Coast credit manager, Chio Suzuki, who was based in Los Angeles, and even more directly by the financial manager of the Portland office, Tadayuki Ito.

Whereas Sumeragi was warm and approachable, Ito was congenitally aloof. Light seemed to bounce off him differently. No, rather, light didn't bounce off him. He absorbed it, like a black hole. Everybody at Blue Ribbon liked Sumeragi—we invited him to every office party. But I don't think we ever invited Ito to anything.

In my mind I called him the Ice Man.

I still had difficulty making eye contact with people, but Ito wouldn't allow me to divert my gaze. He looked directly into my eyes, down into my soul, and it was hypnotizing. Especially when he felt he had the upper hand. Which was almost always. I'd played golf with him once or twice, and I was struck, even after he'd hit a terrible shot, at the way he turned and looked straight at me as he came off the tee. He wasn't a good golfer, but he was so confident, so self-assured, he always gave the impression that his ball was sitting 350 yards away, atop a tuft of grass in the center of the fairway.

And now I remember this in particular. His golf attire, like his business attire, was meticulous. Mine, of course, was not. During one of our matches, the weather was cool, and I was wearing a shaggy mohair sweater. As I approached the first tee Ito asked under his breath if I planned to go skiing later. I stopped, wheeled. He gave me a half smile. It was the first time I'd ever known the Ice Man to try humor. And the last.

This was the man I needed to keep happy. It wouldn't be easy. But I thought: Always do well in his eyes, and credit will continue to expand, thus enabling Blue Ribbon to expand. Stay in his good graces and all will be well. Otherwise . . .

My obsession with keeping Nissho happy, with keeping Ito happy, combined with my refusal to ease up on growth, created a frantic atmosphere around the office. We struggled to make every payment, to Bank of California, to all our other creditors, but that Nissho payment at the end of the month was like passing a kidney stone. As we'd begin scraping together our available cash, writing checks with barely enough to cover them, we'd start to sweat. The Nissho payment was sometimes so big that we'd be dead broke for a day or two. Then every other creditor would have to wait.

Too bad for them, I'd tell Hayes.

I know, I know, he'd say. *Pay Nissho first.*

Hayes didn't like this state of affairs. It was hard on his nerves. "So what do you want to do," I'd ask him, "slow down?" Which would always draw a guilty smile. Silly question.

Occasionally, when our cash reserves were really stretched thin, our account at the bank wouldn't just be empty, it would be overdrawn. Then Hayes and I would have to go down to the bank and explain the situation to Holland. We'd show him our financial statements, point out that our sales were doubling, that our inventory was flying out the door. Our cash flow "situation," we'd say, is merely temporary.

We knew, of course, that living on the float wasn't the way to do things. But we'd always tell ourselves: It's temporary. Besides, everyone did it. Some of the biggest companies in America lived on the float. Banks themselves lived on the float. Holland acknowledged as much. "Sure, boys, I get it," he'd say with a nod. As long as we were upfront with him, as long as we were transparent, he could work with us.

And then came that fateful rainy day. A Wednesday afternoon. The spring of 1975. Hayes and I found ourselves staring into the abyss. We owed Nissho $1 million, our first-ever million-dollar payment, and, hello, we didn't have $1 million lying around. We were about $75,000 short.

I recall that we were sitting in my office, watching raindrops race down the windowpane. Occasionally we'd look through the books, curse the numbers, then look back at the raindrops. "We have to pay Nissho," I said quietly.

"Yes, yes, yes," Hayes said. "But to cover a check this large? We'll have to drain *all* our other bank accounts dry. All. Dry."

"Yes."

We had retail stores in Berkeley, Los Angeles, Portland, New England, each with its own bank account. We'd have to empty them all, divert all that money to the home office account for a day or two—or three. Along with every cent from Johnson's factory in Exeter. We'd have to hold our breath, like walking past a graveyard, until we could replenish those accounts. And still we might not be able to cover that massive check to Nissho. We'd still need a little luck, a payment or two to land from one of the many retailers who owed us money.

"Circular funding," Hayes said.

"Magical banking," I said.

"Son of a bitch," Hayes said, "if you look at our cash flow over the next six months, we're in good shape. It's just this *one payment* to Nissho that's screwing up everything."

"Yes," I said, "if we can get past this one payment, we're home free."

"But this is some payment."

"We've always covered checks to Nissho within a day or two. But this time it might take us—what—three? Four?"

"I don't know," Hayes said, "I honestly don't know."

I followed two raindrops racing down the glass. Neck and neck. *You are remembered for the rules you break.* "Damn the torpedoes," I said. "Pay Nissho."

Hayes nodded. He stood. We looked at each other for one long second. He said he'd tell Carole Fields, our head bookkeeper, what we'd decided. He'd have her start moving the money around.

And come Friday he'd have her cut the check to Nissho.

These are the moments, I thought.

TWO DAYS LATER Johnson was in his new office at the Exeter factory, doing paperwork, when a mob of angry workers suddenly appeared at his door. Their paychecks had bounced, they said. They wanted answers.

Johnson, of course, had no answers to give. He implored them to hold on, there must be some mistake. He phoned Oregon, reached Fields, and told her what was happening. He expected her to say it was all a big misunderstanding, an accounting error. Instead she whispered, "Oooh, shit." Then hung up on him.

A PARTITION WALL separated Fields's office from mine. She ran around the wall and up to my desk. "You'd better sit down," she blurted.

"I *am* sitting down."

"It's all hitting the fan," she said.

"What is?"

"The checks. All the checks."

I called in Hayes. By then he weighed 330 pounds, but he seemed

PHIL KNIGHT

to be shrinking before me as Fields described to us every particular of the Johnson phone call. "We might've really fucked up this time," he said. "What do we do?" I said. "I'll call Holland," Hayes said.

Minutes later Hayes came back into my office, holding up his hands. "Holland says it's fine, no worries, he'll smooth things over with his bosses."

I sighed. Disaster averted.

In the meantime, however, Johnson wasn't waiting for us to get back to him. He phoned his local bank and learned that his account, for some reason, was bone dry. He called in Giampietro, who drove up the road to see an old friend, a man who owned a local box company. Giampietro asked the man for a loan of five thousand dollars, cash. An outrageous request. But the man's box company depended on Blue Ribbon for its survival. If we went out of business, the box company might, too. So the box man became our bag man, forking over fifty crisp hundred-dollar bills.

Giampietro then raced back to the factory and doled out everyone's pay, in cash, like Jimmy Stewart keeping the Bailey Bros. Building & Loan afloat.

HAYES LUMBERED INTO my office. "Holland says we need to get our asses down to the bank. Pronto."

Next thing I knew, we were all sitting in a conference room at the Bank of California. On one side of the table were Holland and two nameless men in suits. They looked like undertakers. On the other side were Hayes and I. Holland, somber, opened. "Gentlemen . . ."

Not good, I thought. "Gentlemen?" I said. "Gentlemen? Perry, it's us."

"Gentlemen, we've decided we no longer want your business at this bank."

Hayes and I stared.

"Does that mean you're throwing us out?" Hayes asked.

"It does indeed," Holland said.

"You can't do that," Hayes said.

"We can and we are," Holland said. "We're freezing your funds, and we will no longer honor any more checks you write on this account."

"Freezing our—! I don't believe this," Hayes said.

"Believe it," Holland said.

I said nothing. I wrapped my arms around my torso and thought, This isn't good, this isn't good, this isn't good.

Never mind the embarrassment, the hassles, the cascade of bad consequences that would follow if Holland threw us out. All I could think of was Nissho. How would they react? How would Ito react? I pictured myself telling the Ice Man that we couldn't give him his million dollars. It chilled me down to my marrow.

I don't remember the end of that meeting. I don't remember leaving the bank, or walking out, or going across the street, or getting on the elevator, or riding it to the top floor. I only recall shaking, violently shaking, as I asked for a word with Mr. Ito.

The next thing I recall is Ito and Sumeragi taking Hayes and me into their conference room. They could sense that we were fragile. They led us to chairs, and they both looked at the floor as I spoke. *Kei*. Much *kei*. "Well," I said, "I have some bad news. Our bank . . . has thrown us out."

Ito looked up. "Why?" he said.

His eyes hardened. But his voice was surprisingly soft. I thought of the wind atop Mount Fuji. I thought of the gentle breeze stirring the ginkgo leaves in the Meiji gardens. I said, "Mr. Ito, do you know how the big trading companies and banks 'live on the float'? Okay, we at Blue Ribbon tend to do that, too, from time to time, including last month. And the fact of the matter is, sir, well, we missed the float. And now the Bank of California has decided to kick us out."

Sumeragi lit a Lucky Strike. One puff. Two.

Ito did the same. One puff. Two. But on the exhale, the smoke didn't seem to come from his mouth. It seemed to emanate from deep down inside him, to curl from his cuffs and shirt collar. He looked into my eyes. He bored into me. "They should not have done that," he said.

My heart stopped midbeat. This was an almost sympathetic thing for Ito to say. I looked at Hayes. I looked back at Ito. I allowed myself to think: We might . . . just . . . get away with this.

Then I realized that I hadn't yet told him the bad part. "Be that as it may," I said, "they did throw us out, Mr. Ito, they did, and the net-net is that I have no bank. And thus I have no money. And I need to make payroll. And I need to pay my other creditors. And if I can't meet those obligations, I am out of business. Today. In which case, not only can I not pay you the million dollars I owe you, sir . . . but I need to ask to borrow another one million dollars."

Ito and Sumeragi slid their eyes toward each other for one half second, then slid them back to me. Everything in the room came to a stop. The dust motes, the molecules of air, paused midflight. "Mr. Knight," Ito said, "before giving you another cent . . . I will need to look at your books."

WHEN I GOT home from Nissho it was about 9:00 p.m. Penny said Holland had phoned. "Holland?" I said.

"Yes," she said. "He left instructions that you should call whenever you got home. He left his home number."

He answered on the first ring. His voice was . . . off. He'd been stiff earlier in the day, while carrying out orders from his bosses, but now he sounded more like a human being. A sad, stressed human being. "Phil," he said, "I feel I ought to tell you . . . we've had to notify the FBI."

I gripped the phone tighter. "Say that again," I whispered. "Say that again, Perry."

"We had no choice."

"What are you telling me?"

"It's—well, it looks to us like fraud."

I WENT INTO the kitchen and fell into a chair. "What is it?" Penny said.

I told her. Bankruptcy, scandal, ruin—the works.

"Is there no hope?" she asked.

"It's all up to Nissho."

"Tom Sumeragi?"

"And his bosses."

"No problem, then. Sumeragi loves you."

She stood. She had faith. She was completely ready for whatever may come. She even managed to turn in.

Not me. I sat up all night, playing out a hundred different scenarios, castigating myself for taking such a risk.

When I finally crawled into bed, my mind wouldn't stop. Lying in the dark I thought over and over: Am I going to jail?

Me? Jail?

I got up, poured myself a glass of water, checked on the boys. They were both sprawled on their tummies, dead to the world. What would they do? What would become of them? Then I went into the den and researched the homestead laws. I was relieved to learn that the Feds couldn't take the house. They could take everything else, but not this little sixteen-hundred-square-foot sanctuary.

I sighed, but the relief didn't last. I started thinking about my life. I scrolled back years, questioning every decision I'd ever made that led to this point. If only I'd been better at selling encyclopedias, I thought. Everything would be different.

I tried to give myself the standard catechism.

What do you know?

But I didn't know anything. Sitting in my recliner I wanted to cry out: *I know nothing!*

I'd always had an answer, some kind of answer, to every problem. But this moment, this night, I had no answers. I got up, found a yellow legal pad, started making lists. But my mind kept drifting; when I looked down at the pad there were only doodles. Check marks, squiggles, lightning bolts.

In the eerie glow of the moon they all looked liked angry, defiant swooshes.

Don't go to sleep one night. What you most want will come to you then.

I MANAGED TO fall asleep for an hour or two, and I spent most of that bleary Saturday morning on the phone, reaching out to people for advice. Everyone said Monday would be the critical day. Perhaps the most critical of my life. I would need to act swiftly and boldly. So, to prepare, I organized a summit for Sunday afternoon.

We all gathered in the conference room at Blue Ribbon. There was Woodell, who must have caught the first flight out of Boston, and Hayes, and Strasser, and Cale flew up from Los Angeles. Someone brought doughnuts. Someone sent out for pizzas. Someone dialed Johnson and put him on the speakerphone. The mood in the room, at first, was somber, because that was my mood. But having my friends around, my team, made me feel better, and as I lightened up, they did, too.

We talked long into the evening, and if we agreed on anything, we agreed there wasn't an easy solution. There usually isn't when the FBI has been notified. Or when you've been ousted by your bank for the second time in five years.

As the summit drew to a close the mood shifted again. The air in the room grew stale, heavy. The pizza looked like poison. A consensus formed. The resolution of this crisis, whatever it might be, is in the hands of others.

And of all those others, Nissho was our best hope.

We discussed tactics for Monday morning. That's when the men from Nissho were due to arrive. Ito and Sumeragi were going to pore through our books, and while there was no telling what they might think of our finances, one thing was pretty much preordained. They were going to see right away that we'd used a big chunk of their financing not to purchase shoes from overseas but to run a secret factory in Exeter. Best case, this would make them mad. Worst case, it would make them lose their minds. If they considered our accounting sleight of hand a full-fledged betrayal, they would abandon us, faster than the bank had, in which case we'd be out of business. Simple as that.

We talked about hiding the factory from them. But everyone around the table agreed that we needed to play this one straight. As in the Onitsuka trial, full disclosure, total transparency, was the only course. It made sense, strategically and morally.

Throughout this summit the phones rang constantly. Creditors from coast to coast were trying to find out what was going on, why our checks were bouncing like Super Balls. Two creditors in particular were livid. One was Bill Shesky, head of Bostonian Shoes. We owed him a cool half million dollars, and he wanted to let us know that he was boarding a plane and coming to Oregon to get it. The second was Bill Manowitz, head of Mano International, a trading company in New York. We owed him one hundred thousand dollars, and he, too, was coming to Oregon to force a showdown. And to cash out.

After the summit adjourned I was the last to leave. Alone, I staggered out to my car. In my lifetime I had finished many races on sore legs, gimpy knees, zero energy, but that night I wasn't altogether sure I had the strength to drive home.

ITO AND SUMERAGI were right on time. Monday morning, 9:00 a.m. sharp, they pulled up to the building, each wearing a dark suit and dark tie, each carrying a black briefcase. I thought of all the samurai movies I'd seen, all the books I'd read about ninjas. This was how it always looked before the ritual killing of the bad shogun.

They walked straight through our lobby and into our conference room and sat down. Without a word of small talk we stacked our books in front of them. Sumeragi lit a cigarette, Ito uncapped a fountain pen. They commenced. Pecking at calculators, scratching at legal pads, drinking bottomless cups of coffee and green tea, they slowly peeled back the layers of our operation and peered inside.

I walked in and out, every fifteen minutes or so, to ask if they needed anything. They never did.

The bank auditor arrived soon after to collect all our cash receipts. A fifty-thousand-dollar check from United Sporting Goods really *had* been in the mail. We showed him: It was right on Carole Fields's desk. This was the late check that set all the dominoes in motion. This, plus the normal day's receipts, covered our shortfall. The bank auditor telephoned United Sporting Goods' bank in Los Angeles and asked that their account be charged immediately, the funds transferred to our account at Bank of California. The Los Angeles bank said no. There were insufficient funds in the United Sporting Goods account.

United Sporting Goods had also been playing the float.

Already feeling a splitting headache coming on, I walked back into the conference room. I could smell it in the air. We'd reached that fateful moment. Leaning over the books, Ito realized what he was looking at and did a slow double-take. Exeter. Secret factory. Then I saw the realization dawn that he was the sucker who'd paid for it.

He looked up at me and pushed his head forward on his neck, as if to say: Really?

I nodded.

And then . . . he smiled. It was only a half smile, a mohair sweater smile, but it meant everything.

I gave him a weak half smile in return, and in that brief wordless exchange countless fates and futures were decided.

* * *

PAST MIDNIGHT, ITO and Sumeragi were still there, still busy with their calculators and legal pads. When they finally left for the day they promised to return early the next morning. I drove home and found Penny waiting up. We sat in the dining room, talking. I gave her an update. We agreed that Nissho was done with their audit; they'd known everything they needed to know before lunch. What followed, and was yet to follow, was simply punishment. "Don't let them push you around like this!" Penny said.

"Are you kidding?" I said. "Right now they can push me around all they want. They're my only hope."

"At least there are no more surprises," she said.

"Yes," I said. "No more shoes to drop."

ITO AND SUMERAGI were back at 9:00 a.m. the next morning, and took up their places in the conference room. I went around the office and told everyone, "It's almost over. Just hang on. Just a little longer. There's nothing else for them to find."

Not long after they'd arrived, Sumeragi stood, stretched, and looked as if he was going to step outside for a smoke. He motioned to me. *A word?* We walked down the hall to my office. "I fear this audit is worse than you realize," he said. "What—why?" I said. "Because," he said, "I delayed . . . I sometimes did not put invoices through right away." "You did what now?" I said.

Hangdog, Sumeragi explained that he'd been worried about us, that he'd tried to help us manage our credit problems by hiding Nissho's invoices in a drawer. He'd held them back, not sent them on through to his accounting people, until he felt we had enough cash to pay them, which in turn made it appear on the Nissho books that their credit exposure to us was much lower than it actually was. In other words, all this time we'd been stressing about paying Nissho on time, and we were *never* paying them on time, because Sumeragi wasn't invoicing us on time, thinking he was *helping*. "This is bad,"

I said to Sumeragi. "Yes," he said, relighting a Lucky Strike, "is bad, Buck. Is very very bad."

I marched him back to the conference room and together we told Ito, who was, of course, appalled. At first he suspected Sumeragi of acting at our behest. I couldn't blame him. A conspiracy was the most logical explanation. In his place I would've thought the same thing. But Sumeragi, who looked as if he was about to prostrate himself before Ito, swore on his life that he'd been acting independently, that he'd gone rogue.

"Why you do such a thing?" Ito demanded.

"Because I think Blue Ribbon could be great success," Sumeragi said, "maybe $20 million account. I shake hands many times with Mr. Steve Prefontaine. I shake hands with Mr. Bill Bowerman. I go many times to Trail Blazer game with Mr. Phil Knight. I even pack orders at warehouse. Nike is my *business child*. Always it is nice to see one's *business child* grow."

"So then," Ito said, "you hide invoices because . . . you . . . *like these men?*"

Deeply ashamed, Sumeragi bowed his head. *"Hai,"* he said. *"Hai."*

I HAD NO idea what Ito might do. But I couldn't stick around to find out. I suddenly had another problem. My two angriest creditors had just landed. Shesky from Bostonian and Manowitz from Mano were both on the ground, in Portland, headed our way.

Quickly, I gathered everyone in my office and gave them their final orders. "Folks—we're going to Code Red. This building, this forty-five-hundred-square-foot building, is about to be swarming with people to whom we owe money. Whatever else we do today, we cannot let any of them bump into each other. Bad enough that we owe them money. If they cross paths in the hall, if one unhappy creditor meets another unhappy creditor, and if they should have a chance to compare notes, they will freak out. They could team up and decide on some sort of collaborative payment schedule! Which would be Armageddon."

We drew up a plan. We assigned a person to each creditor, someone who would keep an eye on him at all times, even escorting him to the restroom. Then we assigned a person to coordinate everything, to be like air traffic control, making sure the creditors and their escorts were always in separate airspace. Meanwhile, I would scurry from room to room, apologizing and genuflecting.

At times the tension was unbearable. At other times it was a bad Marx Brothers movie. In the end, somehow, it worked. None of the creditors met any of the others. Both Shesky and Manowitz left the building that night feeling reassured, even murmuring nice things about Blue Ribbon.

Nissho left a couple hours later. By then Ito had accepted that Sumeragi was acting unilaterally, hiding invoices on his own initiative, unbeknownst to me. And he had forgiven me my sins, including my secret factory. "There are worse things," he said, "than ambition."

ONLY ONE PROBLEM remained. And it was The Problem. All else paled by comparison. The FBI.

Late the next morning Hayes and I drove downtown. We said very little in the car, very little in the elevator ride up to Nissho. We met Ito in his outer office and he said nothing. He bowed. We bowed. Then the three of us rode the elevator silently down to the ground floor and walked across the street. For the second time in a week I saw Ito as a mythic samurai, wielding a jeweled sword. But this time he was preparing to defend—me.

If only I could count on his protection when I went to jail.

We walked into the Bank of California, shoulder to shoulder, and asked to speak with Holland. A receptionist told us to have a seat.

Five minutes passed.

Ten.

Holland came out. He shook Ito's hand. He nodded to me and Hayes and led us into the conference room in the back, the same conference room where he'd lowered the boom days before. Holland said we were going to be joined by a Mr. So-and-So and a Mr. Such-and-Such. We all sat in silence and waited for Holland's cohorts to be released from whatever crypt they were kept in. Finally they arrived and sat on either side of him. No one was sure who should start. It was the ultimate high-stakes game. Only aces or better.

Ito touched his chin and decided he would open. Right away he went all in. All. Fucking. In. "Gentlemen," he said, though he was speaking only to Holland, "it is my understanding that you refuse to handle Blue Ribbon's account any longer?"

Holland nodded. "Yes, that's right, Mr. Ito."

"In that case," Ito said, "Nissho would like to pay off the debt of Blue Ribbon—in full."

Holland stared. "The *full . . . ?*"

Ito grunted. I glowered at Holland. I wanted to say, That's Japanese for: *Did I stutter?*

"Yes," Ito said. "What is the number?"

Holland wrote a number on his pad and slid the paper toward Ito, who glanced quickly down. "Yes," Ito said. "That is what your people have already told my people. And so." He opened his briefcase, removed an envelope, and slid it across the table at Holland. "Here is a check for the full amount."

"It will be deposited first thing in the morning," Holland said.

"It will be deposited *first thing today*!" Ito said.

Holland stammered. "Okay, right, today."

The cohorts looked bewildered, terrified.

Ito swiveled in his chair, took them all in with a subzero gaze. "There is one more thing," he said. "I believe your bank has been negotiating in San Francisco to become one of Nissho's banks?"

"That's right," Holland said.

"Ah. I must tell you that it will be a waste of your time to pursue those negotiations any further."

"Are you sure?" Holland asked.

"I am quite sure."

The Ice Man cometh.

I slid my eyes toward Hayes. I tried not to smile. I tried very hard. I failed.

Then I looked right at Holland. It was all there in his unblinking eyes. He knew the bank had overplayed its hand. He knew the bank's officers had overreacted. I could see, in that moment, there would be no more FBI investigation. He and the bank wanted this matter closed, over, done with. They'd treated a good customer shabbily, and they didn't want to have to answer for their actions.

We would never hear of them, or him, again.

I looked at the suits on either side of Holland. "Gentlemen," I said, standing.

Gentlemen. Sometimes that's Business-ese for: *Take your FBI and shove it.*

WHEN WE WERE all outside the bank, I bowed to Ito. I wanted to kiss him, but I only bowed. Hayes bowed, too, though for a moment I thought he was pitching forward from the stress of the last three days. "Thank you," I said to Ito. "You will never be sorry that you defended us like that."

He straightened his tie. "Such stupidity," he said.

At first I thought he was talking about me. Then I realized he meant the bank. "I do not like stupidity," he said. "People pay too much attention to numbers."

PART TWO

"No brilliant idea was ever born in a conference room," he assured the Dane. "But a lot of silly ideas have died there," said Stahr.

—F. Scott Fitzgerald, *The Last Tycoon*

1975

There was no victory party. There was no victory dance. There wasn't even a quick victory jig in the halls. There wasn't time. We still didn't have a bank, and every company needs a bank.

Hayes made a list of banks with the most deposits in Oregon. They were all much smaller than First National or Bank of California, but oh well. Beggars, choosers, etc.

The first six hung up on us. Number seven, First State Bank of Oregon, didn't. The bank was in Milwaukie, a little town half an hour up the road from Beaverton. "Come on over," said the bank president when I finally got him on the phone. He promised me one million dollars in credit, which was about his bank's limit.

We moved our account that day.

That night, for the first time in about two weeks, I put my head on a pillow and slept.

THE NEXT MORNING I lingered with Penny over breakfast and we talked about the upcoming Memorial Day weekend. I told her I didn't know when I'd craved a holiday so much. I needed rest, and sleep, and good food—and I needed to watch Pre run. She gave me a wry smile. Always mixing business with pleasure.

Guilty.

Pre was hosting a meet that weekend in Eugene, and he'd invited the top runners in the world, including his Finnish archnemesis, Viren. Though Viren had pulled out at the last minute, there was still a gang of amazing runners competing, including one brash marathoner named Frank Shorter, who'd taken gold at the 1972 Games, in Munich, the city of his birth. Tough, smart, a lawyer now living in Colorado, Shorter was starting to become as well known as Pre, and the two were good friends. Secretly I had designs on signing Shorter to an endorsement deal.

Friday night Penny and I drove down to Eugene and took our place with seven thousand screaming, roistering Pre fans. The 5,000-meter race was vicious, furious, and Pre wasn't at his best, everyone could see that. Shorter led going into the last lap. But at the last possible moment, in the last two hundred yards, Pre did what Pre always did. He dug down deep. With Hayward vibrating and swaying, he pulled away and won in 13:23.8, which was 1.6 seconds off his best time.

Pre was most famous for saying, "Somebody may beat me—but they're going to have to bleed to do it." Watching him run that final weekend of May 1975, I'd never felt more admiration for him, or identified with him more closely. Somebody may beat me, I told myself, some banker or creditor or competitor may stop me, but by God they're going to have to bleed to do it.

There was a postrace party at Hollister's house. Penny and I wanted to go, but we had a two-hour drive back to Portland. The kids, the kids, we said as we waved good-bye to Pre and Shorter and Hollister.

The next morning, just before dawn, the phone rang. In the dark I groped for it. *Hello?*

"Buck?"

"Who's this?"

"Buck, it's Ed Campbell . . . down at Bank of California."

"Bank of Cal—?"

Calling in the middle of the night? Surely I was having a bad dream. "Damn it, we don't bank with you anymore—you threw us out."

He wasn't calling about money. He was calling, he said, because he'd heard Pre was dead.

"Dead? That's impossible. We just saw him race. Last night."

Dead. Campbell kept repeating this word, bludgeoning me with it. Dead dead—*dead*. Some kind of accident, he murmured. "Buck, are you there? Buck?"

I fumbled for the light. I dialed Hollister. He reacted just as I had. No, it can't be. "Pre was just *here*," he said. "He left in fine spirits. I'll call you back."

When he did, minutes later, he was sobbing.

AS BEST ANYONE could tell, Pre drove Shorter home from the party, and minutes after dropping Shorter off he'd lost control of his car. That beautiful butterscotch MG, bought with his first Blue Ribbon paycheck, hit some kind of boulder along the road. The car spun high into the air, and Pre flew out. He landed on his back and the MG came crashing down onto his chest.

He'd had a beer or two at the party, but everyone who saw him leave swore that he'd been sober.

He was twenty-four years old. He was the exact age I'd been when I left with Carter for Hawaii. In other words, when my life began. At twenty-four I didn't yet know who I was, and Pre not only knew who he was, the world knew. He died holding every American distance record from 2,000 meters to 10,000 meters, from two miles to six miles. Of course, what he really held, what he'd captured and kept and now would never let go of, was our imaginations.

In his eulogy Bowerman talked about Pre's athletic feats, of course, but insisted that Pre's life and his legend were about larger, loftier things. Yes, Bowerman said, Pre was determined to become the best runner in the world, but he wanted to be so much more. He wanted to break the chains placed on all runners by petty bureaucrats and bean counters. He wanted to smash the silly rules holding back amateur athletes and keeping them poor, preventing them from re- alizing their potential. As Bowerman finished, as he stepped from the podium, I thought he looked much older, almost feeble. Watching him walk unsteadily back to his chair, I couldn't conceive how he'd ever found the strength to deliver those words.

Penny and I didn't follow the cortege to the cemetery. We couldn't. We were too overwrought. We didn't talk to Bowerman, either, and I don't know that I ever talked to him thereafter about Pre's death. Neither of us could bear it.

Later I heard that something was happening at the spot where Pre died. It was becoming a shrine. People were visiting it every day, leaving flowers, letters, notes, gifts—Nikes. Someone should collect it all, I thought, keep it in a safe place. I recalled the many holy sites I'd visited in 1962. Someone needed to curate Pre's rock, and I decided that someone needed to be us. We didn't have money for anything like that. But I talked it over with Johnson and Woodell and we agreed that, as long as we were in business, we'd *find* money for things like that.

1976

N ow that we'd gotten past our bank crisis, now that I was reasonably sure of not going to jail, I could go back to asking the deep questions. What are we trying to build here? What kind of company do we want to be?

Like most companies, we had role models. Sony, for instance. Sony was the Apple of its day. Profitable, innovative, efficient—and it treated its workers well. When pressed, I often said I wanted to be like Sony. At root, however, I still aimed and hoped for something bigger, and vaguer.

I would search my mind and heart and the only thing I could come up with was this word—"winning." It wasn't much, but it was far, far better than the alternative. Whatever happened, I just didn't want to lose. Losing was death. Blue Ribbon was my third child, my business child, as Sumeragi said, and I simply couldn't bear the idea of it dying. It has to live, I told myself. It just has to. That's all I know.

Several times, in those first months of 1976, I huddled with Hayes and Woodell and Strasser, and over sandwiches and sodas we'd kick around this question of ultimate goals. This question of winning and losing. Money wasn't our aim, we agreed. Money wasn't our end game. But whatever our aim or end, money was the only means to get there. More money than we had on hand.

Nissho was loaning us millions, and that relationship felt sound, solidified by the recent crisis. *Best partners you'll ever have.* Chuck Robinson had been right. But to keep up with demand, to continue growing, we needed millions more. Our new bank was loaning us money, which was good, but because they were a small bank we'd already reached their legal limit. At some point in those 1976 Woodell-Strasser-Hayes discussions we started to talk about the most logical arithmetical solution, which was also the most difficult one emotionally.

Going public.

On one level, of course, the idea made perfect sense. Going public would generate a ton of money in a flash. But it would also be highly perilous, because going public often meant losing control. It could mean working for someone else, suddenly being answerable to stockholders, hundreds or maybe thousands of strangers, many of whom would be large investment firms.

Going public could turn us overnight into the thing we loathed, the thing we'd spent our lives running from.

For me there was an added consideration, a semantic one. Defined by shyness, intensely private, I found that phrase itself off-putting: going *public*. No thank you.

And yet, during my nightly run, I'd sometimes ask myself, Hasn't your life been a kind of search for connection? Running for Bowerman, backpacking around the world, starting a company, marrying Penny, assembling this band of brothers at Blue Ribbon's core— hasn't it all been about, one way or another, going public?

In the end, however, I decided, *we* decided, going public wasn't right. It's just not for us, I said, and we said. No way. Never.

Meeting adjourned.

So we set about casting for other ways to raise money.

One way found us. First State Bank asked us to apply for a million-dollar loan, which the U.S. Small Business Administration would then guarantee. It was a loophole, a way for a small bank to gently expand its credit line, because their guaranteed-loan limits were greater than their direct-loan limits. So we did it, mainly to make their life easier.

As is always the case, the process turned out to be more complicated than it first appeared. First State Bank and the Small Business Administration required that Bowerman and I, as majority shareholders, both personally guarantee the loan. We'd done that at First National and at Bank of California, so I didn't see a problem. I was in hock up to my neck, what was one more guarantee?

Bowerman, however, balked. Retired, living on a fixed income, dispirited after the traumas of the last few years, and greatly weakened by the death of Pre, he didn't want any more risk. He feared losing his mountain.

Rather than give his personal guarantee, he offered to give me two-thirds of his stake in Blue Ribbon, at a discounted price. He was bowing out.

I didn't want this. Never mind that I didn't have the money to buy his stake, I didn't want to lose the cornerstone of my company, the anchor of my psyche. But Bowerman was adamant, and I knew better than to argue. So we both went to Jaqua and asked him to help broker the deal. Jaqua was still Bowerman's best friend, but I'd come to think of him as a close friend, too. I still trusted him completely.

Let's not fully dissolve the partnership, I said to him. Though I reluctantly agreed to buy Bowerman's stake (low payments, spread over five years), I begged him to retain a percentage, stay on as a vice president and member of our small board.

Deal, he said. We all shook hands.

WHILE WE WERE busy moving around stakes and dollars, the dollar itself was hemorrhaging value. It was all at once in a death spiral against the Japanese yen. Coupled with rising Japanese labor rates, this was now the most imminent threat to our existence. We'd increased and diversified sources of production, we'd added new factories in New England and Puerto Rico, but we were still doing nearly all our manufacturing in volatile Japan, mostly at Nippon Rubber. A sudden, crippling shortage of supply was a real possibility. Especially given the spike in demand for Bowerman's waffle trainer.

With its unique outer sole, and its pillowy midsole cushion, and its below-market price ($24.95), the waffle trainer was continuing to capture the popular imagination like no previous shoe. It didn't just feel different, or fit different—it looked different. Radically so. Bright red upper, fat white swoosh—it was a revolution in aesthetics. Its look was drawing hundreds of thousands of new customers into the Nike fold, and its performance was sealing their loyalty. It had better traction and cushioning than anything on the market.

Watching that shoe evolve in 1976 from popular accessory to cultural artifact, I had a thought. *People might start wearing this thing to class.*

And the office.

And the grocery store.

And throughout their everyday lives.

It was a rather grandiose idea. Adidas had had limited success converting athletic shoes to everyday wear, with the Stan Smith tennis shoe and the Country running shoe. But neither was nearly as distinctive, or popular, as the waffle trainer. So I ordered our factories to start making the waffle trainer in blue, which would go better with jeans, and that's when it really took off.

We couldn't make enough. Retailers and sales reps were on their knees, pleading for all the waffle trainers we could ship. The soaring pair counts were transforming our company, not to mention the industry. We were seeing numbers that redefined our long-term goals, because they gave us something we'd always lacked—an identity. More than a brand, Nike was now becoming a household word, to such an extent that we would have to change the company name.

Blue Ribbon, we decided, had run its course. We would have to incorporate as Nike, Inc.

And for this newly named entity to stay vibrant, to keep growing, to survive the declining dollar, we'd need as always to ramp up production. Sales reps on their knees—that wasn't sustainable. We'd need to find more manufacturing hubs, outside Japan. Our existing factories in America and Puerto Rico would help, but they weren't nearly enough. Too old, too few, too expensive. So in the spring of 1976 it was finally time to turn to Taiwan.

For our point man in Taiwan I looked to Jim Gorman, a valued employee, long known for his almost fanatical loyalty to Nike. Raised in a series of foster homes, Gorman seemed to find in Nike the family he'd never had, and thus he was always a good sport, always a team player. It was Gorman, for instance, who'd drawn the unpleasant task of driving Kitami to the airport, back in 1972, after that final showdown in Jaqua's conference room. And he did it without complaint. It was Gorman who'd taken over the Eugene store from Woodell, the toughest of acts to follow. It was Gorman who wore subpar Nike spikes in the 1972 Olympic Trials. In every instance, Gorman had done a fine job and never uttered a sour word. He seemed the perfect candidate to take on the latest mission impossible—Taiwan. But first I'd need to give him a crash course on Asia. So I scheduled a trip, just the two of us.

On the flight overseas Gorman proved to be an avid student, a virtual sponge. He grilled me about my experiences, my opinions, my reading, and wrote down every word I said. I felt as if I was back in school, teaching at Portland State, and I liked it. I remembered that the best way to reinforce your knowledge of a subject is to share it, so we both benefited from my transferring everything I knew about Japan, Korea, China, and Taiwan to Gorman's brain.

Shoe producers, I told him, are abandoning Japan en masse. And they're all landing in two places. Korea and Taiwan. Both countries specialize in low-priced footwear, but Korea has elected to go with a few giant factories, whereas Taiwan is building a hundred smaller ones. So that's why we're choosing Taiwan: Our demand is too high, our volume too low, for the biggest factories. And in smaller factories we'll have the dominant position. We'll be in charge.

Of course, the tougher challenge was to get any factory we chose to upgrade its quality.

And then there was the constant threat of political instability. President Chiang Kai-shek had just died, I told Gorman, and after twenty-five years in command he was leaving a nasty power vacuum.

For good measure, you always needed to account for Taiwan's ancient tensions with China.

On and on I talked as we sailed over the Pacific. While taking copious notes, Gorman also came up with new, fresh ideas, which gave me new insights, things to think about. Stepping off the plane in Taichung, our first stop, I was delighted. This guy was intense, energetic, eager to get started. I was proud to be his mentor.

Good choice, I told myself.

By the time we reached the hotel, however, Gorman was wilting. Taichung looked and smelled like the far end of the galaxy. A vast megalopolis of smoking factories, and thousands of people per square foot, it was unlike anything I'd ever seen, and I'd been all over Asia, so of course it overwhelmed poor Gorman. I saw in his eyes that typical first-timer's reaction to Asia, that look of alienation and circuit overload. He looked exactly like Penny when she met me in Japan.

Steady, I told him. Take it one day, one factory, at a time. Follow your mentor's lead.

Over the next week we visited and toured about two dozen factories. Most were bad. Dark, dirty, with workers going through the motions, heads bowed, vacant looks in their eyes. Just outside Taichung, however, in the small town of Douliou, we found a factory that showed promise. It was called Feng Tay, and it was managed by a young man named C. H. Wong. Small, but clean, it had a positive vibe, as did Wong, a shoe dog who lived for his workplace. And in it. When we noticed that one small room off the factory floor was off-limits, I asked what was in there. Home, he said. "That is where my wife and I and our three kids live."

I was reminded of Johnson. I decided to make Feng Tay the cornerstone of our Taiwan effort.

When we weren't touring factories, Gorman and I were being feted by factory owners. They stuffed us with local delicacies, some of which were actually cooked, and plied us with something called a Mao tai, which was a mai tai, but apparently with shoe cream instead of rum. Jet-lagged, Gorman and I both had lost our tolerance. After two Mao tais we were potted. We tried to slow down, but our hosts kept raising their glasses.

To Nike!

To America!

At the final dinner of our Taichung visit Gorman repeatedly excused himself and ran to the men's room, to splash cold water on his face. Every time he left the table I got rid of my Mao tai by pouring it into his water glass. Each time he returned from the men's room there was another toast, and Gorman thought he was playing it safe by raising his water glass.

To our American friends!

To our Taiwanese friends!

After another huge gulp of spiked water, Gorman looked at me, panic-stricken. "I think I'm going to pass out," he said.

"Have some more water," I said.

"Tastes funny."

"Nah."

Despite offloading my booze onto Gorman, I was woozy when I got back to my room. I had trouble getting ready for bed. I had trouble finding the bed. I fell asleep while brushing my teeth. Midbrush.

I woke sometime later and tried to find my extra contact lenses. I found them. Then dropped them on the floor.

There was a knock. Gorman. He walked in and asked me something about our next day's itinerary. He found me on my hands and knees, searching for my contact lenses in a pool of my own sick.

"Phil, you okay?"

"Follow your mentor's lead," I mumbled.

THAT MORNING WE flew to Taipei, the capital, and toured a couple more factories. In the evening we strolled Xinsheng South Road, with its dozens of shrines and temples, churches and mosques. The Road to Heaven, locals called it. Indeed, I told Gorman, Xinsheng means "New Life." When we returned to our hotel I got a strange and unexpected phone call. Jerry Hsieh—pronounced Shay—was "paying his respects."

I'd met Hsieh before. In one of the shoe factories I'd visited the year before. He was working for Mitsubishi and the great Jonas Senter. He'd impressed me with his intensity and work ethic. And youth. Unlike all the other shoe dogs I'd met, he was young, twenty-something, and looked much younger. Like an overgrown toddler.

He said he'd heard we were in the country. Then, like a CIA operative, he added: "I know why you are here . . ."

He invited us to visit him in his office, an invitation that seemed to indicate he was now working for himself, not Mitsubishi.

I wrote down Hsieh's office address and grabbed Gorman. The concierge at our hotel drew us a map—which proved useless. Hsieh's office was in an unmapped part of the city. The worst part. Gorman and I walked down a series of unmarked lanes, up a series of unnumbered alleys. Do you see a street sign? I can barely see the street.

We must have gotten lost a dozen times. Finally, there it was. A stout building of old red brick. Inside we found a precarious staircase. The handrail came off in our hands as we walked up to the third floor, and each stone step had a deep indentation, from contact with a million shoes.

"Enter!" Hsieh shouted when we knocked. We found him sitting in the middle of a room that looked like the nest of a giant rat. Everywhere we looked were shoes, and more shoes, and piles of shoe pieces—soles and laces and tongues. Hsieh jumped to his feet, cleared a space for us to sit. He offered us tea. Then, while the water boiled, he began educating us. *Did you know that every country in the world has many many customs and superstitions about shoes?* He grabbed a shoe from a shelf, held it before our faces. *Did you know that in China, when man marries woman, they throw red shoes on the roof to make sure all goes well on wedding night?* He rotated the shoe in the scant daylight that managed to fight through the grime on his windows. He told us which factory it came from, why he thought it was well made, how it could have been made better. *Did you know that in many countries, when someone starts on a journey, it's actually good luck to throw a shoe at them?* He grabbed another shoe, extended it like Hamlet holding Yorick's skull. He identified its provenance, told us why it was poorly made, why it would soon fall apart, then tossed it aside with disdain. The difference from one shoe to another, he said, nine times out of ten, is the factory. Forget design, forget color, forget all the other things that go into a shoe, it's all about factories.

I listened closely, and took notes, like Gorman on the plane, though the whole time I was thinking: It's a performance. He's putting on a show, trying to sell us. He doesn't realize that we need him more than he needs us.

Now Hsieh went into his pitch. He told us that in exchange for a small fee he'd gladly connect us with the very best factories in Taiwan.

This had the potential to be big. We could use someone on the ground, to pave our way, to make introductions, to help Gorman acclimate. An Asian Giampietro. We haggled over commission per pair, for a few minutes, but it was a friendly haggling. Then we shook hands.

Deal? Deal.

We sat down again and drew up an agreement to establish a Taiwan-based subcompany. What to call it? I didn't want to use Nike. If we ever wanted to do business in the People's Republic of China, we couldn't be associated with China's sworn enemy. It was a faint hope, at best, an impossible dream. But still. So I picked Athena. The Greek goddess who brings *nike*. Athena Corp. And thus I preserved the unmapped, unnumbered Road to Heaven. Or a shoe dog's idea of heaven.

A country with two billion feet.

I SENT GORMAN home ahead of me. Before leaving Asia, I told him, I needed to make one quick stop in Manila. Personal errand, I said vaguely.

I went to Manila to visit a shoe factory, a very good one. Then, closing an old loop, I spent the night in MacArthur's suite.

You are remembered for the rules you break.

Maybe.

Maybe not.

IT WAS THE Bicentennial Year, that strange moment in America's cultural history, that 365-day lollapalooza of self-examination and civics lessons and seminightly fireworks. From January 1 to December 31 of that year, you couldn't change the channel without hitting upon a movie or documentary about George Washington or Ben Franklin or Lexington and Concord. And invariably, embedded in the patriotic programming, there would be yet another "Bicentennial Minute," a public service announcement in which Dick Van Dyke or Lucille Ball or Gabe Kaplan would recount some episode that took place on this date during the Revolutionary era. One night it might be Jessica Tandy talking about the felling of the Liberty Tree. The next night it might be President Gerald Ford exhorting all Americans to "keep the Spirit of '76 alive." It was all somewhat corny, a little bit sentimental—and immensely moving. The yearlong swell of patriotism brought out an already strong love of country in me. Tall ships sailing into New York Harbor, recitations of the Bill of Rights and Declaration of Independence, fervent talk of liberty and justice—it all refreshed my gratitude about being an American. And being free. And not being in jail.

AT THE 1976 Olympic Trials, held again that June in Eugene, Nike had a chance, a fantastic chance, to make a good show. We'd never had that chance with Tiger, whose spikes weren't top caliber. We'd never had that chance with the first generation of Nike products. Now, at last, we had our own stuff, and it was really good: top-quality marathon shoes and spikes. We were buzzing with excitement as we left Portland. Finally, we said, we're going to have a Nike-shod runner make an Olympic team.

It was going to happen.

It needed to happen.

Penny and I drove to Eugene, where we met up with Johnson, who was photographing the event. Despite our excitement about the trials, we talked most about Pre as we took our seats in the packed bleachers. It was clear that Pre was on everyone else's mind, too. We heard his name coming from every direction, and his spirit seemed to hover like the low clouds roiling above the track. And if you were tempted to forget him, even for a moment, you got another bracing reminder when you looked at the runners' feet. Many were wearing Pre Montreals. (Many more were wearing Exeter-made products like the Triumph and the Vainqueur. Hayward that day looked like a Nike showroom.) It was well known that these trials would have been the start of Pre's epic comeback. After being knocked down in Munich, he'd have risen again, no doubt, and the rising would have begun right here, right now. Each race prompted the same thoughts, the same image: Pre bursting ahead of the pack.

Pre diving through the tape. We could *see* it. We could *see* him flush with victory.

If only, we kept saying, our voices choking, if only.

At sunset the sky turned red, white, and a deep blackish blue. But it was still bright enough to read by as the runners in the 10,000 meters gathered at the starting line. Penny and I tried to clear our minds as we stood, hands clasped as if in prayer. We were counting on Shorter, of course. He was extremely talented, and he'd been the last person to see Pre alive—it made sense that he'd be the one to carry Pre's torch. But we also had Nikes on Craig Virgin, a brilliant young runner from the University of Illinois, and on Garry Bjork-lund, a lovable veteran from Minnesota, who was trying to come back from surgery to remove a loose bone in his foot.

The gun went off, the runners shot forward, all bunched tight, and Penny and I were bunched tight, too, oohing and aahing with every stride. There wasn't an inch of separation in the pack until the halfway mark, when Shorter and Virgin violently pushed ahead. In the jostling, Virgin accidentally stepped on Bjorklund and sent his Nike flying. Now Bjorklund's tender, surgically repaired foot was bare, exposed, smacking the hard track with every stride. And yet Bjorklund didn't stop. He didn't falter. He didn't even slow down. He just kept running, faster and faster, and that blazing show of courage won over the crowd. I think we cheered for him as loudly as we'd cheered for Pre the year before.

Entering the final lap, Shorter and Virgin were in front. Penny and I were jumping up and down. "We're going to get two," we said, "we're going to get two!" And then we got three. Shorter and Virgin took first and second, and Bjorklund plunged ahead of Bill Rodgers at the tape to take third. I was covered with sweat. Three Olympians . . . in Nikes!

The next morning, rather than take a victory lap at Hayward, we set up camp at the Nike store. While Johnson and I mingled with customers, Penny manned the silk-screen machine and churned out Nike T-shirts. Her craftsmanship was exquisite; all day long people came in to say they'd seen someone wearing a Nike T-shirt on the street and they just had to have one for themselves. Despite our continual melancholy about Pre, we allowed ourselves to feel joy, because it was becoming clear that Nike was doing more than making a good show. Nike was dominating those trials. Virgin took the 5,000 meters in Nikes. Shorter won the marathon in Nikes. Slowly, in the shop, in the town, we heard people whispering, *Nike Nike Nike*. We heard our name more than the name of any athlete. Besides Pre.

Saturday afternoon, walking into Hayward to visit Bowerman, I heard someone behind me say, "Jeez, Nike is *really* kicking Adidas's ass." It might have been the highlight of the weekend, of the year, followed closely by the Puma sales rep I spotted moments later, leaning against a tree and looking suicidal.

Bowerman was there strictly as a spectator, which was strange for him, and us. And yet he was wearing his standard uniform: the ratty sweater, the low ball cap. At one point he formally requested a meeting in a small office under the east grandstand. The office wasn't really an office, more like a closet, where the groundskeepers stored their rakes and brooms and a few canvas chairs. There was barely room for the coach and Johnson and me, never mind the others invited by the coach: Hollister, and Dennis Vixie, a local podiatrist who worked with Bowerman as a shoe consultant. As we shut the door I noticed Bowerman didn't look like himself. At Pre's funeral he'd seemed old. Now he seemed lost. After a minute of small talk he started bellowing. He complained that he wasn't getting any "respect" anymore from Nike. We'd built him a home lab, and supplied him with a lasting machine, but he said that he was constantly asking in vain for raw materials from Exeter.

Johnson looked horrified. "What materials?" he asked.

"I ask for shoe uppers and my requests are ignored!" Bowerman said.

Johnson turned to Vixie. "I sent you the uppers!" he said. "Vixie—didn't you get them?"

Vixie looked perplexed. "Yes, I got them."

Bowerman took off his ball cap, put it back on, took it off. "Yeah, well," he grumbled, "but you didn't send the *outer soles*."

Johnson's face reddened. "I sent those, too! Vixie?"

"Yes," Vixie said, "we got them."

Now we all turned to Bowerman, who was pacing, or trying to. There was no room. The office was dark, but I could still tell that my old coach's face was turning red. "Well . . . we didn't get them on time!" he shouted, and the tines of the rakes trembled. This wasn't about uppers and outer soles. This was about retirement. And time. Like Pre, time wouldn't *listen* to Bowerman. Time wouldn't *slow down*. "I'm not going to put up with this bullshit anymore," he huffed, and stormed out, leaving the door swinging open.

I looked at Johnson and Vixie and Hollister. They all looked at me. It didn't matter if Bowerman was right or wrong, we'd just have to find a way to make him feel needed and useful. If Bowerman isn't happy, I said, Nike isn't happy.

A FEW MONTHS later, muggy Montreal was the setting for Nike's grand debut, our Olympic coming-out party. As those 1976 Games opened, we had athletes in several high-profile events wearing Nikes. But our highest hopes, and most of our money, were pinned on Shorter. He was the favorite to win gold, which meant that Nikes, for the first time ever, were going to cross an Olympic finish line ahead of all other shoes. This was an enormous rite of passage for a running-shoe company. You really weren't a legitimate, card-carrying running-shoe company until an Olympian ascended to the top medal stand in your gear.

I woke up early that Saturday—July 31, 1976. Right after my morning coffee I took up my position in my recliner. I had a sandwich at my elbow, cold sodas in the fridge. I wondered if Kitami was watching. I wondered if my former bankers were watching. I wondered if my parents and sisters were watching. I wondered if the FBI was watching.

The runners approached the starting line. With them I crouched forward. I probably had as much adrenaline in my system as Shorter had in his. I waited for the pistol, and for the inevitable close-up of Shorter's feet. The camera zoomed in. I stopped breathing. I slid out of my recliner onto the floor and crawled toward the TV screen. No, I said. No, I cried out in anguish. "No. NO!"

He was wearing . . . *Tigers*.

I watched in horror as the great hope of Nike took off in the shoes of our enemy.

I stood, walked back to my recliner, and watched the race unfold, talking to myself, mumbling to myself. Slowly the house grew dark. Not dark enough to suit me. At some point I drew the curtains, turned off the lights. But not the TV. I would watch, all two hours and ten minutes, to the bitter end.

I'm still not sure I know exactly what happened. Apparently, Shorter became convinced that his Nike shoes were fragile and wouldn't hold up for the whole twenty-six miles. (Never mind that they'd performed perfectly well at the Olympic Trials.) Maybe it was nerves. Maybe it was superstition. He wanted to use what he'd always used. Runners are funny that way. In any case, at the last moment he switched back to the shoes that he wore when he won the gold in 1972.

And I switched from soda to vodka. Sitting in the dark, clutching a cocktail, I told myself it was no big deal, in the grand scheme of things. Shorter didn't even win. An East German surprised him and took the gold. Of course I was lying to myself, it was a very big deal, and not because of the disappointment or the lost marketing oppor-tunity. If watching Shorter go off in shoes other than mine could affect me so deeply, it was now official: Nike was more than just a shoe. I no longer simply made Nikes; Nikes were making me. If I saw an athlete choose another shoe, if I saw anyone choose another shoe, it wasn't just a rejection of the brand alone, but of me. I told myself to be reasonable, not everyone in the world was going to wear Nike. And I won't say that I became upset every time I saw someone walking down the street in a running shoe that wasn't mine.

But it definitely registered.

And I didn't care for it.

At some point that night I phoned Hollister. He was devastated, too. There was raw anger in his voice. I was glad. I wanted people working for me who would feel that same burn, that same gut-punch rejection.

Happily, there were fewer such rejections all the time. At the close of fiscal 1976 we doubled our sales—$14 million. A startling number, which financial analysts noted, and wrote about. And yet we were still cash-poor. I kept borrowing every nickel I could, plowing it into growth, with the explicit or tacit blessing of people I trusted. Woodell, Strasser, Hayes.

In early 1976 the four of us had talked tentatively about going public, and tabled the idea. Now, at the close of 1976, we took up the idea again, more seriously. We analyzed the risks, weighed the cons, considered the pros. Again we decided: No.

Sure, sure, we said, we'd love to have that quick infusion of capital. Oh, the things we could do with that money! The factories we could lease! The talent we could hire! But going public would change our culture, make us beholden, make us corporate. That's not our play, we all agreed.

Weeks later, strapped for money again, our bank accounts at zero, we took another look at the idea.

And rejected it again.

Wanting to settle the matter once and for all, I put the subject at the top of the agenda for our biannual gathering, a retreat we'd taken to calling the Buttface.

* * *

JOHNSON COINED THE phrase, we think. At one of our earliest retreats he muttered: "How many multimillion-dollar companies can you yell out, 'Hey, Buttface,' and the entire management team turns around?" It got a laugh. And then it stuck. And then it became a key part of our vernacular. Buttface referred to both the retreat and the retreaters, and it not only captured the informal mood of those retreats, where no idea was too sacred to be mocked, and no person was too important to be ridiculed, it also summed up the company spirit, mission and ethos.

The first few Buttfaces took place at various Oregon resorts. Otter Crest. Salishan. Ultimately we came to prefer Sunriver, an idyllic spot in sunny central Oregon. Typically, Woodell and Johnson would fly out from the East Coast, and we'd all drive out to Sunriver late Friday. We'd reserve a bunch of cabins, seize a conference room, and spend two or three days shouting ourselves hoarse.

I can see myself so clearly at the head of a conference table, shouting, being shouted at—laughing until my voice was gone. The problems confronting us were grave, complex, seemingly insurmountable, made more so by the fact we were separated from each other by three thousand miles, at a time when communication wasn't easy or instant. And yet we were always laughing. Sometimes, after a really cathartic guffaw, I'd look around the table and feel overcome by emotion. Camaraderie, loyalty, gratitude. Even love. Surely love. But I also remember feeling shocked that *these* were the men I'd assembled. These were the founding fathers of a multimillion-dollar company that sold *athletic* shoes? A paralyzed guy, two morbidly obese guys, a chain-smoking guy? It was bracing to realize that, in this group, the one with whom I had the most in common was . . . Johnson. And yet, it was undeniable. While everyone else was laughing, rioting, he'd be the sane one, sitting quietly in the middle of the table reading a book.

The loudest voice at every Buttface always seemed to be Hayes.

And the craziest. Like his girth, his personality was ever expanding, adding new phobias and enthusiasms. For instance, by this time Hayes had developed a curious obsession with heavy equipment. Backhoes, bulldozers, cherry pickers, cranes, they fascinated him. They . . . turned him on, there's no other way to say it. At an early Buttface we were leaving a local bar when Hayes spied a bulldozer in the field behind the lodge. He discovered, to his astonishment, the keys had been left inside, so he hopped in and moved the earth all around the field, and in the parking lot, quitting only when he narrowly missed crushing several cars. Hayes on a bulldozer, I thought: As much as the swoosh, *that* might be our logo.

I always said that Woodell made the trains run on time, but it was Hayes who laid down the tracks. Hayes set up all the esoteric accounting systems without which the company would have ground to a halt. When we first went from manual to automated accounting, Hayes acquired the first primitive machines, and by constantly mending them, modifying them, or pounding them with his big hammy fists, he kept them uncannily accurate. When we first started doing business outside the United States, foreign currencies became a devilishly tricky problem, and Hayes set up an ingenious currency-hedging system, which made the spread more reliable, more predictable.

Despite our hijinks, despite our eccentricities, despite our physical limitations, I concluded in 1976 that we were a formidable team. (Years later a famous Harvard business professor studying Nike came to the same conclusion. "Normally," he said, "if one manager at a company can think tactically *and* strategically, that company has a good future. But boy are you lucky: More than half the Buttfaces think that way!")

Undoubtedly we looked, to any casual observer, like a sorry, motley crew, hopelessly mismatched. But in fact we were more alike than different, and that gave a coherence to our goals and our efforts. We were mostly Oregon guys, which was important. We had an inborn need to prove ourselves, to show the world that we weren't hicks and hayseeds. And we were nearly all merciless self-loathers, which kept the egos in check. There was none of that smartest-guy-in-the-room foolishness. Hayes, Strasser, Woodell, Johnson, each would have been the smartest guy in any room, but none believed it of himself, or the next guy. Our meetings were defined by contempt, disdain, and heaps of abuse.

Oh, what abuse. We called each other terrible names. We rained down verbal blows. While floating ideas, and shooting down ideas, and hashing out threats to the company, the last thing we took into account was someone's feelings. Including mine. Especially mine. My fellow Buttfaces, my employees, called me Bucky the Bookkeeper, constantly. I never asked them to stop. I knew better. If you showed any weakness, any sentimentality, you were dead.

I remember a Buttface when Strasser decided we weren't being "aggressive" enough in our approach. Too many bean counters in this company, he said. "So before this meeting starts I want to interject something. I've prepared here a *counter* budget." He waved a big binder. "This right here is what we should be doing with our money."

Of course everyone wanted to see his numbers, but no one more than the numbers guy, Hayes. When we discovered that the numbers didn't add up, not one column, we started howling.

Strasser took it personally. "It's the essence I'm getting at," he said. "Not the specifics. The *essence*."

The howling grew louder. So Strasser picked up his binder and threw it against the wall. "Fuck all you guys," he said. The binder burst open, pages flew everywhere, and the laughter was deafening. Even Strasser couldn't help himself. He had to join in.

Little wonder that Strasser's nickname was Rolling Thunder. Hayes, meanwhile, was Doomsday. Woodell was Weight. (As in Dead Weight.) Johnson was Four Factor, because he tended to exaggerate and therefore everything he said needed to be divided by four. No one took it personally. The only thing truly not tolerated at a Buttface was a thin skin.

And sobriety. At day's end, when everybody had a scratchy throat from all the abusing and laughing and problem-solving, when our yellow legal pads were filled with ideas, solutions, quotations, and lists upon lists, we'd shift ground to the bar at the lodge and continue the meeting over drinks. Many drinks.

The bar was called the Owl's Nest. I love to close my eyes and remember us storming through the entrance, scattering all other patrons. Or making friends of them. We'd buy drinks for the house, then commandeer a corner and continue laying into each other about some problem or idea or harebrained scheme. Say the problem was midsoles not getting from Point A to Point B. Round and round we'd go, everyone speaking at once, a chorale of name-calling and finger-pointing, all made louder, and funnier, and somehow clearer, by the booze. To anyone in the Owl's Nest, to anyone in the corporate world, it would have looked inefficient, inappropriate. Even scandalous. But before the bartender gave last call, we'd know full well *why* those midsoles weren't getting from Point A to Point B, and the person responsible would be contrite, and put on notice, and we'd have ourselves a creative solution.

The only person who didn't join us in these late-night revels was Johnson. He'd typically go for a head-clearing run, then retreat to his room and read in bed. I don't think he ever set foot in the Owl's Nest. Or knew where it was. We'd always have to spend the first part of the next morning updating him on what we'd decided in his absence.

In the Bicentennial Year alone we were struggling with a number of unusually stressful problems. We needed to find a larger warehouse on the East Coast. We needed to transfer our sales-distribution center, from Holliston, Massachusetts, to a new forty-thousand-square-foot space in Greenland, New Hampshire, which was sure to be a logistical nightmare. We needed to hire an advertising agency to handle the increasing volume of print ads. We needed to either fix or get shut of our underperforming factories. We needed to smooth out glitches in our Futures Program. We needed to hire a director of promotions. We needed to form a Pro Club, a sort of reward system for our top NBA stars, to cement their loyalty and keep them in the Nike fold. We needed to approve new products, like the Arsenal, a soccer-baseball cleat with leather upper and vinyl poly-foam tongue, and the Striker, a multipurpose cleat good for soccer, baseball, football, softball, and field hockey. And we needed to decide on a new logo. Aside from the swoosh, we had a lowercase script name, *nike*, which was problematic—too many people thought it was *like*, or *mike*. But it was too late in the day to change the name of the company, so making the letters more readable seemed a good idea. Denny Strickland, creative director at our advertising agency, had designed a block-lettered NIKE, all caps, and nested it inside a swoosh. We spent days considering it, debating it.

Above all, we needed to decide, once and for all, this "going public" question. In those earliest Buttfaces, a consensus began to form. If we couldn't sustain growth, we couldn't survive. And despite our fears, despite the risks and downsides, going public was the best way to sustain growth.

And yet, in the midst of those intense discussions, in the middle of one of the most trying years in the company's history, those Buttface meetings were nothing but a joy. Of all those hours spent at Sunriver, not one minute felt like work. It was us against the world, and we felt damned sorry for the world. That is, when we weren't righteously pissed off at it. Each of us had been misunderstood, misjudged, dismissed. Shunned by bosses, spurned by luck, rejected by society, shortchanged by fate when looks and other natural graces were handed out. We'd each been forged by early failure. We'd each given ourselves to some quest, some attempt at validation or meaning, and fallen short.

Hayes couldn't become a partner because he was too fat.

Johnson couldn't cope in the so-called normal world of nine-to-five.

Strasser was an insurance lawyer who hated insurance—and lawyers.

Woodell lost all his youthful dreams in one fluke accident.

I got cut from the baseball team. And I got my heart broken.

I identified with the born loser in each Buttface, and vice versa, and I knew that together we could become winners. I still didn't know exactly what winning meant, other than not losing, but we seemed to be getting closer to a defining moment when that question would be settled, or at least more sharply defined. Maybe going public would be that moment.

Maybe going public would finally ensure that Nike would live on.

If I had any doubts about Blue Ribbon's management team in 1976, they were mainly about me. Was I doing right by the Buttfaces, giving them so little guidance? When they did well I'd shrug and deliver my highest praise: Not bad. When they erred I'd yell for a minute or two, then shake it off. None of the Buttfaces felt the least threatened by me—was that a good thing? *Don't tell people how to do things, tell them what to do and let them surprise you with their results.* It was the right tack for Patton and his GIs. But did that make it right for a bunch of Buttfaces? I worried. Maybe I should be more hands-on. Maybe we should be more structured.

But then I'd think: Whatever I'm doing, it must be working, because mutinies are few. In fact, ever since Bork, no one had thrown a genuine tantrum, about anything, not even what they were paid, which is unheard of in any company, big or small. The Buttfaces knew I wasn't paying myself much, and they trusted that I was paying them what I could.

Clearly the Buttfaces liked the culture I'd created. I trusted them, wholly, and didn't look over their shoulders, and that bred a powerful two-way loyalty. My management style wouldn't have worked for people who wanted to be guided, every step, but this group found it liberating, empowering. I let them be, let them do, let them make their own mistakes, because that's how I'd always liked people to treat me.

At the end of a Buttface weekend, consumed with these and other thoughts, I'd drive back to Portland in a trance. Halfway there I'd come out of the trance and start thinking about Penny and the boys. The Buttfaces were like family, but every minute I spent with them was at the cost of my other family, my real family. The guilt was palpable. Often I'd walk into my house and Matthew and Travis would meet me at the door. "Where have you been?" they'd ask. "Daddy was with his friends," I'd say, picking them up. They'd stare, confused. "But Mommy told us you were working."

It was around this time, as Nike rolled out its first children's shoes, Wally Waffle and Robbie Road Racer, that Matthew announced he would never wear Nikes so long as he lived. His way of expressing anger about my absences, as well as other frustrations. Penny tried to make him understand that Daddy wasn't absent by choice. Daddy was trying to build something. Daddy was trying to ensure that he and Travis would one day be able to attend college.

I didn't even bother to explain. I told myself it didn't matter what I said. Matthew never understood, and Travis always understood—they seemed born with these unvarying default positions. Matthew seemed to harbor some innate resentment toward me, while Travis seemed congenitally devoted. What difference would a few more words make? What difference would a few more hours make?

My fatherhood style, my management style. I was forever questioning, Is it good—or merely good enough?

Time and again I'd vow to change. Time and again I'd tell myself: *I will spend more time with the boys.* Time and again I'd keep that promise—for a while. Then I'd fall back to my former routine, the only way I knew. Not hands-off. But not hands-on.

This might have been the one problem I couldn't solve by brainstorming with my fellow Buttfaces. Vastly trickier than how to get midsoles from Point A to Point B was the question of Son A and Son B, how to keep them happy, while keeping Son C, Nike, afloat.

1977

His name was M. Frank Rudy, he was a former aerospace engineer, and he was a true original. One look at him told you he was a nutty professor, though it wasn't until years later that I learned the full extent of his nuttiness. (He kept a meticulous diary of his sex life and bowel movements.) He had a business partner, Bob Bogert, another brainiac, and they had a Crazy Idea, and together they were going to pitch us—that's the sum total of what I knew that morning in March 1977 as we settled around the conference table. I wasn't even sure how these guys reached us, or how they'd arranged this meeting.

"Okay, fellas," I said, "what've you got?"

It was a beautiful day, I remember. The light outside the room was a buttery pale yellow, and the sky was blue for the first time in months, so I was distracted, a little spring feverish, as Rudy leaned his weight on the edge of the conference table and smiled. "Mr. Knight, we've come up with a way to inject . . . *air* . . . into a running shoe."

I frowned and dropped my pencil. "Why?" I said.

"For greater cushioning," he said. "For greater support. For the ride of a *lifetime*."

I stared. "You're kidding me, right?"

I'd heard a lot of silliness from a lot of different people in the shoe business, but this. Oh. Brother.

Rudy handed me a pair of soles that looked as if they'd been teleported from the twenty-second century. Big, clunky, they were clear thick plastic and inside were—bubbles? I turned them over. "Bubbles?" I said.

"Pressurized air bags," he said.

I set down the soles and gave Rudy a closer look, a full head-to-toe. Six-three, lanky, with unruly dark hair, bottle-bottom glasses, a lopsided grin, and a severe vitamin D deficiency, I thought. Not enough sunshine. Or else a long-lost member of the Addams Family.

He saw me appraising him, saw my skepticism, and wasn't the least fazed. He walked to the blackboard, picked up a piece of chalk, and began writing numbers, symbols, equations. He explained at some length why an air shoe would work, why it would never go flat, why it was the Next Big Thing. When he finished I stared at the blackboard. As a trained accountant I'd spent a good part of my life looking at blackboards, but this Rudy fella's scribbles were something else. Indecipherable.

Humans have been wearing shoes since the Ice Age, I said, and the underlying design hasn't changed all that much in forty thousand years. There hadn't really been a breakthrough since the late 1800s, when cobblers started lasting left and right shoes differently, and rubber companies started making soles. It didn't seem all too likely that, at this late date in history, something so new, so revolutionary, was going to be dreamed up. "Air shoes" sounded to me like jet packs and moving sidewalks. Comic book stuff.

Rudy still wasn't discouraged. He kept at it, unflappable, earnest. Finally he shrugged and said that he understood. He'd tried to pitch Adidas and they'd been skeptical, too. Abracadabra. That was all I needed to hear.

I asked if I could fit his air soles into my running shoes and give them a try. "They don't have a moderator," he said. "They'd be loose and wobbly."

"I don't care about that," I said.

I squeezed the soles into my shoes, slipped the shoes back on, laced them up. Not bad, I said, bouncing up and down.

SHOE DOG

I went for a six-mile run. They were indeed unstable. But they were also one heck of a ride.

I ran back to the office. Still covered with sweat, I ran straight up to Strasser and told him: "I think we might have something here."

THAT NIGHT STRASSER and I went to dinner with Rudy and Bogert. Rudy explained more of the science behind the air soles, and this second time around it started to make sense. I told him there was a possibility we could do business. Then I turned it over to Strasser to close.

I'd hired Strasser for his legal mind, but by 1977 I'd discovered his true talent. Negotiating. The first few times I asked him to work out a contract with sports agents, the toughest negotiators in the world, he more than held his own. I was amazed. So were the agents. Every time, Strasser walked away with more than we'd ever hoped. No one scared him, no one matched him in a clash of wills. By 1977 I was sending him into every negotiation with total confidence, as if I were sending in the Eighty-Second Airborne.

His secret, I think, was that he just didn't care what he said or how he said it or how it went over. He was totally honest, a radical tactic in any negotiation. I recall one tug-of-war Strasser had over Elvin Hayes, the Washington Bullets all-star, whom we badly wanted to sign again. Elvin's agent told Strasser, "You should give Elvin your whole damn company!"

Strasser yawned. "You want it? Help yourself. We've got ten grand in the bank.

"Final offer, take it or leave it."

The agent took it.

Now, seeing great potential in these "air soles," Strasser offered Rudy ten cents for every pair of soles that we sold, and Rudy demanded twenty, and after weeks of haggling they settled somewhere in the middle. We then shipped Rudy and his partner back to Exeter, which was becoming our de facto Research and Development Department.

Of course, when Johnson met Rudy, he did exactly what I'd done. He slipped some air soles into his running shoes and trotted six brisk miles, after which he phoned me. "This could be huge," he said.

"That's what I thought," I said.

But Johnson worried that the bubble would cause friction. His foot felt hot, he said. He had the start of a blister. He suggested putting air in the midsole as well, to level out the ride. "Don't tell me," I said, "tell your new roommate, Mr. Rudy."

FRESH OFF HIS successful closing with Rudy, we gave Strasser another critical assignment. Sign college basketball coaches. Nike had a solid stable of NBA players, and sales of basketball shoes were rising briskly, but we had virtually no college teams. Not even the University of Oregon. Unthinkable.

The coach, Dick Harter, told us in 1975 that he'd left the decision up to his players, and the team vote was 6–6. So the team stayed with Converse.

The next year the team voted for Nike, 9–3, but Harter said it was still too close, so he was staying with Converse.

What the?

I told Hollister to lobby the players steadily over the next twelve months. Which he did. And the 1977 vote was 12–0 for Nike.

The next day I met Harter in Jaqua's office, and he told us he still wasn't ready to sign.

Why not?

"Where's my twenty-five hundred dollars?" he said.

"Ah," I said. "Now I get it."

I mailed Harter a check. At last my Ducks would wear Nikes on the hardboards.

At almost this same odd moment in time, a second strange shoe inventor showed up on our doorstep. His name was Sonny Vaccaro, and he was just as unique as Frank Rudy. Short, round, with constantly darting eyes, he spoke in a soupy voice with an Americanized Italian accent, or an Italianized American accent, I couldn't place it. He was a shoe dog, for sure, but a shoe dog straight out of *The Godfather*. When he first arrived at Nike he carried with him several shoes of his own invention, which set off gales of laughter around the conference room. The guy was no Rudy. And yet in the course of conversation he claimed to be chummy with every college basketball coach in the country. Somehow, years before, he'd founded a popular high school all-star game, the Dapper Dan Classic, and it was a big hit, and through it he'd gotten to know all the coaching royalty.

"Okay," I told him, "you're hired. You and Strasser hit the road, go out and see if you can crack that college basketball market."

All the great basketball schools—UCLA, Indiana, North Carolina, and so on—had long-standing deals with Adidas or Converse. So who was left? And what could we offer? We hurriedly dreamed up an "Advisory Board," another version of our Pro Club, our NBA reward system—but it was small beer. I fully expected Strasser and Vaccaro to fail. And I expected to see neither of them for a year, at least.

One month later Strasser was standing in my office, beaming. And shouting. And ticking off names. Eddie Sutton, Arkansas! Abe Lemmons, Texas! Jerry Tarkanian, UNLV! Frank McGuire, South Carolina! (I leaped out of my chair. McGuire was a legend: He'd defeated Wilt Chamberlain's Kansas team to win the national championship for North Carolina.) We hit pay dirt, Strasser said.

Plus, almost as a throw-in, he mentioned two under-the-radar youngsters: Jim Valvano at Iona and John Thompson at Georgetown.

(A year or two later he did the same thing with college football coaches, landing all the greats, including Vince Dooley and his national champion Georgia Bulldogs. Herschel Walker in Nikes—yes.)

We rushed out a press release, announcing that Nike had these schools under contract. Alas, the press release had a bad typo. Iona was spelled "Iowa." Lute Olson, coach at Iowa, phoned immediately. He was irate. We apologized and said we'd send a correction the next day.

He got quiet. "Well now wait wait," he said, "what's this *Advisory Board* anyway . . . ?"

The Harter Rule, in full effect.

OTHER ENDORSEMENTS WERE a greater struggle. Our tennis effort had started so promisingly, with Nastase, but then we'd hit that speed-bump with Connors, and now Nastase was dumping us. Adidas had offered him one hundred thousand dollars a year, including shoes, clothes, and rackets. We had the right to match, but it was out of the question. "Fiscally irresponsible," I said to Nasty's agent, and everyone else who would listen. "No one will ever see a sports endorsement deal that big ever again!"

So there we were in 1977 without a horse in tennis. We quickly hired a local pro to be a consultant, and that summer he and I went to Wimbledon. On our first day in London we met with a group of American tennis officials. "We've got some great young players," they said. "Elliot Telscher may be the best. Gottfried is also outstanding. Whatever you do, just stay away from the kid playing out on Court 14."

"Why?"

"He's a hothead."

I went straight to Court 14. And fell madly, hopelessly in love with a frizzy-haired high schooler from New York City named John McEnroe.

AT THE SAME time we were signing deals with athletes and coaches and nutty professors, we were coming out with the LD 1000, a running shoe that featured a dramatically flared heel. The heel flared so much, in fact, that from certain angles it looked like a water ski.

The theory was that a flared heel would lessen torque on the leg and reduce pressure on the knee, thus lowering the risk of tendinitis and other running-related maladies. Bowerman designed it, with heavy input from Vixie the podiatrist. Customers loved it.

At first. Then came the issues. If a runner didn't land just right, the flared heel could cause pronation, knee problems, or worse. We issued a recall and braced ourselves for a public backlash—but it never came. On the contrary, we heard nothing but gratitude. No other shoe company was trying new things, so our efforts, successful or not, were seen as noble. All innovation was hailed as progressive, forward-thinking. Just as failure didn't deter us, it didn't seem to diminish the loyalty of our customers.

Bowerman, however, got very down on himself. I tried to console him by reminding him that there was no Nike without him, so he should continue to invent, create, fearlessly. The LD 1000 was like a literary genius's novel that didn't quite come together. It happened to the best of them. No reason to stop writing.

My pep talks didn't work. And then I made the mistake of mentioning the air sole we had in development. I told Bowerman about Rudy's oxygenated innovation, and Bowerman scoffed. "Pff—air shoes. That'll never work, Buck."

He sounded a bit—jealous?

I considered it a good sign. His competitive juices were already flowing again.

MANY AFTERNOONS I'D sit around the office with Strasser, trying to figure out why some lines were selling and some not, which led to broader discussions of what people thought of us, and why. We didn't have focus groups, or market research—we couldn't afford them—so we tried to intuit, divine, read tea leaves. Clearly people liked the look of our shoes, we agreed. Clearly they liked our story: Oregon firm founded by running geeks. Clearly they liked what wearing a pair of Nikes said about them. We were more than a brand; we were a statement.

Some of the credit went to Hollywood. We had a guy out there giving Nikes to stars, all kinds of stars, big, little, rising, fading. Every time I turned on the TV our shoes were on a character in some hit show—*Starsky & Hutch*, *The Six Million Dollar Man*, *The Incredible Hulk*. Somehow, our Hollywood liaison got a pair of Senorita Cortezes into the hands of Farrah Fawcett, who wore them in a 1977 episode of *Charlie's Angels*. That was all it took. One quick shot of Farrah in Nikes and every store in the nation was sold out of Senorita Cortezes by noon the next day. Soon the cheerleaders at UCLA and USC were jumping and leaping in what was commonly called the Farrah Shoe.

All of which meant more demand . . . and more problems meeting demand. Our manufacturing base was broader. Besides Japan, we now had several factories in Taiwan and two smaller factories in Korea, plus Puerto Rico and Exeter, but still we couldn't keep up. Also, the more factories we brought online, the more strain it put on our cash.

Occasionally our problems had nothing to do with cash. In Korea, for instance, the five biggest factories were so massive, and the competition among them so cutthroat, we knew we were going to get knocked off soon. Sure enough, one day I received in the mail a perfect replica of our Nike Bruin, including the trademark swoosh. Imitation is flattery, but knockoff is theft, and this theft was diabolical. The detail and workmanship, without any input from our people, was startlingly good. I wrote the president of the factory and demanded he cease and desist or I'd have him thrown in jail for a hundred years.

And by the way, I added, how would you like to work with us?

I signed a contract with his factory in the summer of 1977, which ended our knockoff problem for the moment. More important, it gave us the capacity to shift production in a huge way, if need be.

It also ended once and for all our dependence on Japan.

* * *

THE PROBLEMS WERE never going to stop, I realized, but for the moment we had more momentum than problems. To build on this momentum we rolled out a new ad campaign with a sexy new slogan: "There is no finish line." It was the idea of our new ad agency and its CEO, John Brown. He'd just opened his own shop in Seattle, and he was young, bright, and of course the opposite of an athlete. That was all we seemed to hire in those days. Besides Johnson and myself, Nike was a haven for the sedentary. Still, nonjock or not, Brown managed to dream up a campaign and a tagline that perfectly captured Nike's philosophy. His ad showed a single runner on a lonely country road, surrounded by tall Douglas firs. Oregon, clearly. The copy read: "Beating the competition is relatively easy. Beating yourself is a never-ending commitment."

Everyone around me thought the ad was bold, fresh. It didn't focus on the product, but on the spirit behind the product, which was something you never saw in the 1970s. People congratulated me on that ad as if we'd achieved something earth-shattering. I'd shrug. I wasn't being modest. I still didn't believe in the power of advertising. At all. A product, I thought, speaks for itself, or it doesn't. In the end, it's only quality that counts. I couldn't imagine that any ad campaign would ever prove me wrong or change my mind.

Our advertising people, of course, told me I was wrong, wrong, a thousand percent wrong. But again and again I'd ask them: Can you say definitively that people are buying Nikes because of your ad? Can you show it to me in black-and-white numbers?

Silence.

No, they'd say . . . we can't say that *definitively*.

So then it's a little hard to get enthused, I'd say—isn't it?

Silence.

I OFTEN WISHED I had more time to kick back and debate the niceties of advertising. Our semidaily crises were always bigger and more pressing than what slogan to print under a picture of our shoes. In the second half of 1977 the crisis was our debenture holders. They were suddenly clamoring for a way to cash in. By far the best way for them to do so would be a public offering, which, we tried to explain to them, was not an option. They didn't want to hear that.

I turned once more to Chuck Robinson. He'd served with distinction as lieutenant commander on a battleship in World War II. He'd built Saudi Arabia's first steel mill. He'd helped negotiate the grain deal with the Soviets. Chuck knew business cold, better than anyone I'd ever met, and I'd been wanting his advice for quite some time. But over the last few years he'd been the number two man under Henry Kissinger at the State Department, and thereby "off-limits" to me, according to Jaqua. Now, with Jimmy Carter newly elected, Chuck was on Wall Street and available once again for consultations. I invited him out to Oregon.

I'll never forget his first day in our office. I caught him up on the developments of the last few years and thanked him for his invaluable counsel about Japanese trading companies. Then I showed him our financial statements. He flipped through them, started to laugh. He couldn't stop laughing. "Compositionally," he said, "you *are* a Japanese trading company—90 percent debt!"

"I know."

"You can't live like this," he said.

"Well . . . I guess that's why you're here."

As the first order of business, I invited him to be on our board of directors. To my surprise, he agreed. Then I asked his opinion about going public.

He said going public wasn't an option. It was mandatory. I needed to solve this cash flow problem, he said, attack it, wrestle it to the ground, or else I could lose the company. Hearing his assessment was frightening, but necessary.

For the first time ever I saw going public as inevitable, and I couldn't help it, the realization made me sad. Of course we stood to make a great deal of money. But getting rich had never factored in my decisions, and it mattered even less to the Buttfaces. So when I brought it up at the next meeting and told them what Chuck had said, I didn't ask for another debate. I just put it to a vote.

Hayes was for.

Johnson was against.

Strasser, too. "It'll spoil the culture," he kept saying, over and over.

Woodell was on the fence.

If there was one thing we all agreed on, however, it was the lack of barriers. Nothing stood in the way of going public. Sales were extraordinary, word of mouth was positive, legal disputes were behind us. We had debt, but for the moment it was manageable. At the start of the 1977 Christmas season, as the brightly colored lights appeared on the houses in my neighborhood, I recall thinking during one of my nightly runs: Everything is about to change. It's just a matter of time.

And then came the letter.

AN UNIMPOSING LITTLE thing. Standard white envelope. Embossed return address. *U.S. Customs Service, Washington, DC.* I opened it and my hands started to shake. It was a bill. For $25 million.

I read it, and reread it. I couldn't make heads or tails. As best I could determine, the federal government was saying that Nike owed customs duties dating back three years, by virtue of something called the "American Selling Price," an old duty-assessing method. American Selling—what? I called Strasser into my office and thrust the letter at him. He read it, laughed. "This can't be real," he said, tugging his beard. "My reaction exactly," I said.

We passed it back and forth and agreed it had to be a mistake. Because if it was real, if we actually did owe $25 million to the government, we were out of business. Just like that. All this talk of going public had been a colossal waste of time. Everything since 1962 had been a waste of time. There is no finish line? This right here, *this* is the finish line.

Strasser made a few phone calls and came back to me the next day. This time he wasn't laughing. "It might be real," he said.

And its origin was sinister. Our American competitors, Converse and Keds, plus a few small factories—in other words, what was left of the American shoe industry—were all behind it. They'd lobbied Washington, in an effort to slow our momentum, and their lobbying had paid off, better than they'd ever dared hope. They'd managed to convince customs officials to effectively hobble us by enforcing this American Selling Price, an archaic law that dated back to the protectionist days, which preceded—some say prompted—the Great Depression.

Essentially the American Selling Price law, or ASP, said that import duties on nylon shoes must be 20 percent of the manufacturing cost of the shoe—unless there's a "similar shoe" manufactured by a competitor in the United States. In which case, the duty must be 20 percent of the competitor's *selling price*. So all our competitors needed to do was make a few shoes in the United States, get them declared "similar," then price them sky high—and boom. They could send our import duties sky high, too.

And that's just what they did. One dirty little trick, and they'd managed to spike our import duties by 40 percent—retroactively. Customs was saying we owed them import duties dating back years, to the tune of $25 million. Dirty trick or not, Strasser told me customs wasn't joking around. We owed them $25 million, and they wanted it. Now.

I put my head on my desk. A few years earlier, when my fight had been with Onitsuka, I told myself the problem was rooted in cultural differences. Some part of me, shaped by World War II, wasn't all that surprised to be at odds with a former foe. Now I was in the position of the Japanese, at war with the United States of America. With my own government.

This was one conflict I never imagined, and desperately didn't want, and yet I couldn't duck it. Losing meant annihilation. What the government was demanding, $25 million, was very nearly our sales number for all of 1977. And even if we could somehow give them a year's worth of revenue, we couldn't *continue* to pay import duties that were 40 percent higher.

So there was only one thing to do, I told Strasser with a sigh. "We'll have to fight this with everything we've got."

I DON'T KNOW why this crisis hit me harder, mentally, than all the others. I tried to tell myself, over and over, We've been through bad times, we'll get through this.

But this one just felt different.

I tried to talk to Penny about it, but she said I didn't actually talk, I grunted and stared off. "Here comes the wall," she'd say, exasperated, and a little frightened. I should have told her, That's what men do when they fight. They put up walls. They pull up the drawbridge. They fill in the moat.

But from behind my rising wall I didn't know how. I lost the ability in 1977 to speak. It was either silence or rage with me. Late at night, after talking on the phone with Strasser, or Hayes, or Woodell, or my father, I couldn't see any way out. I could only see myself folding up this business I'd worked so hard to build. So I'd erupt—at the telephone. Instead of hanging up, I'd slam the receiver down, then slam it down again, harder and harder, until it shattered. Several times I beat the living tar out of that telephone.

After I'd done this three times, maybe four, I noticed the repairman from the telephone company eyeing me. He replaced the phone, checked to make sure there was a dial tone, and as he was packing up his tools he said very softly: "This is . . . really . . . immature."

I nodded.

"You're supposed to be a grown-up," he said.

I nodded again.

If a phone repairman feels the need to chastise you, I told myself, your behavior probably needs modifying. I made promises to myself that day. I vowed that from then on I'd meditate, count backward, run twelve miles a night, whatever it took to hold it together.

HOLDING IT TOGETHER wasn't the same thing as being a good father. I'd always promised myself that I'd be a better father to my sons than my father had been to me—meaning I'd give them more explicit approval, more attention. But in late 1977, when I evaluated myself honestly, when I looked at how much time I was spending away from the boys, and how distant I was even when I was home, I gave myself low marks. Going strictly by the numbers, I could only say that I was 10 percent better than my father had been with me.

At least I'm a better provider, I told myself.

And at least I keep telling them their bedtime stories.

Boston, April 1773. Along with scores of angry colonists, protesting the rise of import duties on their beloved tea, Matt and Travis History snuck aboard three ships in Boston Harbor and threw all the tea overboard . . .

The minute their eyes were closed, I would sneak out of the room and settle into my recliner and reach for the phone. *Hey, Dad. Yeah. How you doing? . . . Me? Not so good.*

Over the last ten years this had been my nightcap, my salvation. But now, more than ever, I lived for it. I craved things I could only get from my old man, though I'd have been hard-pressed to name them.

Reassurance?

Affirmation?

Comfort?

On December 9, 1977, I got them all, in a burst. Sports, of course, were the cause.

The Houston Rockets were playing the Los Angeles Lakers that night. At the start of the second half, Lakers guard Norm Nixon missed a jumper, and his teammate Kevin Kunnert, a seven-foot beanpole out of Iowa, fought for the rebound with Houston's Kermit Washington. In the tussle, Washington pulled down Kunnert's shorts, and Kunnert retaliated with an elbow. Washington then socked Kunnert in the head. A fight broke out. As Houston's Rudy Tomjanovich ran over to defend his teammates, Washington turned and threw a devastating haymaker, breaking Tomjanovich's nose, and jaw, and separating his skull and facial bones from his skin. Tomjanovich fell to the floor as if hit with a shotgun blast. His massive body struck the ground with a sickening smack. The sound echoed throughout the upper reaches of the L.A. Forum, and for several seconds Tomjanovich lay there, motionless, in an ever-widening puddle of his own blood.

I hadn't heard anything about it until I talked to my father that night. He was breathless. I was surprised that he'd watched the game, but everyone in Portland was basketball crazy that year, because our Trail Blazers were the defending NBA champs. Still, it wasn't the game, per se, that had him breathless. After telling me about the fight, he cried, "Oh, Buck, Buck, it was one of the most incredible things I have ever seen." Then there was a long pause and he added, "The camera kept zooming in and you could see quite clearly . . . on Tomjanovich's shoes . . . the swoosh! They kept zooming in on *the swoosh*."

I'd never heard such pride in my father's voice. Sure, Tomjanovich was in a hospital fighting for his life, and sure his facial bones were floating around his head—but Buck Knight's logo was in the national spotlight.

That might have been the night the swoosh became real to my father. Respectable. He didn't actually use the word "proud." But I hung up the phone feeling as if he had.

It almost makes this all worthwhile, I told myself.

Almost.

* * *

SALES HAD BEEN climbing geometrically, year after year, ever since the first few hundred pairs I sold out of my Valiant. But as we closed out 1977 . . . sales were going berserk. Nearly $70 million. So Penny and I decided to buy a bigger house.

It was a strange thing to do, in the midst of an apocalyptic fight with the government. But I liked the idea of acting *as if* things were going to work out.

Fortune favors the brave, that sort of thing.

I also liked the idea of a change of scenery.

Maybe, I thought, it will initiate a change of luck.

We were sad to leave the old house, of course. Both boys had taken their first steps there, and Matthew had lived for that swimming pool. He was never so at peace as when frolicking in the water. I recall Penny shaking her head and saying, "One thing's for certain. That boy will never drown."

But both boys were getting so big, they desperately needed more room, and the new place had plenty. It sat on five acres high above Hillsboro, and every room felt spacious and airy. From the first night we knew we'd found our home. There was even a built-in niche for my recliner.

To honor our new address, our new start, I tried to keep a new schedule. Unless I was out of town, I tried to attend all the youth basketball games, and youth soccer games, and Little League games. I spent whole weekends teaching Matthew to swing a bat, though both of us wondered why. He refused to keep his back foot still. He refused to listen. He argued with me constantly.

The ball's moving, he said, why shouldn't I?

Because it's harder to hit that way.

That was never a good enough reason for him.

Matthew was more than a rebel. He was, I discovered, more than a contrarian. He positively couldn't abide authority, and he perceived authority lurking in every shadow. Any opposition to his will was oppression and thus a call to arms. In soccer, for instance, he played like an anarchist. He didn't compete against the opponent so much as against the rules—the structure. If the other team's best player was coming toward him on a breakaway, Matthew would forget the game, forget the ball, and just go for the kid's shins. Down went the kid, out came the parents, and pandemonium would ensue. During one Matthew-sparked melee, I looked at him and realized he didn't want to be there any more than I did. He didn't like soccer. For that matter, he didn't care for sports. He was playing, and I was watching him play, out of some sense of obligation.

Over time his behavior had a suppressive effect on his younger brother. Though Travis was a gifted athlete and loved sports, Matthew had turned him off. One day little Travis simply retired. He would no longer go out for any teams. I asked him to reconsider, but the only thing he had in common with Matthew, and maybe his father, was a stubborn streak. Of all the negotiations in my life, those with my sons have been the most difficult.

On New Year's Eve, 1977, I went around my new house, putting out the lights, and I felt a kind of fissure deep within the bedrock of my existence. My life was about sports, my business was about sports, my bond with my father was about sports, and neither of my two sons wanted anything to do with sports.

Like the American Selling Price, it all seemed so unjust.

1978

Strasser was our five-star general, and I was ready to follow him into any fray, any fusillade. In our fight with Onitsuka his outrage had comforted and sustained me, and his mind had been a formidable weapon. In this new fight with the Feds he was doubly outraged. Good, I thought. He stomped around the offices like a pissed-off Viking, and his stomps were music to my ears.

We both knew, however, that rage wasn't going to be enough. Nor was Strasser alone. We were taking on the United States of America. We needed *a few* good men. So Strasser reached out to a young Portland lawyer, a friend of his named Richard Werschkul.

I don't remember ever being introduced to Werschkul. I don't remember anyone asking me to meet him or hire him. I just remember suddenly being *aware* of Werschkul, extremely conscious of his presence, all the time. The way you're aware of a big woodpecker in your front yard. Or on your head.

For the most part Werschkul's presence was welcome. He had the kind of go-go motor we liked, and the credentials we always looked for. Stanford undergrad, University of Oregon Law. He also had a compelling personality, a presence. Dark, wiry, sarcastic, bespectacled, he possessed an uncommonly deep, plummy baritone, like Darth Vader with a head cold. Overall he gave the impression of a man with a plan, and the plan didn't include surrender or sleep.

On the other hand, he also had an eccentric streak. We all did, but Werschkul had what Mom Hatfield might have called a "wild hair." There was always something about him that didn't quite . . . fit. For instance, though he was a native Oregonian, he had a baffling East Coast air. Blue blazers, pink shirts, bow ties. Sometimes his accent suggested summers in Newport, rowing for Yale—a string of polo ponies. Surpassing strange in a man who knew his way around the Willamette Valley. And while he could be very witty, even silly, he could change on a dime and become scary serious.

Nothing made him more serious than the topic of Nike vs. U.S. Customs.

Some inside Nike worried about Werschkul's seriousness, fearing it bordered on obsession. Fine by me, I thought. Obsessives were the only ones for the job. The only ones for me. Some questioned his stability. But when it came to stability, I asked, who among us will throw the first stone?

Besides, Strasser liked him, and I trusted Strasser. So when Strasser suggested that we promote Werschkul, and move him to Washington, D.C., where he'd be closer to the politicians we'd need on our side, I didn't hesitate. Neither, of course, did Werschkul.

ABOUT THE SAME time we dispatched Werschkul to Washington, I sent Hayes to Exeter to check on things at the factory, and to see how Woodell and Johnson were getting along. Also on his agenda was the purchase of something called a rubber mill. Allegedly it would help us do a better job of dictating the quality of our outer soles and midsoles. More, Bowerman wanted it for his experiments, and my policy was still WBW: Whatever Bowerman Wants. If Bowerman requisitions a Sherman tank, I told Woodell, don't ask questions. Just dial the Pentagon.

But when Hayes asked Woodell about "these rubber mill gizmos," and where to find one, Woodell shrugged. Never heard of them.

Woodell referred Hayes to Giampietro, who knew everything worth knowing about rubber mills, of course, and days later Hayes found himself trekking with Giampietro into the backwoods of Maine, to the little town of Saco, and an auction of industrial equipment.

Hayes wasn't able to find a rubber mill at the auction, but he did fall in love with the auction site, an old redbrick factory on an island in the Saco River. The factory was something out of Stephen King, but that didn't spook Hayes. It spoke to him. I guess it was to be expected that a man with a bulldozer fetish would become enamored of a rusted-out factory. The surprising part was, the factory happened to be for sale. Price: $500,000. Hayes offered the factory owner $100,000, and they settled on $200,000.

"Congratulations," Hayes and Woodell said when they phoned that afternoon.

"For what?"

"For only slightly more than the cost of a rubber mill you are the proud owner of a whole damn factory," they said.

"The heck are you talking about?"

They filled me in. Like Jack telling his mother about the magic beans, they mumbled when they got to the part about the price. And about the factory needing tens of thousands of dollars in repairs.

I could tell they'd been drinking, and later Woodell would confess that, after stopping at a huge discount liquor outlet in New Hampshire, Hayes whooped: "At prices like this? A man can't afford *not* to drink!"

I rose from my chair and yelled into the phone, "You dummies! What do I need with a *nonworking* factory in *Saco, Maine*?"

"Storage?" they said. "And one day it could be a complement to our factory in Exeter."

In my best John McEnroe I screamed, "You cannot be *serious*! Don't you dare!"

"Too late. We already bought it."

Dial tone.

I sat down. I didn't even feel mad. I was too upset to be mad. The Feds were dunning me for $25 million I didn't have and my men were running around the country writing checks for hundreds of thousands of dollars more, without even asking me. Suddenly I became calm. Quasi-comatose. I told myself, Who cares? When the government comes in, when they repossess everything, lock, stock, and barrel, let *them* figure out what to do with a nonworking factory in Saco, Maine.

Later Hayes and Woodell called back and said they'd only been kidding about buying the factory. "Pulling your chain," they said. "But you do need to buy it. You must."

Okay, I said wearily. Okay. Whatever you dummies think best.

WE WERE ON track in 1979 for sales of $140 million. Better yet, our quality was rising apace. People in the trade, industry insiders, were writing articles, praising us for "finally" putting out a better shoe than Adidas. Personally, I thought the insiders were late to the party. Other than a few early stumbles, our quality had been tops for years. And we'd never lagged in innovation. (Plus, we had Rudy's air soles in the pipeline.)

Aside from our war with the government, we were in great shape.

Which seemed like saying: Aside from being on death row, life was grand.

Another good sign. We kept outgrowing our headquarters. We moved again that year, to a forty-thousand-square-foot building all our own, in Beaverton. My private office was sleek, and huge, bigger than our entire first headquarters next to the Pink Bucket.

And utterly empty. The interior decorator decided to go Japanese minimalist—with one touch of the absurd that everyone found hilarious. She thought it would be a hoot to set beside my desk a leather chair that was a giant baseball mitt. "Now," she said, "you can sit there every day and think about your . . . sports things."

I sat in the mitt, like a foul ball, and looked out the window. I should have reveled in that moment, savored the humor and the irony. Getting cut from my high school baseball team had been one of the great hurts of my life, and now I was sitting in a giant mitt, in a swank new office, presiding over a company that sold "sports things" to professional baseball players. But instead of cherishing how far we'd come, I saw only how far we had to go. My window looked onto a beautiful stand of pines, and I definitely couldn't see the forest for the trees.

I didn't understand what was happening, in the moment, but now I do. The years of stress were taking their toll. When you see only problems, you're not seeing clearly. At just the moment I needed to be my sharpest, I was approaching burnout.

I OPENED THE final Buttface of 1978 with a rah-rah speech, trying to fire up the troops, but especially myself. "Gentlemen," I said, "our industry is made up of Snow White and the Seven Dwarfs! And next year . . . finally . . . one of the dwarfs is going to get into Snow White's pants!"

As if the metaphor needed further explanation, I explained that Adidas was Snow White. And our time, I thundered, is coming!

But first we needed to start selling clothes. Aside from the plain numerical fact that Adidas sold more apparel than shoes, apparel gave them a psychological edge. Apparel helped them lure bigger athletes into sweeter endorsement deals. Look at all we can give you, Adidas would say to an athlete, pointing to their shirts and pants and other gear. And they could say the same thing when they sat down with sporting goods stores.

Besides, if we ever resolved our fight with the Feds, and if we ever wanted to go public, Wall Street wouldn't give us the respect we deserved if we were just a shoe company. We needed to be diverse, which meant developing a solid line of apparel—which meant finding someone darned good to put in charge of it. At the Buttface I announced that someone would be Ron Nelson.

"Why him?" Hayes asked.

"Uh, well," I said, "for starters, he's a CPA . . ."

Hayes waved his arms over his head. "Just what we need," he said, "another accountant."

He had me there. I did seem to hire nothing but accountants. And lawyers. It wasn't that I had some bizarre affection for accountants and lawyers, I just didn't know where else to look for talent. I reminded Hayes, not for the first time, that there's no shoe school, no University of Footwear from which we could recruit. We needed to hire people with sharp minds, that was our priority, and accountants and lawyers had at least proved that they could master a difficult subject. And pass a big test.

Most had also demonstrated basic competence. When you hired an accountant, you knew he or she could count. When you hired a lawyer, you knew he or she could talk. When you hired a marketing expert, or product developer, what did you know? Nothing. You couldn't predict what he or she could do, or if he or she could do anything. And the typical business school graduate? He or she didn't want to start out with a bag selling shoes. Plus, they all had zero experience, so you were simply rolling the dice based on how well they did in an interview. We didn't have enough margin for error to roll the dice on anyone.

Besides, as accountants went, Nelson was a standout. He'd become a manager in just five years, which was ridiculously fast. And he'd been valedictorian at his high school. (Alas, we didn't find out until later that he went to high school in eastern Montana; his class had five people.)

On the minus side of the ledger, because he'd become an accountant so fast, Nelson was young. Maybe too young to handle something as big as the launch of an apparel line. But I told myself that his youth wouldn't be a critical factor, because starting an apparel line was relatively easy. After all, there wasn't any technology or physics involved. As Strasser had once quipped, "There's no such thing as air shorts."

Then, during one of my first meetings with Nelson, right after I'd hired him, I noticed . . . he had absolutely no sense of style. The more I looked him over, up and down, side to side, the more I realized that he might have been the worst dresser I'd ever met. Worse than Strasser. Even Nelson's car, I noticed one day in the parking lot, was a hideous shade of brown. When I mentioned this to Nelson, he laughed. He had the nerve to brag that every car he'd ever owned had been the same brown.

"I might have made a mistake with Nelson," I confided to Hayes.

I WAS NO fashion plate. But I knew how to wear a decent suit. And because my company was launching an apparel line, I now started paying closer attention to what I wore, and what those around me wore. On the second front I was appalled. Bankers and investors, reps from Nissho, all kinds of people we needed to impress, were passing through our new halls, and whenever they saw Strasser in his Hawaiian shirts, or Hayes in his bulldozer-driving outfits, they did triple-takes. Sometimes our eccentricity was funny. (A top executive at Foot Locker said, "We think of you guys as gods—until we see your cars.") But most times it was embarrassing. And potentially damaging. Thus, around Thanksgiving, 1978, I instituted a strict company dress code.

The reaction wasn't terribly enthusiastic. Corporate bullshit, many grumbled. I was mocked. Mostly I was ignored. To even a casual observer, it became clear that Strasser started dressing *worse*. When he showed up to work one day in baggy-seated Bermuda shorts, as if he were walking a Geiger counter down the beach, I couldn't stand by. This was rank insubordination.

I intercepted him in the halls and called him out. "You need to wear a coat and tie!" I said.

"We're not a coat-and-tie company!" he shot back.

"We are now."

He walked away from me.

In the coming days Strasser continued to dress with a studied, confrontational casualness. So I fined him. I instructed the bookkeeper to deduct seventy-five dollars from Strasser's next paycheck.

He threw a fit, of course. And he plotted. Days later he and Hayes came to work in coats and ties. But preposterous coats and ties. Stripes and plaids, checks with polka dots, all of it rayon and polyester—and burlap? They meant it as a farce, but also as a protest, a gesture of civil disobedience, and I was in no mood for two fashion Gandhis staging a dress-in. I disinvited them both from the next Buttface. Then I ordered them both to go home and not to come back until they could behave, and dress, like adults.

"And—you're fined again!" I yelled at Strasser.

"Then you're fucked!" he yelled back.

Just then, at that exact moment, I turned. Coming toward me was Nelson, dressed worse than the lot of them. Polyester bell-bottoms, a pink silk shirt open to his navel. Strasser and Hayes were one thing, but where the heck did this new guy get off protesting my dress code? After I'd *just hired* him? I pointed at the door and sent him home, too. From the confused, horrified look on his face I realized he wasn't protesting. He was just naturally unstylish.

My new head of apparel.

I retreated that day to my baseball-mitt chair and stared out the window for a long, long time. Sports things.

I knew what was coming. And, oh, it came.

A few weeks later Nelson stood before us and made his formal presentation of the first-ever line of Nike apparel. Beaming with pride, grinning with excitement, he laid all the new clothes on the conference table. Soiled workout shorts, ragged T-shirts, wrinkled hoodies—each putrid item looked as if it had been donated to, or pilfered from, a Dumpster. The topper: Nelson pulled each item from a dirty brown paper bag, which looked as if it also contained his lunch.

At first we were in shock. None of us knew what to say. Finally, someone chuckled. Strasser, probably. Then someone haw-hawed. Woodell, maybe. Then the dam burst. Everyone was laughing, rocking back and forth, falling out of their chairs. Nelson saw that he'd goofed, and in a panic he started stuffing the clothes back into the paper bag, which ripped apart, which made everyone laugh harder. I was laughing, too, harder than anyone, but at any moment I felt as if I might start sobbing.

Shortly after that day I transferred Nelson to the newly formed production department, where his considerable accounting talents helped him do a great job. Then I quietly shifted Woodell to apparel. He did his typically flawless job, assembling a line that gained immediate attention and respect in the industry. I asked myself why I didn't just let Woodell do everything.

Including my job. Maybe he could fly back east and get the Feds off my back.

AMID ALL THIS turmoil, amid all this uncertainty about the future, we needed a morale booster, and we got it at the tail end of 1978, when we finally brought out the Tailwind. Developed in Exeter, made in Japan, the brainchild of M. Frank Rudy was more than a shoe. It was a work of postmodern art. Big, shiny, bright silver, filled with Rudy's patented air soles, it featured twelve different product innovations. We hyped it to the heavens, with a splashy ad campaign, and tied the launch to the Honolulu Marathon, where many runners would be wearing it.

Everyone flew out to Hawaii for the launch, which turned into a drunken bacchanal, and a mock coronation of Strasser. I was transitioning him from legal to marketing, moving him out of his comfort zone, as I liked to do with everyone now and then, to prevent them from growing stale. Tailwind was Strasser's first big project, so he felt like Midas. "Nailed it," he kept saying, and who could begrudge him a bit of chest-thumping. After its wildly successful debut, Tailwind became a sales monster. Within ten days we thought it might have a chance of eclipsing the waffle trainer.

Then the reports began to trickle in. Customers were returning the shoe to stores, in droves, complaining that the thing was blowing up, falling apart. Autopsies on the returned shoes revealed a fatal design flaw. Bits of metal in the silver paint were rubbing against the shoe's upper, acting like microscopic razors, slicing and shredding the fabric. We issued a recall, of sorts, and offered full refunds, and half of the first generation of Tailwinds ended up in recycling bins.

What began as a morale booster ended up being a body blow to everyone's confidence. Each person reacted in his own way. Hayes drove in frantic circles on a bulldozer. Woodell stayed longer each day at the office. I toggled dazedly between my baseball mitt and my recliner.

In time we all agreed to pretend it was no big deal. We'd learned a valuable lesson. Don't put twelve innovations into one shoe. It asks too much of the shoe, to say nothing of the design team. We reminded each other that there was honor in saying, "Back to the drawing board." We reminded each other of the many waffle irons Bowerman had ruined.

Next year, we all said. You'll see. Next year. The dwarf is going to get Snow White.

But Strasser couldn't get past it. He started drinking, showing up late to work. His mode of dress was now the least of my problems. This might have been his first real failure, ever, and I'll always remember those dreary winter mornings, seeing him shamble into my office with the latest bad news about his Tailwind. I recognized the signs. He, too, was approaching burnout.

The only person who wasn't depressed about the Tailwind was Bowerman. In fact, its catastrophic debut helped pull him out of the slump in which *he'd* been mired since retiring. How he loved being able to tell me, to tell us all, "Told you so."

*   *   *

OUR FACTORIES IN Taiwan and Korea were humming along, and we opened new ones that year in Heckmondwike, England, and Ireland. Industry watchers pointed to our new factories, and our sales, and said we were unstoppable. Few imagined we were broke. Or that our head of marketing was wallowing in a depression. Or that our founder and president was sitting in a giant baseball mitt with a long face.

The burnout spread around the office like mono. And while we were all burning out, our man in Washington was flaming out.

Werschkul had done everything we'd asked of him. He'd button-holed politicians. He'd petitioned, lobbied, pleaded our cause with passion, if not always with sanity. Day after day he'd run up and down the halls of Congress, handing out free pairs of Nikes. Swag, with a side of swoosh. (Knowing that representatives were legally bound to report gifts worth more than $35, Werschkul always included an invoice for $34.99.) But every pol told Werschkul the same thing. Give me something in writing, son, something I can study. Give me a breakdown of your case.

So Werschkul spent months writing a breakdown—and in the process suffered a breakdown. What was supposed to be a summary, a brief, had ballooned into an exhaustive history, The Decline and Fall of the Nike Empire, which ran to *hundreds* of pages. It was longer than Proust, longer than Tolstoy, and not a fraction as readable. It even had a title. Without a shred of irony Werschkul called it: *Werschkul on American Selling Price, Volume I.*

When you thought about it, when you really thought about it, what really scared you was that *Volume I.*

I sent Strasser back east to rein in Werschkul, check him into a psych ward if necessary. Just calm the kid down, I said. That first night they went to a local pub in Georgetown for a cocktail or three, and at the end of the night Werschkul wasn't any calmer. On the contrary. He got up on a table and delivered his stump speech to the patrons. He went full Patrick Henry. "Give me Nike or give me death!" The patrons were ready to vote for the latter. Strasser tried to coax Werschkul down off the chair, but Werschkul was just getting warmed up. "Don't you people realize," he shouted, "that freedom is on trial here? FREEDOM! Did you know that Hitler's father was a customs inspector?"

On the plus side, I think Werschkul scared Strasser straight. He seemed like the old Strasser when he returned and told me about Werschkul's mental condition.

We had a good laugh, a healing laugh. Then he handed me a copy of *Werschkul on American Selling Price, Volume I*. Werschkul had even had it bound. In leather.

I looked at the title: *WASP*. How perfect. How Werschkul.

"Are you going to read it?" Strasser said.

"I'll wait for the movie," I said, plopping it on my desk.

I knew right then that I'd have to start flying back to Washington, D.C., take on this fight myself. There was no other way.

And maybe it would cure my burnout. Maybe the cure for any burnout, I thought, is to just work harder.

1979

He occupied a teeny office at the Treasury Department, a space about the size of my mother's linen closet. There was barely room for his government-issued gunmetal-gray desk, let alone the matching chair for infrequent visitors.

He pointed to this chair. Sit, he said.

I sat. I looked around in disbelief. This was the home base of the man who kept sending us those bills for $25 million? I looked now at him, this beady-eyed bureaucrat. What creature did he remind me of? Not a worm. No, he was bigger than that. Not a snake. He was less simple than that. Then I had it. Johnson's pet octopus. I recalled Stretch dragging the helpless crab back to its lair. Yes, this bureaucrat was a kraken. A micro-kraken. A bureau-kraken.

Smothering these thoughts, burying all my hostility and fear, I screwed a fake smile onto my face and tried in a friendly tone to explain that this whole thing was a gigantic misunderstanding. Even the bureau-kraken's colleagues within the Treasury Department sided with our position. I handed him a document. "You have right here," I said, "a memo stating that the American Selling Price does not apply to Nike shoes. The memo comes from Treasury."

"Hmm," the bureau-kraken said. He looked it over, pushed it back at me. "That's not binding on Customs."

Not binding? I gritted my teeth. "But this whole case," I said, "is

335

nothing but the result of a dirty trick played by our competitors. We're being penalized for our success."

"We don't see it that way."

"By we . . . who do you mean?"

"The U.S. government."

I found it hard to believe this . . . man . . . was speaking for the U.S. government, but I didn't say that. "I find it hard to believe that the U.S. government would want to stifle free enterprise," I said. "That the U.S. government would want to be a party to this kind of deceit and trickery. That the U.S. government, my government, would want to bully a little company in Oregon. Sir, with all respect, I've been all over the world, I've seen corrupt governments in undeveloped countries act this way. I've seen thugs push around businesses, with arrogance, with impunity, and I can't believe my own government would behave in such a fashion."

The bureau-kraken said nothing. A faint smirk flickered across his thin lips. It struck me all at once that he was grotesquely unhappy, as all functionaries are. When I started to speak again, his unhappiness manifested itself in a restless, manic energy. He jumped up and paced. Back and forth he danced behind his desk. Then he sat down. Then he did it again. It wasn't the pacing of a thinker, but the agitation of a caged animal. Three mincing steps left, three halting limps right.

Sitting again, he cut me off midsentence. He explained that he didn't care what I said, or what I thought, or whether any of this was "fair," or "American." (He made air quotes with his bony "fingers.") He just wanted his money. *His* money?

I wrapped my arms around myself. Ever since the onset of burnout, this old habit was becoming more pronounced. I often looked in 1979 as if I were trying to keep myself from flying apart, trying to keep my contents from spilling out. I wanted to make another point, to rebut something the bureau-kraken had just said, but I didn't trust myself to speak. I feared that my limbs might go flailing, that I might begin screaming. That I might beat the living tar out of his telephone. We made quite a pair, him with his frantic pacing, me with my frenzied self-hugging.

It became clear that we were at an impasse. I had to do something. So I commenced kissing up. I told the bureau-kraken that I respected his position. He had a job to do. It was a very important job. It must not be easy, enforcing burdensome fees, dealing with complaints all the time. I looked around his office-cell, as if to sympathize. However, I said, if Nike was forced to pay this exorbitant sum of money, the straight truth was, it would put us out of business.

"So?" he said.

"So?" I said.

"Yeah," he said. "So . . . what? Mr. Knight, it's my responsibility to collect import duties for the U.S. Treasury. For me, that's as far as it goes. Whatever happens . . . happens."

I hugged myself so tight, I must have looked as if I was wearing an invisible straitjacket.

Then I released myself, stood. Gingerly, I picked up my briefcase. I told the bureau-kraken that I wasn't going to accept his decision, and I wasn't going to give up. If necessary I would visit every congressman and senator and privately plead my case. I suddenly had the greatest sympathy for Werschkul. No wonder he'd come unhinged. *Don't you know that Hitler's father was a customs inspector?*

"Do what you gotta do," the bureau-kraken said. "Good day."

He turned back to his files. He checked his watch. Getting close to five. Not much time before the workday ended to ruin someone else's life.

I BEGAN, MORE or less, commuting to Washington. Every month I'd meet with politicians, lobbyists, consultants, bureaucrats, anyone who might help. I immersed myself in that strange political underworld, and read everything I could about customs.

I even skimmed *WASP, Volume I.*

Nothing was working.

Late in the summer of 1979 Werschkul got me an appointment with one of Oregon's senators, Mark O. Hatfield. Well respected, well connected, Hatfield was chairman of the Senate Appropriations Committee. With one phone call he might be able to get the bureau-kraken's bosses to clear up that $25 million discrepancy. So I spent days preparing, studying for the meeting, and huddled several times with Woodell and Hayes.

"Hatfield's just got to see it our way," Hayes said. "He's respected on both sides of the aisle. Saint Mark, some call him. He has no truck with abuse of power. He went toe-to-toe with Nixon on Watergate. And he fought like a tiger to get funding for dams on the Columbia."

"Sounds like our best shot," Woodell said.

"Maybe our last shot," I said.

The night I arrived in Washington, Werschkul and I had dinner and rehearsed. Like two actors running lines, we went through every possible argument Hatfield might throw at us. Werschkul kept referring to *WASP, Volume I.* Sometimes he'd even reference *Volume II.* "Forget that," I said. "Let's just keep it simple."

The next morning we walked slowly up the steps of the U.S. Senate Office Building, and I looked up at that magnificent façade, at all the columns and all the shiny marble, and the big flag overhead, and I had to pause. I thought of the Parthenon, the Temple of Nike. I knew that this, too, would be one of the seminal moments of my life. No matter how it turned out, I didn't want to let it pass without embracing it, acknowledging it. So I stared at the columns. I admired the sunlight bouncing off the marble. I stood there for the longest time . . .

"You coming?" Werschkul said.

It was a blazing summer day. My hand, the one gripping my briefcase, was drenched with sweat. My suit was soaked through. I looked as if I'd walked through a rainstorm. How was I going to meet a U.S. senator in this condition? How was I going to shake his hand?

How was I going to think straight?

We entered Hatfield's outer office, and one of his aides led us into a waiting room. A bullpen. I thought of the births of my two sons. I thought of Penny. I thought of my parents. I thought of Bowerman. I thought of Grelle. I thought of Pre. I thought of Kitami. I thought of James the Just.

"The senator will see you now," the aide said.

She led us into a large, refreshingly cool office. Hatfield came out from behind his desk. He welcomed us collegially, as fellow Oregonians, and led us to a sitting area by his window. We all sat. Hatfield smiled, Werschkul smiled. I mentioned to Hatfield that we were distantly related. My mother, I believed, was his third cousin. We talked a bit about Roseburg.

Then we all cleared our throats and the air conditioner soughed. "Ah, well, Senator," I said, "the reason we've come to see you today—"

He held up his hand. "I know all about your situation. My staff has read *Werschkul on American Selling Price*, and briefed me on it. What can I do to help?"

I stopped, stunned. I turned to Werschkul, whose face was the color of his pink bow tie. We'd spent so much time rehearsing this negotiation, preparing to convince Hatfield of the rightness of our cause, we weren't ready for the possibility of . . . success. We leaned into each other. In half whispers we talked about different ways Hatfield might help. Werschkul thought he should write a letter to the president of the United States, or maybe the head of customs. I wanted him to pick up the phone. We couldn't agree. We started to argue. The air conditioner seemed to be laughing at us. Finally, I shushed Werschkul, shushed the air conditioner, turned to Hatfield. "Senator," I said, "we were not prepared for you to be so obliging today. The truth is, we don't know what we want. We'll have to get back to you."

I walked out, not looking back to see if Werschkul was coming.

* * *

I FLEW HOME in time to preside over two milestones. In downtown Portland we opened a thirty-five-hundred-square-foot retail palace, which was instantly mobbed. The lines at the cash registers were endless. People were clamoring to try on . . . everything. I had to jump in and help. For a moment I was back in my parents' living room, measuring feet, fitting runners with the right shoes. It was a ball, a blast, and a timely reminder of why we were in this.

Then we moved offices again. We needed still more space, and we found it in a forty-six-thousand-square-foot building with all the amenities—steam room, library, gym, and more conference rooms than I could count. Signing the lease, I remembered those nights, driving around with Woodell. I shook my head. But I had no sense of victory. "It can all disappear tomorrow," I whispered.

We were big, there was no denying it. To make sure we weren't *too big* for our britches, as Mom Hatfield would have said, we moved the way we'd always moved. All three hundred employees came in on the weekend and packed up their belongings into their own cars. We provided pizza and beer, and some of the warehouse guys loaded the heavier stuff into vans, and then we all slowly caravanned down the road.

I told the warehouse guys to leave the baseball-mitt chair behind.

IN THE FALL of 1979 I flew to Washington for a second meeting with the bureau-kraken. This time he wasn't so feisty. Hatfield had been in touch. As had Oregon's other senator, Bob Packwood, chairman of the Senate Finance Committee, which had review authority on Treasury. "I'm *sick* . . . and *tired*," said the bureau-kraken, pointing one of his tentacles at me, "of hearing from your high-placed *friends*."

"Oh, sorry," I said. "That mustn't be any fun. But you'll be hearing from them until this situation is resolved."

"Do you realize," he hissed, "that I don't need this job? Do you know that my wife . . . has . . . *money*! I don't need to work, you know."

"Good for you. And her." The sooner you retire, I thought, the better.

But the bureau-kraken would never retire. In years to come, through Republican and Democratic administrations, he'd remain. On and on. Like death and taxes. In fact, one day in the distant future, he'd be among the small coterie of bureaucrats to give the disastrous green light that would send federal agents storming the compound at Waco.

WITH THE BUREAU-KRAKEN rattled, I was momentarily able to turn my attention back to our other existential threat, production. The same conditions that brought down Japan—fluctuating currency, rising labor costs, government instability—were beginning to coalesce in Taiwan and Korea. The time had come, yet again, to seek new factories, new countries. The time had come to think of China.

The question wasn't how to get into China. One shoe company or another was going to get in, eventually, and then all the others would follow. The question was how to get in first. The first to get in would have a competitive advantage that could last decades, not only in China's production sector, but in its markets, and with its political leaders. What a coup that would be. In our first meetings on the subject of China we'd always say: One billion people. Two. Billion. Feet.

We had one bona fide China expert on our team. Chuck. Besides having worked alongside Henry Kissinger, he sat on the board of the Allen Group, an auto-parts manufacturer with designs on the Chinese market. Its CEO was Walter Kissinger, Henry's brother. Chuck told us that Allen, in its exhaustive research into China, had discovered a very impressive China hand named David Chang. Chuck knew China, and he knew people who knew China, but no one knew China like David Chang.

"Put it this way," Chuck said. "When Walter Kissinger wanted to get into China, and couldn't, he didn't call Henry. He called Chang."

I lunged for the phone.

THE CHANG DYNASTY at Nike didn't start well. For starters, he was preppy. I'd thought Werschkul was preppy, until I met Chang. Blue blazer, gold buttons, heavily starched gingham shirt, regimental necktie—and he wore it all effortlessly. Shamelessly. He was the paisley-hearted love child of Ralph Lauren and Laura Ashley.

I took him around the office, introduced him to everyone, and he showed a remarkable talent for saying the absolute wrong thing. He met Hayes, who was 330 pounds, and Strasser, who was 320, and Jim Manns, our new CFO, who was a Mounds bar away from 350. Chang made a crack about our "half ton of upper management."

So much heft, he said, *at an athletic company*?

No one laughed. "Maybe it's your delivery," I told him, hurrying him along.

We went down the hall and bumped into Woodell, whom I'd recently called back from the East Coast. Chang reached down, shook Woodell's hand. "Skiing accident?" he said.

"What?" Woodell said.

"When you getting out of that chair?" Chang asked.

"Never, you dumb shit."

I sighed. "Well," I told Chang, "there's nowhere to go from here but up."

1980

We all gathered in the conference room and Chang gave us his bio. He was born in Shanghai, and raised in opulence. His grandfather was the third-largest soy sauce manufacturer in northern China, and his father had been the third-highest-ranking member of the Chinese Ministry of Foreign Affairs. When Chang was a teenager, however, the revolution came. The Changs fled to the United States, to Los Angeles, where Chang attended Hollywood High. He often thought he'd go back, and his parents did also. They kept in close touch with friends and family in China, and his mother remained extremely close with Soong Ching-ling, the godmother of the revolution.

In the meantime Chang attended Princeton, and studied architecture, and moved to New York. He landed a job at a good architectural firm, where he worked on the Levittown project. Then he set up his own firm. He was making decent money, doing good work, but bored stiff. He wasn't having any fun, and he didn't feel he was accomplishing anything real.

One day a Princeton friend complained about being unable to get a visa for Shanghai. Chang helped his friend get the visa, and helped him set up appointments with business contacts, and found that he enjoyed it. Being an emissary, a go-between, was a better use of his time and talents.

Even with his help, Chang cautioned, getting into China was

extremely difficult. The process was laborious. "You can't just apply for permission to visit China," he said. "You have to formally request that the Chinese government invite you. Bureaucracy doesn't begin to describe it."

I closed my eyes and pictured, somewhere on the other side of the world, a Chinese version of the bureau-kraken.

I also thought of the ex-GIs who'd explained Japanese business practices to me when I was twenty-four. I'd followed their advice, to the letter, and never regretted it. So, under Chang's direction, we put together a written presentation.

It was long. It was almost as long as *Werschkul on American Selling Price, Volume I*. We, too, had it bound.

Often we asked each other: Is anyone actually going to read this thing?

Oh well, we said. This is how Chang says it's done.

We sent it off to Beijing without hope.

AT THE FIRST Buttface of 1980 I announced that, though we'd gained the upper hand with the Feds, it might go on forever if we didn't do something bold, something outrageous. "I've given this a lot of thought," I said, "and I think what we need to do is . . . American Selling Price *ourselves*."

The Buttfaces laughed.

Then they stopped laughing and looked at each other.

We spent the rest of the weekend kicking it around. Was it possible? Nah, it couldn't be. Could we? Oh, no way. But . . . maybe?

We decided to give it a try. We launched a new shoe, a running shoe with nylon uppers, and called it One Line. It was a knockoff, dirt cheap, with a simple logo, and we manufactured it in Saco, at Hayes's ancient factory. We priced it low, just above cost. Now customs officials would have to use this "competitor" shoe as a new reference point in deciding our import duty.

That was the jab. That was just to get their attention. Then we threw the left hook. We produced a TV commercial telling the story of a little company in Oregon, fighting the big bad government. It opened on a runner doing his lonely road work, as a deep voice extolled the ideals of patriotism, liberty, the American way. And fighting tyranny. It got people pretty fired up.

Then we threw the haymaker. On February 29, 1980, we filed a $25 million antitrust suit in the U.S. District Court for the Southern District of New York, alleging that our competitors, and assorted rubber companies, through underhanded business practices, had conspired to take us out.

We sat back, waited. We knew it wouldn't take long, and indeed it didn't. The bureau-kraken cracked up. He threatened to go nuclear, whatever that meant. It didn't matter. He didn't matter. His bosses, and his bosses' bosses, didn't want this fight anymore. Our competitors, and their accomplices in the government, realized that they'd underestimated our will.

Immediately they initiated settlement talks.

DAY IN, DAY out, our lawyers would phone. From some government office, some blue-chip law firm, some conference room on the East Coast, meeting with the other side, they'd tell me the latest settlement offer being floated, and I'd reject it out of hand.

One day the lawyers said we could settle the whole thing, with no fuss, no courtroom drama, for the tidy sum of $20 million.

Not a chance, I said.

Another day they phoned and said we could settle for $15 million.

Don't make me laugh, I said.

As the number crept lower, I had several heated conversations with Hayes, and Strasser, and my father. They wanted me to settle, be done with this. "What's your ideal number?" they'd ask. Zero, I'd say.

I didn't want to pay one penny. Even one penny would be unfair.

But Jaqua, and Cousin Houser, and Chuck, who were all consulting on the case, sat me down one day and explained that the government needed something to save face. They couldn't walk away from this fight with nothing. As negotiations ground to a halt, I met one-on-one with Chuck. He reminded me that until this fight was behind us, we couldn't think about going public, and if we didn't go public we continued to risk losing everything.

I became petulant. I moaned about fairness. I talked about holding out. I said maybe I didn't *want* to go public—ever. Yet again I expressed my fear that going public would change Nike, ruin it, by turning over control to others. What would happen to the culture of Oregon Track, for instance, if it was subject to shareholder votes or corporate raider demands? We'd gotten a little taste of that scenario with the small group of debenture holders. Scaling up and letting in *thousands* of shareholders—it would be a thousand times worse. Above all, I couldn't bear the thought of one titan buying up shares, becoming a behemoth on the board. "I don't want to lose control," I said to Chuck. "That's my greatest fear."

"Well . . . there might be a way to go public without losing any control," he said.

"What?"

"You could issue two classes of stock—class A and class B. The public would get class Bs, which would carry one vote per share. The founders and inner circle, and your convertible debenture holders, would get class As, which would entitle them to name three-quarters of the board of directors. In other words, you raise enormous sums of money, turbocharge your growth, but ensure that you keep control."

I looked at him, dumbstruck. "Can we really do that?"

"It's not easy. But the *New York Times* and the *Washington Post* and a couple of others have done it. I think you can do it."

Maybe it wasn't satori, or *kensho*, but it was instant enlightenment.

In a flash. The breakthrough I'd been seeking for years. "Chuck," I said, "that sounds like . . . the answer."

At the next Buttface I explained the concept of class A and class B, and everyone had the same reaction. At long last. But I cautioned the Buttfaces: Whether or not this was the solution, we needed to do something, right now, fix our cash flow problem once and for all, because our window was closing. I could suddenly see a recession on the horizon. Six months, a year at the max. If we waited, tried to go public then, the market would give us far less than we were worth.

I asked for a show of hands. Going public . . . all in favor?

It was unanimous.

The moment we resolved our longstanding cold war with our competitors and the Feds, we would initiate a public offering.

THE SPRING FLOWERS were up by the time our lawyers and government officials had settled on a number: $9 million. It still sounded way too high, but everyone told me to pay it. Take the deal, they kept saying. I spent an hour staring out my window, mulling. The flowers and the calendar said it was spring, but that day the clouds were eye-level, dishwater gray, and the wind was cold.

I groaned. I grabbed the phone and dialed Werschkul, who had taken the role of lead negotiator. "Let's do it."

I told Carole Fields to cut the check. She brought it to me for my signature. We looked at each other and of course we were both thinking about the time I'd written that check for $1 million, which I couldn't cover. Now I was writing a check for $9 million, and there was no way it was going to bounce. I looked at the signature line. "Nine million," I whispered. I could still remember selling my 1960 MG with racing tires and a twin cam for eleven hundred dollars. Like yesterday. *Lead me from the unreal to the real.*

* * *

THE LETTER ARRIVED at the start of summer. The Chinese government requests the pleasure of a visit . . .

I spent a month deciding who would go. It has to be the A Team, I thought, so I sat with a yellow legal pad in my lap, making lists of names, scratching them out, making new lists.

Chang, of course.

Strasser, naturally.

Hayes, surely.

I notified everyone who was going on the trip to get their papers and passports and affairs in order. Then I spent the days leading up to our departure reading, cramming on Chinese history. The Boxer Rebellion. The Great Wall. Opium Wars. Ming dynasty. Confucius. Mao.

And darned if I was going to be the only student. I made a syllabus for all members of our traveling party.

In July 1980 we boarded a plane. Beijing, here we come. But first, Tokyo. I thought it would be a good idea to stop there along the way. Just to check in. Sales were starting to grow again in the Japanese market. Also, Japan would be a nice way to ease everyone into China, which was going to be a challenge for all of us. Baby steps. Penny and Gorman—I'd learned my lesson.

Twelve hours later, walking the streets of Tokyo, alone, my mind kept spinning back to 1962. My Crazy Idea. Now I was back, on the verge of taking that idea into a mammoth new market. I thought of Marco Polo. I thought of Confucius. But I also thought of all the games I'd seen through the years—football, basketball, baseball—when one team had a big lead in the final seconds, or innings, and relaxed. Or tightened. And therefore lost.

I told myself to stop looking back, keep my gaze forward.

We ate a few wonderful Japanese dinners, and visited a few old friends, and after two or three days, rested and ready, we were all set to go. Our flight to Beijing was the next morning.

We had one last meal together in the Ginza, washed down with several cocktails, and everyone turned in early. I took a hot shower, phoned home, and poured myself into bed. A few hours later I woke to frantic knocking. I looked at the clock on the nightstand. Two a.m. "Who's there?"

"David Chang! Let me in!"

I went to the door and found Chang looking very un-Chang. Rumpled, harried, regimental tie askew. "Hayes isn't going!" he said.

"What are you talking about?"

"Hayes is downstairs in the bar and he says he can't do it, he cannot get on that plane."

"Why not?"

"He's having some kind of panic attack."

"Yes. He has phobias."

"What kind of phobias?"

"He has . . . all the phobias."

I started to get dressed, to go down to the bar. Then I remembered who it was we were dealing with. "Go to bed," I said to Chang. "Hayes will be there in the morning."

"But—"

"He'll be there."

First thing in the morning, dull-eyed, deathly pale, Hayes was standing in the lobby.

Of course, he made sure to pack enough "medicine" for his next attack. Hours later, going through customs in Beijing, I heard behind me a great commotion. The room was bare, with plywood partitions, and on the other side of one partition several Chinese officers were shouting. I went around the partition and found two officers, agitated, pointing at Hayes and his open suitcase.

I walked over. Strasser and Chang walked over. Lying atop Hayes's giant underwear were twelve quarts of vodka.

No one said anything for the longest time. Then Hayes heaved a sigh.

"That's for me," he said. "You guys are on your own."

* * *

OVER THE NEXT twelve days we traveled all over China, in the company of government handlers. They took us to Tiananmen Square and made sure we stopped a long time in front of the giant portrait of Chairman Mao, who had died four years earlier. They took us to the Forbidden City. They took us to the Ming tombs. We were fascinated, of course, and curious—too curious. We made our handlers excruciatingly uncomfortable with all our questions.

At one stop I looked around and saw hundreds of people in Mao suits and flimsy black shoes, which seemed made of construction paper. But a few children were wearing canvas sneakers. That gave me hope.

What we wanted to see, of course, were factories. Our handlers reluctantly agreed. They took us by train to remote towns, far from Beijing, where we saw vast and terrifying industrial complexes, small metropolises of factories, each one more outdated than the last. Old, rusted, decrepit, these factories made Hayes's ancient Saco ruin look state-of-the-art.

Above all, they were filthy. A shoe would roll off the assembly line with a stain, a swath of grime, and nothing would be done. There was no overarching sense of cleanliness, no real quality control. When we pointed out a defective shoe, the officials running the factories would shrug and say: "Perfectly functional."

Never mind aesthetics. The Chinese didn't see why the nylon or canvas in a pair of shoes needed to be the same shade in the left shoe and the right. It was common practice for a left shoe to be light blue and a right shoe to be dark blue.

We met with scores of factory officials, and local politicians, and assorted dignitaries. We were toasted, feted, queried, monitored, talked at, and almost always welcomed warmly. We ate pounds of sea urchin and roasted duck, and at many stops we were treated to thousand-year-old eggs. I could taste every one of those thousand years.

Of course we were served many Mao tais. After all my trips to Taiwan, I was prepared. My liver was seasoned. What I wasn't prepared for was how much Hayes would like them. With each sip he smacked his lips and asked for more.

Near the end of our visit we took a nineteen-hour train ride to Shanghai. We could've flown, but I insisted on the train. I wanted to see, to experience the countryside. Within the first hour the men were cursing me. The day was dripping hot and the train was not air-conditioned.

There was one old fan in the corner of our train car, the blades barely moving the hot dust around. To get cool, Chinese passengers thought nothing of stripping down to their underwear, and Hayes and Strasser thought this gave them license to do the same. If I live to be two hundred years old, I won't forget the sight of those leviathans walking up and down the train car in their T-shirts and BVDs. Nor will any Chinese man or woman who was on the train that day.

Before leaving China we had a final errand or two in Shanghai. The first was to secure a deal with the Chinese track-and-field federation. This meant securing a deal with the government's Ministry of Sports. Unlike the Western world, where every athlete made his own deal, China itself negotiated endorsement deals for all its athletes. So, in an old Shanghai schoolhouse, in a classroom with seventy-five-year-old furniture and a huge portrait of Chairman Mao, Strasser and I met with the ministry representative. The first several minutes the representative lectured us on the beauties of communism. He kept saying that the Chinese like to do business with "like-minded people." Strasser and I looked at each other. Like-minded? What gives? Then the lecture abruptly stopped. The representative leaned forward and in a low voice that struck me as a Chinese version of uber agent Leigh Steinberg he asked: "How much you offering?"

Within two hours we had ourselves a deal. Four years later, in Los Angeles, the Chinese track-and-field team would walk into an

Olympic stadium for the first time in nearly two generations wearing American shoes and warm-ups.

Nike shoes and warm-ups.

Our final meeting was with the Ministry of Foreign Trade. As with all previous meetings, there were several rounds of long speeches, mainly by officials. Hayes was bored during the first round. By the third round he was suicidal. He started playing with the loose threads on the front of his polyester dress shirt. Suddenly he became annoyed with the threads. He took out his lighter. As the deputy minister of foreign trade was hailing us as worthy partners, he stopped and looked up to see that Hayes had set himself on fire. Hayes beat on the flame with his hands, and managed to put it out, but only after ruining the moment, and the speaker's mojo.

It didn't matter. Just before getting on the plane home we signed deals with two Chinese factories, and officially became the first American shoemaker in twenty-five years to be allowed to do business in China.

It seems wrong to call it "business." It seems wrong to throw all those hectic days and sleepless nights, all those magnificent triumphs and desperate struggles, under that bland, generic banner: business. What we were doing felt like so much more. Each new day brought fifty new problems, fifty tough decisions that needed to be made, right now, and we were always acutely aware that one rash move, one wrong decision could be the end. The margin for error was forever getting narrower, while the stakes were forever creeping higher—and none of us wavered in the belief that "stakes" didn't mean "money." For some, I realize, business is the all-out pursuit of profits, period, full stop, but for us business was no more about making money than being human is about making blood. Yes, the human body needs blood. It needs to manufacture red and white cells and platelets and redistribute them evenly, smoothly, to all the right places, on time, or else. But that day-to-day business of the human body isn't our mission as human beings. It's a basic process that enables our higher aims, and life always strives to transcend the basic processes of living—and at some point in the late 1970s, I did, too. I redefined winning, expanded it beyond my original definition of not losing, of merely staying alive. That was no longer enough to sustain me, or my company. We wanted, as all great businesses do, to create, to contribute, and we dared to say so aloud. When you make something, when you improve something, when you deliver something, when you add some new thing or service to the lives of strangers, making them happier, or healthier, or safer, or better, and when you do it all crisply and efficiently, smartly, the way everything should be done but so seldom is—you're participating more fully in the whole grand human drama. More than simply alive, you're helping others to live more fully, and if that's business, all right, call me a businessman.

Maybe it will grow on me.

THERE WAS NO time to unpack. There was no time to get over our post-China jet lag, which was profound. As we returned to Oregon, the process of going public was in full swing. Big choices needed to be made. Especially: who was going to manage the offering.

Public offerings don't always succeed. On the contrary, when mismanaged, they turn into train wrecks. So this was a critical decision right out of the blocks. Chuck, having worked at Kuhn, Loeb, still had strong relationships with their people, and thought they'd be best. We interviewed four or five other firms but in the end decided to go with Chuck's instincts. He hadn't steered us wrong yet.

Next we had to create a prospectus. It took fifty drafts, at least, to get it looking and sounding the way we wanted.

Finally, at the tail end of summer, we handed all our paperwork to the Securities and Exchange Commission, and at the start of September we released the formal announcement. Nike will be creating 20 million shares of class A stock and 30 million shares of class B.

The price of the stock, we told the world, would be somewhere between eighteen and twenty-two dollars a share. TBD.

Of 50 million shares, total, almost 30 million would be held in reserve, and about 2 million class Bs would be sold to the public. Of the roughly 17 million remaining class A shares, the preexisting shareholders, or insiders, meaning me, Bowerman, the debenture holders, and the Buttfaces, would own 56 percent.

I personally would own about 46 percent. It needed to be that much, we all agreed, because the company needed to be run by one person, to speak with one firm and steady voice—come what may. There could be no chance of alliances or breakaway factions, no existential struggles for control. To the outsider the division of shares might have seemed disproportionate, unbalanced, unfair. To the Buttfaces it was a necessity. There wasn't a word of dissent or complaint. Ever.

WE HIT THE road. Days before the offering we went out to sell potential investors on the worthiness of our product, our company, our brand. Ourselves. After China, we weren't in any mood to travel, but there was no other way. We had to do what Wall Street calls a dog-and-pony show. Twelve cities, seven days.

First stop, Manhattan. Breakfast meeting with a roomful of hard-eyed bankers, who represented thousands of potential investors. Hayes rose first and said a few introductory words. He summed up the numbers succinctly. He was quite good. Forceful, sober. Johnson then stood and spoke about the shoes themselves, what made them different and special, how they'd come to be so innovative. He was never better.

I closed. I talked about the company's origins, its soul and spirit. I had a note card with a few words scribbled on it, but I didn't look at it once. I had no uncertainty about what I wanted to say. I'm not sure I could've explained myself to a roomful of strangers, but I had no trouble explaining Nike.

I started with Bowerman. I talked about running for him at Oregon, then forming a partnership with him as a kid in my mid-twenties. I talked about his brains, his bravery, his magic waffle iron. I talked about his booby-trapped mailbox. It was a funny story, and it never failed to get a laugh, but it had a point. I wanted to let these New Yorkers know that though we hailed from Oregon, we were not to be trifled with.

The cowards never started and the weak died along the way. That leaves us, ladies and gentlemen. Us.

That first night we gave the same presentation at a formal dinner, in Midtown, before twice as many bankers. Cocktails were served beforehand. Hayes had one too many. This time, when he stood to speak, he decided to improvise, to free-style. "I've been around these guys a *long* time," he said, laughing, "the core of the company, you might say, and I'm here to tell you, haha, they're all chronic unemployables."

Dry coughs.

A throat in the back was cleared.

A lone cricket chirped. Then died.

Somewhere, far off, one person laughed like a loon. To this day I think it was Johnson.

Money was no laughing matter to these people, and a public offering of this size was not the occasion for jokes. I sighed, looked down at my note card. If Hayes had driven a bulldozer through the room, it could hardly have been worse. Later that night I took him aside and told him I thought it was best if he didn't speak anymore. Johnson and I would handle the formal presentations. But we'd still need him for the Q and A sessions.

Hayes looked at me, blinked once. He understood. "I thought you were going to send me home," he said. "No," I said, "you need to be part of this."

We continued to Chicago, then Dallas, then Houston, then San Francisco. We went on to Los Angeles, then Seattle. At each stop we grew more tired, almost weepy with fatigue. Johnson and I especially. A strange sentimentality was stealing over us. On the airplanes, in the hotel bars, we talked about our salad days. His endless letters. *Please send encouraging words.* My silence. We talked about the name Nike coming to him in a dream. We talked about Stretch, and Giampietro, and the Marlboro Man, and all the different times I'd jerked him back and forth across the country. We talked about the day he was almost strung up by his Exeter employees, when their paychecks had bounced. "After all that," Johnson said one day in the back of a town car, headed to the next meeting, "and now we're the toasts of Wall Street."

I looked at him. Things do change. But he hadn't. He now reached into his bag, took out a book, and began to read.

The road show ended the day before Thanksgiving. I vaguely remember a turkey, some cranberries, my family around me. I vaguely remember being aware that it was an anniversary of sorts. I'd first flown to Japan on Thanksgiving Day, 1962.

Over dinner my father had a thousand questions about the public offering. My mother had none. She said she'd always known it would happen, ever since the day she bought a pair of seven-dollar Limber Ups. They were understandably feeling reflective, congratulatory, but I quickly hushed them, begged them not to be premature. The game was still on. The race was afoot.

WE CHOSE A date for the offering. December 2, 1980. The last remaining hurdle was settling on a price.

The night before the offering Hayes came into my office. "The guys at Kuhn, Loeb are recommending twenty dollars per share," he said.

"Too low," I said. "It's insulting."

Well, it can't be too high, he cautioned. We want the damn thing to sell.

The whole process was crazy-making, because it was imprecise. There *was* no *right* number. It was all a matter of opinion, feeling, selling. *Selling*—that's what I'd been doing for much of these last eighteen years, and I was tired of it. I didn't want to sell anymore. Our stock was worth twenty-two dollars a share. That was the number. We'd earned that number. We deserved to be on the high end of the price range. A company called Apple was also going public that same week, and selling for twenty-two dollars a share, and we were worth as much as them, I said to Hayes. If a bunch of Wall Street guys didn't see it that way, I was ready to walk away from the deal.

I glared at Hayes. I knew what he was thinking. Here we go again. *Pay Nissho first.*

THE NEXT MORNING Hayes and I drove downtown to our law firm. A clerk showed us into the senior partner's office. A paralegal dialed Kuhn, Loeb in New York, then clicked a button on a speaker in the middle of the big walnut desk. Hayes and I stared at the speaker. Disembodied voices filled the room. One of the voices grew louder, clearer. "Gentlemen . . . good morning."

"Good morning," we said.

The loud voice took the lead. It gave a long and careful explanation of Kuhn, Loeb's reasoning on the stock price, which was jabberwocky. And so, the loud voice said, we can't go any higher than twenty-one dollars.

"No," I said. "Our number is twenty-two."

We heard the other voices murmuring. They came up to twenty-one-fifty. "I'm afraid," said the loud voice, "that's our final offer."

"Gentlemen, twenty-two is our number."

Hayes stared at me. I stared at the speaker.

Cracking silence. We could hear heavy breaths, pops, scrapes. Papers being shuffled. I closed my eyes and let all that white noise wash over me. I relived every negotiation in my life to that point.

So, Dad, you remember that Crazy Idea I had at Stanford . . . ?

Gentlemen, I represent Blue Ribbon Sports of Portland, Oregon.

You see, Dot, I love Penny. And Penny loves me. And if things continue in this vein, I see us building a life together.

"I'm sorry," the loud voice said angrily. "We'll have to call you back."

Click.

We sat. We said nothing. I took long deep breaths. The clerk's face slowly melted.

Five minutes passed.

Fifteen minutes.

Sweat ran down Hayes's forehead and neck.

The phone rang. The clerk looked at us, to make sure we were ready. We nodded. He pressed the button on the speaker.

"Gentlemen," the loud voice said. "We have a deal. We'll send it out to market this Friday."

I drove home. I remember the boys were outside playing. Penny was standing in the kitchen. "How was your day?" she said.

"Hm. Okay."

"Good."

"We got our price."

She smiled. "Of course you did."

I went for a long run.

Then I took a hot, hot shower.

Then I had a quick dinner.

Then I tucked in the boys and gave them a story.

The year was 1773. Privates Matt and Travis were fighting under the command of General Washington. Cold, tired, hungry, their uniforms in tatters, they camped for the winter at Valley Forge, Pennsylvania. They slept in log huts, wedged between two mountains: Mount Joy and Mount Misery. Morning till night, bitter cold winds sliced through the mountains and barreled through the chinks in the huts. Food was scarce; only a third of the men had shoes.

Whenever they walked outside, they left bloody footprints in the snow. Thousands died. But Matt and Travis held on.

Finally, spring came. The troops got word that the British had retreated, and the French were coming to the aid of the colonists. Privates Matt and Travis knew from then on that they could live through anything. Mount Joy, Mount Misery.

The end.

Good night, boys.

Night, Dad.

I turned out the light and went and sat in front of the TV with Penny. Neither of us was really watching. She was reading a book and I was doing calculations in my head.

By this time next week Bowerman would be worth $9 million.

Cale—$6.6 million.

Woodell, Johnson, Hayes, Strasser—each about $6 million.

Fantasy numbers. Numbers that meant nothing. I never knew that numbers could mean so much, and so little, at the same time.

"Bed?" Penny said.

I nodded.

I went around the house, turning off lights, checking doors. Then I joined her. For a long time we lay in the dark. It wasn't over. Far from it. The first part, I told myself, is behind us. But it's only the first part.

I asked myself: What are you feeling?

It wasn't joy. It wasn't relief. If I felt *anything*, it was . . . regret?

Good God, I thought. Yes. Regret.

Because I honestly wished I could do it all over again.

I fell asleep for a few hours. When I woke it was cold and rainy. I went to the window. The trees were dripping water. Everything was mist and fog. The world was the same as it had been the day before, as it had always been. Nothing had changed, least of all me. And yet I was worth $178 million.

I showered, ate breakfast, drove to work. I was at my desk before anyone else.

NIGHT

We love going to the movies. We always have. But tonight we have a dilemma. We've seen all the violent movies, which Penny likes best, so we're going to have to venture outside our comfort zone, try something different. A comedy, maybe.

I leaf through the paper. "How about *The Bucket List*—at the Century? Jack Nicholson and Morgan Freeman?"

She frowns: I guess.

It's Christmastime, 2007.

THE BUCKET LIST turns out to be anything but a comedy. It's a movie about mortality. Two men, Nicholson and Freeman, both terminally ill with cancer, decide to spend their remaining days doing all the fun things, the crazy things, they've always wanted to do, to make the most of their time before they kick the bucket. An hour into the movie, there's not a chuckle to be had.

There are also many strange, unsettling parallels between the movie and my life. First, Nicholson always makes me think of *One Flew Over the Cuckoo's Nest*, which makes me think of Kesey, which takes me back to my days at the University of Oregon. Second, high on the bucket list of Nicholson's character is seeing the Himalayas, which transports me to Nepal.

Above all, Nicholson's character employs a personal assistant—a sort of surrogate son—named Matthew. He even looks a bit like my son. Same scruffy goatee.

When the movie ends, when the lights come up, Penny and I are both relieved to stand and return to the bright glare of real life.

The theater is a new sixteen-screen colossus in the heart of Cathedral City, just outside Palm Springs. These days we spend much of the winter there, hiding from the chilly Oregon rains. Walking through the lobby, waiting for our eyes to adjust, we spot two familiar faces. At first we can't place them. We're still seeing Nicholson and Freeman in our minds. But these faces are equally familiar—equally famous. Now we realize. It's Bill and Warren. Gates and Buffett.

We stroll over.

Neither man is what you'd call a *close* friend, but we've met them several times, at social events and conferences. And we have common causes, common interests, a few mutual acquaintances. "Fancy meeting you here!" I say. Then I cringe. Did I really just say that? Is it possible that I'm *still* shy and awkward in the presence of celebrities?

"I was just thinking about you," one of them says.

We shake hands, all around, and talk mostly about Palm Springs. Isn't this place lovely? Isn't it wonderful to get out of the cold? We talk about families, business, sports. I hear someone behind us whisper, "Hey, look, Buffett and Gates—who's that other guy?"

I smile. As it should be.

In my head I can't help doing some quick math. At the moment I'm worth $10 billion, and each of these men is worth five or six times more. *Lead me from the unreal to the real.*

Penny asks if they enjoyed the movie. Yes, they both say, looking down at their shoes, though it was a bit depressing. What's on your bucket lists? I nearly ask, but I don't. Gates and Buffett seem to have done everything they've ever wanted in this life. They have no bucket lists, surely.

Which makes me ask myself: Have I?

* * *

AT HOME PENNY picks up her needlepoint and I pour myself a glass of wine. I pull out a yellow legal pad to look at my notes and lists for tomorrow. For the first time in a while . . . it's blank.

We sit in front of the eleven o'clock news, but my mind is far, far away. Drifting, floating, time-traveling. A familiar feeling of late.

I'm apt to spend long stretches of the day walking around in my childhood. For some reason I think a lot about my grandfather, Bump Knight. He had nothing, less than nothing. And yet he managed to scrimp and save and buy a brand-new Model T, in which he moved his wife and five kids from Winnebago, Minnesota, all the way to Colorado, then on to Oregon. He told me that he didn't bother to get his driver's license, he just up and went. Descending the Rockies in that rattling, shuddering piece of tin, he repeatedly scolded it. "Whoa, WHOA, you son of a bitch!" I heard this story so many times from him, and from aunts and uncles and cousins, I feel as though I was there. In a way, I was.

Bump later bought a pickup, and he loved putting us grandkids in the back of it, driving us into town on errands. Along the way he'd always stop by Sutherlin Bakery and buy us a dozen glazed doughnuts—each. I need only look up at the blue sky or the white ceiling (any blank screen will do) and I see myself, dangling my bare feet over his truck bed, feeling the fresh green wind on my face, licking glaze off a warm doughnut. Could I have risked as much, dared as much, walked the razor's edge of entrepreneurship between safety and catastrophe, without the early foundation of that feeling, that bliss of safety and contentment? I don't think so.

After forty years I've stepped down as Nike CEO, leaving the company in good hands, I think, and good shape, I trust. Sales last year, 2006, were $16 billion. (Adidas was $10 billion, but who's counting?) Our shoes and clothes are in five thousand stores worldwide, and we have ten thousand employees. Our Chinese operation in Shanghai alone has seven hundred. (And China, our second-largest market, is now our largest producer of shoes. I guess that 1980 trip paid off.)

The five thousand employees at the world headquarters in Beaverton are housed on an Edenic collegiate campus, with two hundred acres of wooded wilderness, laced by rolling streams, dotted by pristine ball fields. The buildings are named after the men and women who have given us more than their names and endorsements. Joan Benoit Samuelson, Ken Griffey Jr., Mia Hamm, Tiger Woods, Dan Fouts, Jerry Rice, Steve Prefontaine—they've given us our identity.

As chairman I still go most days to my office. I look around at all those buildings, and I don't see buildings, I see temples. Any building is a temple if you make it so. I think often of that momentous trip when I was twenty-four. I think of myself standing high above Athens, gazing at the Parthenon, and I never fail to experience the sensation of time folding in on itself.

Amid the campus buildings, along the campus walkways, there are enormous banners: action photos of the super athletes, the legends and giants and titans who've elevated Nike to something more than a brand.

Jordan.

Kobe.

Tiger.

Again, I can't help but think of my trip around the world.

The River *Jordan*.

Mystical *Kobe*, Japan.

That first meeting at Onitsuka, pleading with the executives for the right to sell *Tigers* . . .

Can this all be a coincidence?

I think of the countless Nike offices around the world. At each one, no matter the country, the phone number ends in 6453, which spells out Nike on the keypad. But, by pure chance, from right to left it also spells out Pre's best time in the mile, to the tenth of a second: 3:54.6.

I say by pure chance, but is it really? Am I allowed to think that some coincidences are more than coincidental? Can I be forgiven for thinking, or hoping, that the universe, or some guiding daemon, has been nudging me, whispering to me? Or else just playing with me? Can it really be nothing but a fluke of geography that the oldest shoes ever discovered are a pair of nine-thousand-year-old sandals . . . salvaged from a cave in Oregon?

Is there nothing to the fact that the sandals were discovered in 1938, the year I was born?

I ALWAYS FEEL a thrill, a shot of adrenaline, when I drive through the intersection of the campus's two main streets, each named after a Nike Founding Father. All day, every day, the security guard at the front gate gives visitors the same directions. *What you wanna do is take Bowerman Drive all the way up to Del Hayes Way* . . . I also take great pleasure in strolling past the oasis at the center of campus, the Nissho Iwai Japanese Gardens. In one sense our campus is a topographical map of Nike's history and growth; in another it's a diorama of my life. In yet another sense it's a living, breathing expression of that vital human emotion, maybe the most vital of all, after love. Gratitude.

The youngest employees at Nike seem to have it. In abundance. They care deeply about the names on the streets and buildings, and about the bygone days. Like Matthew begging for his bedtime story, they clamor for the old tales. They crowd the conference room whenever Woodell or Johnson visits. They've even formed a discussion group, an informal think tank, to preserve that original sense of innovation. They call themselves The Spirit of 72, which fills my heart.

But it's not just the young people within the company who honor the history. I think back to July 2005. In the middle of some event, I can't recall which, LeBron James asks for a private word.

"Phil, can I see you a moment?"

"Of course."

"When I first signed with you," he says, "I didn't know all that much about the history of Nike. So I've been studying up."

"Oh?"

"You're the founder."

"Well. Cofounder. Yes. It surprises a lot of people."

"And Nike was born in 1972."

"Well. Born—? Yes. I suppose."

"Right. So I went to my jeweler and had them find a Rolex watch from 1972."

He hands me the watch. It's engraved: *With thanks for taking a chance on me.*

As usual, I say nothing. I don't know what to say.

It wasn't much of a chance. He was pretty close to a sure thing. But taking a chance on people—he's right. You could argue that's what it's all been about.

I GO OUT to the kitchen, pour another glass of wine. Returning to my recliner, I watch Penny needlepoint for a while and the mental images come tumbling faster and faster. As if I'm needlepointing memories.

I watch Pete Sampras crush every opponent at one of his many Wimbledons. After the final point he tosses his racket into the stands—to me! (He overshoots and hits the man behind me, who sues, of course.)

I see Pete's archrival, Andre Agassi, win the U.S. Open, unseeded, and come to my box after the final shot, in tears. "We did it, Phil!"

We?

I smile as Tiger drains the final putt at Augusta—or is it St. Andrews? He hugs me—and holds on for many seconds longer than I expect.

I roll my mind back over the many private, intimate moments I've shared with him, and with Bo Jackson, and with Michael Jordan.

Staying at Michael's house in Chicago, I pick up the phone next to the bed in the guestroom and discover that there's a voice on the line. *May I help you?* It's room service. Genuine, round-the-clock, whatever-your-heart-desires room service.

I set down the phone, my mouth hanging open.

They're all like sons, and brothers—family. No less. When Tiger's father, Earl, dies, the church in Kansas holds fewer than one hundred, and I'm honored to be included. When Jordan's father is murdered, I fly to North Carolina for the funeral and discover with a shock that a seat is reserved for me in the front row.

All of which leads me back, of course, to Matthew.

I think of his long, difficult search for meaning, for identity. For me. His search often looked so familiar, even though Matthew didn't have my luck, or my focus. Nor my insecurity. Maybe if he'd had a little more insecurity . . .

In his quest to find himself, he dropped out of college. He experimented, dabbled, rebelled, argued, ran away. Nothing worked. Then, at last, in 2000, he seemed to enjoy being a husband, a father, a philanthropist. He got involved in Mi Casa, Su Casa, a charity building an orphanage in El Salvador. On one of his visits there, after a few days of hard, satisfying work, he took a break. He drove with two friends to Ilopango, a deep-water lake, to go scuba diving.

For some reason he decided to see how deep he could go. He decided to take a risk that even his risk-addicted father would never take.

Something went wrong. At 150 feet my son lost consciousness.

If I were to think about Matthew in his final moments, fighting for air, I believe my imagination could get me very close to how he must have felt. After the thousands of miles I've logged as a runner, I know that feeling of fighting for that next breath. But I won't let my imagination go there, ever.

Still, I've talked to the two friends who were with him. I've read everything I've been able to get my hands on about diving accidents. When things go wrong, I've learned, a diver often feels something called "the martini effect." He thinks everything is okay. Better than okay. He feels euphoric. That must have happened to Matthew, I tell myself, because at the last second he pulled out his mouthpiece. I choose to believe this euphoria scenario, to believe that my son didn't suffer at the end. That my son was happy. I choose, because it's the only way I can go on.

Penny and I were at the movies when we found out. We'd gone to the five o'clock showing of *Shrek 2*. In the middle of the movie we turned and saw Travis standing in the aisle. Travis. *Travis?*

He was whispering to us in the dark. "You guys need to come with me."

We walked up the aisle, out of the theater, from darkness to light. As we emerged he said, "I just got a phone call from El Salvador . . ."

Penny fell to the floor. Travis helped her up. He put his arm around his mother and I staggered away, to the end of the hallway, tears streaming. I recall seven strange unbidden words running through my head, over and over, like a fragment of some poem: *So this is the way it ends.*

BY THE NEXT morning the news was everywhere. Internet, radio, newspapers, TV, all blaring the bare facts. Penny and I pulled the blinds, locked the doors, cut ourselves off. But not before our niece Britney moved in with us. To this day I believe that she saved our lives.

Every Nike athlete wrote, emailed, phoned. Every single one. But the first was Tiger. His call came in at 7:30 a.m. I will never, ever forget. And I will not stand for a bad word spoken about Tiger in my presence.

Another early caller was Alberto Salazar, the ferociously competitive distance runner who won three straight New York City Marathons in Nikes. I will always love him for many things, but above all for that show of concern.

He's a coach now, and recently he brought a few of his runners to Beaverton. They were having a light workout, in the middle of Ronaldo Field, when someone turned and saw Alberto on the ground, gasping for air. A heart attack. He was legally dead for fourteen minutes, until paramedics revived him and rushed him to St. Vincent's.

I know that hospital well. My son Travis was born there, my mother died there, twenty-seven years after my father. In his final six months I was able to take my father on a long trip, to put to rest the eternal question of whether he was proud, to show him that *I* was proud of *him*. We went around the world, saw Nikes in every country we visited, and with every appearance of a swoosh his eyes shone. The pain of his impatience, his hostility to my Crazy Idea—it had faded. It was long gone. But not the memory.

Fathers and sons, it's always been the same, since the dawn of time. "My dad," Arnold Palmer once confided to me at the Masters, "did all he could to discourage me from being a professional golfer." I smiled. "You don't say."

Visiting Alberto, walking into the lobby of St. Vincent's, I was overcome with visions of both my parents. I felt them at my elbow, at my ear. Theirs was a strained relationship, I believe. But, as with an iceberg, everything was below the surface. In their house on Claybourne Street, the tension was concealed, and calm and reason almost always prevailed, because of their love for us. Love wasn't spoken, or shown, but it was there, always. My sisters and I grew up knowing that both parents, different as they were from each other, and from us, cared. That's their legacy. That's their lasting victory.

I walked to the cardiac unit, saw the familiar sign on the door: *No Admittance*. I sailed past the sign, through the door, down the hall, and found Alberto's room. He lifted his head off the pillow, managed a pained smile. I patted his arm and we had a good talk. Then I saw that he was fading. "See you soon," I said. His hand shot out and grabbed mine. "If something happens to me," he said, "promise me you'll take care of Galen."

His athlete. The one he'd been training. Who was just like a son to him.

I got it. Oh, how I got it.

"Of course," I said. "Of course. Galen. Consider it done."

I walked out of the room, barely hearing the beeping machines, the laughing nurses, the patient groaning down the hall. I thought of that phrase, "It's just business." It's never just business. It never will be. If it ever does become just business, that will mean that business is very bad.

TIME FOR BED, Penny says, packing up her needlepoint.

Yes, I tell her. I'll be along in a minute.

I keep thinking of one line in *The Bucket List*. "You measure yourself by the people who measure themselves by you." I forget if it was Nicholson or Freeman. The line is so true, so very true. And it transports me to Tokyo, to the offices of Nissho. I was there not long ago for a visit. The phone rang. "For you," the Japanese receptionist said, extending the receiver. "Me?" It was Michael Johnson, the three-time gold medalist, holder of the world record in the 200 meters and 400 meters. He did it all in our shoes. He happened to be in Tokyo, he said, and heard I was, too. "Do you want to have dinner?" he asked.

I was flattered. But I told him I couldn't. Nissho was having a banquet for me. I invited him to come. Hours later we were sitting together on the floor, before a table covered with shabu-shabu, toasting each other with cup after cup of sake. We laughed, cheered, clinked glasses, and something passed between us, the same thing that passes between me and most of the athletes I work with. A transference, a camaraderie, a sort of *connection*. It's brief, but it nearly always happens, and I know it's part of what I was searching for when I went around the world in 1962.

To study the self is to forget the self. *Mi casa, su casa.*

Oneness—in some way, shape, or form, it's what every person I've ever met has been seeking.

I THINK OF others who didn't make it this far. Bowerman died on Christmas Eve, 1999, in Fossil. He'd gone back to his hometown, as we always suspected he would. He still owned his house on the mountaintop above campus, but he chose to quit it, to move with Mrs. Bowerman to a Fossil retirement home. He needed to be where he started—did he tell someone that? Or am I imagining him muttering it to himself?

I remember when I was a sophomore, we had a dual meet with Washington State, in Pullman, and Bowerman made the bus driver go through Fossil so he could show us. I immediately thought of that sentimental detour when I heard that he'd lain down on the bed and never got up.

It was Jaqua who phoned. I was reading the paper, the Christmas tree blinking blinking blinking. You always remember the strangest details from such moments. I choked into the phone, "I'll have to call you back," then walked upstairs to my den. I turned out all the lights. Eyes shut, I replayed a million different moments, including that long-ago lunch at the Cosmopolitan Hotel.

Deal?

Deal.

An hour passed before I could go back downstairs. At some point that night I gave up the Kleenex and just draped a towel over my shoulder. A move I learned from another beloved coach—John Thompson.

Strasser passed suddenly, too. Heart attack, 1993. He was so young, it was a tragedy, all the more so because it came after we'd had a falling out. Strasser had been instrumental in signing Jordan, in building up the Jordan brand and wrapping it around Rudy's air soles. Air Jordan changed Nike, took us to the next level, and the next, but it changed Strasser, too. He felt that he should no longer be taking orders from anyone, including me. Especially me. We clashed, too many times, and he quit.

It might have been okay if he'd just quit. But he went to work for Adidas. An intolerable betrayal. I never forgave him. (Though I did recently—happily, proudly—hire his daughter, Avery. Twenty-two years old, she works in Special Events, and she's said to be thriving. It's a blessing and a joy to see her name in the company directory.) I wish Strasser and I had patched things up before he died, but I don't know that it was possible. We were both born to compete, and we were both bad at forgiving. For both of us, betrayal was extra potent kryptonite.

I felt that same sense of betrayal when Nike came under attack for conditions in our overseas factories—the so-called sweatshop controversy. Whenever reporters said a factory was unsatisfactory, they never said how much better it was than the day we first went in. They never said how hard we'd worked with our factory partners to upgrade conditions, to make them safer and cleaner. They never said these factories weren't ours, that we were renters, one among many tenants. They simply searched until they found a worker with complaints about conditions, and they used that worker to vilify us, and only us, knowing our name would generate maximum publicity.

Of course my handling of the crisis only made it worse. Angry, hurt, I often reacted with self-righteousness, petulance, anger. On some level I knew my reaction was toxic, counterproductive, but I couldn't stop myself. It's just not easy to remain even-keeled when you wake up one day, thinking you're creating jobs and helping poor countries modernize and enabling athletes to achieve greatness, only to find yourself being burned in effigy outside the flagship retail store in your own hometown.

The company reacted as I did. Emotionally. Everyone was reeling. Many late nights in Beaverton, you'd find all the lights on, and soul-searching conversations taking place in various conference rooms and offices. Though we knew that much of the criticism was unjust, that Nike was a symbol, a scapegoat, more than the true culprit, all of that was beside the point. We had to admit: We could do better.

We told ourselves: We must do better.

Then we told the world: Just watch. We'll make our factories shining examples.

And we did. In the ten years since the bad headlines and lurid exposés, we've used the crisis to reinvent the entire company.

For instance. One of the worst things about a shoe factory used to be the rubber room, where uppers and soles are bonded. The fumes are choking, toxic, cancer-causing. So we invented a water-based bonding agent that gives off no fumes, thereby eliminating 97 percent of the carcinogens in the air. Then we gave this invention to our competitors, handed it over to anyone who wanted it.

They all did. Nearly all of them now use it.

One of many, many examples.

We've gone from a target of reformers to a dominant player in the factory reform movement. Today the factories that make our products are among the best in the world. An official at the United Nations recently said so: Nike is the gold standard by which we measure all apparel factories.

Out of the sweatshop crisis also came the Girl Effect, a massive Nike effort to break the generational cycles of poverty in the bleakest corners of the world. Along with the United Nations and other corporate and government partners, the Girl Effect is spending tens of millions of dollars in a smart, tough, global campaign to educate and connect and lift up young girls. Economists, sociologists, not to mention our own hearts, tell us that, in many societies, young girls are the most economically vulnerable, and vital, demographic. So helping them helps all. Whether striving to end child marriage in Ethiopia, or building safe spaces for teenage girls in Nigeria, or launching a magazine and radio show that deliver powerful, inspiring messages to young Rwandans, the Girl Effect is changing millions of lives, and the best days of my week, month, year, are those when I receive the glowing reports from its front lines.

I'd do anything to go back, to make so many different decisions, which might or might not have averted the sweatshop crisis. But I can't deny that the crisis has led to miraculous change, inside and outside Nike. For that I must be grateful.

Of course, there will always be the question of wages. The salary of a Third World factory worker seems impossibly low to Americans, and I understand. Still, we have to operate within the limits and structures of each country, each economy; we can't simply pay whatever we wish to pay. In one country, which shall be nameless, when we tried to raise wages, we found ourselves called on the carpet, summoned to the office of a top government official and ordered to stop. We were disrupting the nation's entire economic system, he said. It's simply not right, he insisted, or feasible, that a shoe worker makes more than a medical doctor.

Change never comes as fast as we want it.

I think constantly of the poverty I saw while traveling the world in the 1960s. I knew then that the only answer to such poverty is entry-level jobs. Lots of them. I didn't form this theory on my own. I heard it from every economics professor I ever had, at both Oregon and Stanford, and everything I saw and read thereafter backed it up. International trade always, *always* benefits both trading nations.

Another thing I often heard from those same professors was the old maxim: "When goods don't pass international borders, soldiers will." Though I've been known to call business war without bullets, it's actually a wonderful bulwark against war. Trade is the path of coexistence, cooperation. Peace feeds on prosperity. That's why, haunted as I was by the Vietnam War, I always vowed that someday Nike would have a factory in or near Saigon.

By 1997 we had four.

I was very proud. And when I learned that we were to be honored and celebrated by the Vietnamese government as one of the nation's top five generators of foreign currency, I felt that I simply had to visit.

What a wrenching trip. I don't know if I'd appreciated the full depth of my hatred for the war in Vietnam until I returned twenty-five years after the peace, until I joined hands with our former antagonists. At one point my hosts graciously asked what they could do for me, what would make my trip special or memorable. I got a lump in my throat. I didn't want them to go to any trouble, I said.

But they insisted.

Okay, I said, okay, I'd like to meet eighty-six-year-old General Võ Nguyên Giáp, the Vietnamese MacArthur, the man who single-handedly defeated the Japanese, the French, the Americans, and the Chinese.

My hosts stared in amazed silence. Slowly they rose and excused themselves and stood off in a corner, conversing in frantic Vietnamese.

After five minutes they came back. Tomorrow, they said. One hour.

I bowed deeply. Then counted the minutes until the big meeting.

The first thing I noticed as General Giáp entered the room was his size. This brilliant fighter, this genius tactician who'd organized the Tet Offensive, who'd planned those miles and miles of underground tunnels, this giant of history, came up to my shoulders. He was, *maybe*, five foot four.

And humble. No corncob pipe for Giáp.

I remember that he wore a dark business suit, like mine. I remember that he smiled as I did—shyly, uncertainly. But there was an intensity about him. I'd seen that kind of glittery confidence in great coaches, and great business leaders, the elite of the elite. I never saw it in a mirror.

He knew I had questions. He waited for me to ask them.

I said simply: "How did you do it?"

I thought I saw the corners of his mouth flicker. A smile? Maybe?

He thought. And thought. "I was," he said, "a professor of the jungle."

THOUGHTS OF ASIA always lead back to Nissho. Where on earth would we have been without Nissho? And without Nissho's former CEO, Masuro Hayami. I got to know him well after Nike went public. We couldn't help but bond: I was his most profitable client, and his most avid pupil. And he was perhaps the wisest man I ever knew.

Unlike many other wise men, he drew great peace from his wisdom. I fed off that peace.

In the 1980s, whenever I went to Tokyo, Hayami would invite me for the weekend to his beach house, near Atami, the Japanese Riviera. We'd always leave Tokyo late Friday, by rail, and have a cognac along the way. Within an hour we'd be at the Izu Peninsula, where we'd stop at some marvelous restaurant for dinner. The next morning we'd play golf, and Saturday night we'd have a Japanese-style barbecue in his backyard. We'd solve all the world's problems, or I'd give him my problems and he'd solve them.

On one trip we ended the evening in Hayami's hot tub. I recall, above the foaming water, the sound of the distant ocean slapping the shore. I recall the cool smell of the wind through the trees— thousands and thousands of coastal trees, dozens of species not found in any Oregon forest. I recall the jungle crows cawing in the distance as we discussed the infinite. Then the finite. I complained about my business. Even after going public, there were so many problems. "We have so much opportunity, but we're having a terrible time getting managers who can seize those opportunities. We try people from the outside, but they fail, because our culture is so different."

Mr. Hayami nodded. "See those bamboo trees up there?" he asked.

"Yes."

"Next year . . . when you come . . . they will be one foot higher."
I stared. I understood.

When I returned to Oregon I tried hard to cultivate and grow
the management team we had, slowly, with more patience, with an
eye toward more training and more long-term planning. I took the
wider, longer view. It worked. The next time I saw Hayami, I told
him. He merely nodded, once, *hai*, and looked off.

ALMOST THREE DECADES ago Harvard and Stanford began
studying Nike, and sharing their research with other universities,
which has created many opportunities for me to visit different colleges, to take part in stimulating academic discussions, to continue
to learn. It's always a happy occasion to be walking a campus, but
also bracing, because while I find students today much smarter
and more competent than in my time, I also find them far more
pessimistic. Occasionally they ask in dismay: "Where is the U.S.
going? Where is the world going?" Or: "Where are the new entrepreneurs?" Or: "Are we doomed as a society to a worse future
for our children?"

I tell them about the devastated Japan I saw in 1962. I tell them
about the rubble and ruins that somehow gave birth to wise men
like Hayami and Ito and Sumeragi. I tell them about the untapped
resources, natural and human, that the world has at its disposal, the
abundant ways and means to solve its many crises. All we have to do,
I tell the students, is work and study, study and work, hard as we can.

Put another way: We must all be professors of the jungle.

I TURN OUT the lights, walk upstairs to bed. Curled up with a book
beside her, Penny has drifted off. That chemistry, that in-sync feeling
from Day One, Accounting 101, remains. Our conflicts, such as they

are, have centered mostly on work versus family. Finding a balance. Defining that word "balance." At our most trying moments, we've managed to emulate those athletes I most admire. We've held on, pressed through. And now we've endured.

I slide under the covers, gingerly, so as not to wake her, and I think of others who've endured. Hayes lives on a farm in the Tualatin Valley, 108 rolling acres, with a ridiculous collection of bulldozers and other heavy equipment. (His pride and joy is a John Deere JD-450C. It's bright school-bus yellow and as big as a one-bedroom condo.) He has some health problems, but he bulldozes ahead.

Woodell lives in central Oregon with his wife. For years he flew his own private airplane, giving the middle finger to everyone who said he'd be helpless. (Above all, flying private meant he never again had to worry about an airline losing his wheelchair.)

He's one of the best storytellers in the history of Nike. My favorite, naturally, is the one about the day we went public. He sat his parents down and told them the news. "What does that mean?" they whispered. "It means your original eight-thousand-dollar loan to Phil is worth $1.6 million." They looked at each other, looked at Woodell. "I don't understand," his mother said.

If you can't trust the company your son works for, who can you trust?

When he retired from Nike, Woodell became head of the Port of Portland, managing all the rivers and the airports. A man immobilized, guiding all that motion. Lovely. He's also the leading shareholder and director of a successful microbrewery. He always did like his beer.

But whenever we get together for dinner, he tells me, of course, his greatest joy and proudest accomplishment is his college-bound son, Dan.

Woodell's old antagonist, Johnson, lives slap in the middle of a Robert Frost poem, somewhere in the wilderness of New Hampshire. He's converted an old barn into a five-story mansion, which he calls his

Fortress of Solitude. Twice divorced, he's filled the place to the rafters with dozens of reading chairs, and thousands and thousands of books, and he keeps track of them all with an extensive card catalog. Each book has its own number and its own index card, listing author, date of publication, plot summary—and its precise location in the fortress.

Of course.

Scampering and prancing around Johnson's spread are countless wild turkeys and chipmunks, most of whom he's named. He knows them all so well, so intimately, he can tell you when one is late in hibernating. Beyond, in the distance, nestled in a field of tall grass and swaying maples, Johnson has built a second barn, a sacred barn, which he's painted and lacquered and furnished and filled with over-flow from his personal library, plus pallets of used books he buys at library sales. He calls this book utopia "Horders," and he keeps it lighted, open, free, twenty-four hours a day, for any and all who need a place to read and think.

That's Full-time Employee Number One.

In Europe, I'm told, there are T-shirts that read, *Where is Jeff Johnson?* Like the famous opening line from Ayn Rand, *Who is John Galt?* The answer is, Right where he should be.

WHEN IT CAME rolling in, the money affected us all. Not much, and not for long, because none of us was ever driven by money. But that's the nature of money. Whether you have it or not, whether you want it or not, whether you like it or not, it will try to define your days. Our task as human beings is not to let it.

I bought a Porsche. I tried to buy the Los Angeles Clippers, and wound up in a lawsuit with Donald Sterling. I wore sunglasses every-where, indoors and out. There's a photo of me in a ten-gallon gray cowboy hat—I don't know where or when or why. I had to get it all out of my system. Even Penny wasn't immune. Overcompensating for the insecurity of her childhood, she walked around with thousands of dollars in her purse. She bought hundreds of staples, like rolls of toilet paper, at a time.

It wasn't long before we were back to normal. Now, to the extent that she and I ever think about money, we focus our efforts on a few specific causes. We give away $100 million each year, and when we're gone we'll give away most of what's left.

At the moment we're in the midst of building a gleaming new basketball facility at the University of Oregon. The Matthew Knight Arena. The logo at half court will be Matthew's name in the shape of a torii gate. *From the profane to the sacred* . . . We're also finishing construction on a new athletic facility, which we plan to dedicate to our mothers, Dot and Lota. On a plaque next to the entrance will go an inscription: *Because mothers are our first coaches.*

Who can say how differently everything would have turned out if my mother hadn't stopped the podiatrist from surgically removing that wart and hobbling me for an entire track season? Or if she hadn't told me I could run *fast*? Or if she hadn't bought that first pair of Limber Ups, putting my father in his place?

Whenever I go back to Eugene, and walk the campus, I think of her. Whenever I stand outside Hayward Field, I think of the silent race she ran. I think of all the many races that each of us have run. I lean against the fence and look at the track and listen to the wind, thinking of Bowerman with his string tie blowing behind him. I think of Pre, God love him. Turning, looking over my shoulder, my heart leaps. Across the street stands the William Knight Law School. A very serious-looking edifice. No one ever jackasses around in there.

I CAN'T SLEEP. I can't stop thinking about that blasted movie, *The Bucket List*. Lying in the dark, I ask myself again and again, What's on yours?

Pyramids? Check.

Himalayas? Check.

Ganges? Check.

So . . . nothing?

I think about the few things I want to do. Help a couple of universities change the world. Help find a cure for cancer. Besides that, it's not so much things I want to do as things I'd like to say. And maybe unsay.

It might be nice to tell the story of Nike. Everyone else has told the story, or tried to, but they always get half the facts, if that, and none of the spirit. Or vice versa. I might start the story, or end it, with regrets. The hundreds—maybe thousands—of bad decisions. I'm the guy who said Magic Johnson was "a player without a position, who'll never make it in the NBA." I'm the guy who tabbed Ryan Leaf as a better NFL quarterback than Peyton Manning.

It's easy to laugh those off. Other regrets go deeper. Not phoning Hiraku Iwano after he quit. Not getting Bo Jackson renewed in 1996. Joe Paterno.

Not being a good enough manager to avoid layoffs. Three times in ten years—a total of fifteen hundred people. It still haunts.

Of course, above all, I regret not spending more time with my sons. Maybe, if I had, I could've solved the encrypted code of Matthew Knight.

And yet I know that this regret clashes with my secret regret—that I can't do it all over again.

God, how I wish I could relive the whole thing. Short of that, I'd like to share the experience, the ups and downs, so that some young man or woman, somewhere, going through the same trials and ordeals, might be inspired or comforted. Or warned. Some young entrepreneur, maybe, some athlete or painter or novelist, might press on.

It's all the same drive. The same dream.

It would be nice to help them avoid the typical discouragements. I'd tell them to hit pause, think long and hard about how they want to spend their time, and with whom they want to spend it for the next forty years. I'd tell men and women in their midtwenties not to settle for a job or a profession or even a career. Seek a calling. Even if you don't know what that means, seek it. If you're following your calling, the fatigue will be easier to bear, the disappointments will be fuel, the highs will be like nothing you've ever felt.

I'd like to warn the best of them, the iconoclasts, the innovators, the rebels, that they will always have a bull's-eye on their backs. The better they get, the bigger the bull's-eye. It's not one man's opinion; it's a law of nature.

I'd like to remind them that America isn't the entrepreneurial Shangri-La people think. Free enterprise always irritates the kinds of trolls who live to block, to thwart, to say no, sorry, no. And it's always been this way. Entrepreneurs have always been outgunned, outnumbered. They've always fought uphill, and the hill has never been steeper. America is becoming less entrepreneurial, not more. A Harvard Business School study recently ranked all the countries of the world in terms of their entrepreneurial spirit. America ranked behind Peru.

And those who urge entrepreneurs to never give up? Charlatans. Sometimes you have to give up. Sometimes knowing when to give up, when to try something else, is genius. Giving up doesn't mean stopping. Don't ever stop.

Luck plays a big role. Yes, I'd like to publicly acknowledge the power of luck. Athletes get lucky, poets get lucky, businesses get lucky. Hard work is critical, a good team is essential, brains and determination are invaluable, but luck may decide the outcome. Some people might not call it luck. They might call it Tao, or Logos, or Jñāna, or Dharma. Or Spirit. Or God.

Put it this way. The harder you work, the better your Tao. And since no one has ever adequately defined Tao, I now try to go regularly to mass. I would tell them: Have faith in yourself, but also have faith in faith. Not faith as others define it. Faith as you define it. Faith as faith defines itself in your heart.

In what format do I want to say all this? A memoir? No, not a memoir. I can't imagine how it could all fit into one unified narrative.

Maybe a novel. Or a speech. Or a series of speeches. Maybe just a letter to my grandkids.

I peer into the dark. So maybe there is something on my bucket list after all?

Another Crazy Idea.

Suddenly my mind is racing. People I need to call, things I need to read. I'll have to get in touch with Woodell. I should see if we have any copies of those letters from Johnson. There were so many! Somewhere in my parents' house, where my sister Joanne still lives, there must be a box with my slides from my trip around the world.

So much to do. So much to learn. So much I don't know about my own life.

Now I really can't sleep. I get up, grab a yellow legal pad from my desk. I go to the living room and sit in my recliner.

A feeling of stillness, of immense peace, comes over me.

I squint at the moon shining outside my window. The same moon that inspired the ancient Zen masters to worry about nothing. In the timeless, clarifying light of that moon, I begin to make a list.

ACKNOWLEDGMENTS

I've spent a fair portion of my life in debt. As a young entrepreneur I became distressingly familiar with that feeling of going to sleep each night, waking up each day, owing many people a sum far greater than I could repay.

Nothing, however, has made me feel quite so indebted as the writing of this book.

Just as there's no end to my gratitude, there seems no proper, logical place to begin to express it. And so. At Nike, I wish to thank my assistant, Lisa McKillips, for doing everything—I mean everything—perfectly, cheerfully, and always with her dazzling smile; old friends Jeff Johnson and Bob Woodell for making me remember, and being patient when I remembered it different; historian Scott Reames for deftly sifting facts from myths; and Maria Eitel for applying her expertise to weightiest matters.

Of course, my biggest and most emphatic thanks to the 68,000 Nike employees worldwide for their daily efforts and their dedication, without which there would be no book, no author, no nothing.

At Stanford, I wish to thank the mad genius and gifted teacher Adam Johnson for his golden example of what it means to be a working writer and a friend; Abraham Verghese, who instructs as he writes—quietly, effortlessly; and numberless graduate students I met with while sitting in the back row of writing classes—each inspired me with his or her passion for language and craft.

ACKNOWLEDGMENTS

At Scribner, thanks to the legendary Nan Graham for her stead-fast support; Roz Lippel, Susan Moldow, and Carolyn Reidy for their bracing, energizing enthusiasm; Kathleen Rizzo for keeping production moving smoothly forward while always maintaining a sublime calm; above all, thanks to my supremely talented and razor-sharp editor, Shannon Welch, who gave me the affirmation I needed, when I needed it, without either of us fully appreciating how much I needed it. Her early note of praise and analysis and precocious wisdom was everything.

Randomly, in no order, thanks to the many pals and colleagues who were so lavish with their time, talent, and advice, including super agent Bob Barnett, poet-administrator extraordinaire Eavan Boland, Grand Slam memoirist Andre Agassi, and number artist Del Hayes. A special and profound thank-you to memoirist-novelist-journalist-sportswriter-muse-friend J. R. Moehringer, whose generosity and good humor and enviable storytelling gifts I relied on through the many, many drafts of this book.

Last, I wish to thank my family, all of them, but particularly my son Travis, whose support and friendship meant—and mean—the world. And, of course, a full-throated, full-hearted thanks to my Penelope, who waited. And waited. She waited while I journeyed, and she waited while I got lost. She waited night after night while I made my maddeningly slow way home—usually late, the dinner cold—and she waited the last few years while I relived it all, aloud, and in my head, and on the page, even though there were parts she didn't care to relive. From the start, going on half a century, she's waited, and now at last I can hand her these hard-fought pages and say, about them, about Nike, about everything: "Penny, I couldn't have done it without you."